# Representation in
# State Legislatures

MALCOLM E. JEWELL

# Representation in State Legislatures

THE UNIVERSITY PRESS OF KENTUCKY

**Library of Congress Cataloging in Publication Data**

Jewell, Malcolm Edwin, 1928-
    Representation in state legislatures.

    Bibliography: p.
    Includes index.
    1. Legislative bodies—United States—States.
2. Representative government and representation
—United States—States.    I. Title.
JK2488.J39        328.73'0734        82-40174
ISBN 0-8131-1463-2

Scholarly publisher for the Commonwealth,
serving Berea College, Centre College of Kentucky,
Eastern Kentucky University, The Filson Club,
Georgetown College, Kentucky Historical Society,
Kentucky State University, Morehead State University,
Murray State University, Northern Kentucky University,
Transylvania University, University of Kentucky,
University of Louisville, and Western Kentucky University.

*Editorial and Sales Offices:* Lexington, Kentucky 40506-0024

# Contents

# List of Tables

# Acknowledgments

During the 1978–1979 academic year I held a University Research Professorship at the University of Kentucky, which made possible the trips to nine states for legislative interviews.

My most important debt is to the 221 legislators who were willing to be interviewed. In many cases my visit to the state came when there were many demands on their time, but most of those I contacted agreed to take the time for an interview. They talked frankly to me about their role as representatives and provided me with materials related to that job.

I am indebted to Helen M. Ingram and to Deborah Gona, as well as to members of the Network of State Polls, for making available unpublished data. Information on the 1978 congressional election survey was made available by the Inter-University Consortium for Political and Social Research. The data were originally collected by the Center for Political Studies of the Institute for Social Research, the University of Michigan, under grants from the National Science Foundation.

I want to thank several colleagues who reviewed the manuscript for me and who provided unusually valuable suggestions: Samuel C. Patterson, Richard F. Fenno, Jr., and Alan Rosenthal.

Naturally the various persons and institutions that were interviewed, reviewed the manuscript, and provided data and funding share no responsibility for the results reported in this book.

# 1. Representation in State Legislatures

In late 1978 and early 1979 I spent many weeks in the capitals of nine American states talking to legislators about how they represent their constituents. The question may appear to be a simple one, but the answers I received show that representation has many dimensions and that legislators approach it differently, depending on the state and the particular district they represent as well as their own perceptions and political styles. I found that there is no average legislator and no set of answers to the questions about representation that might be considered typical. But examples of a couple of interviews will suggest the range of meanings that are associated with the term *representation.*

Late one afternoon, after the Ohio House had adjourned for the day, I found a legislator who was prepared to talk at some length about his job. A thirty-nine-year-old Republican lawyer, he was just starting his fourth term in the House. When I began asking him about his district, he described it as "a microcosm of the state." At the center of the district is a small but heavily industrialized city, surrounded by small towns and rural areas. His district includes almost all the county, but one rural township has been lopped off to achieve population equality. He would prefer to represent the whole county: "Splitting up counties is damaging because people think in terms of counties. I'm unusually lucky to have a district that is almost identical to the county, but those persons who live in the part of the county attached to another district really don't have any influence on that district."

Noting that he was elected without opposition in 1978 and won with over 60 percent in each of the three previous elections, I suggest that the district appears to be very secure for Republican candidates. He quickly replies: "That is deceptive." The success of Republican candidates, including himself, is due to an unusually hard-working Republican organization that seeks and gets support from groups—such as union members and blacks—whom the Republicans usually fail to contact. "Even though I ran unopposed, I spent ten days after the election at the factory gates, thanking people for voting for me."

I ask him how he develops visibility and how he maintains contact with constituents.

Anything I say is news, being the only representative in the county, like members in most rural counties. But I have the advantage of a more sophisticated media than most rural legislators have, including a newspaper, two radio stations, and a TV station.

Every other week I have a press conference in the city, and then repeat it in a couple of the small towns. These are open to the press and the public, but mostly just the press comes. I report on bills that have been passed, and my stand on them, and on my activities in the legislature and in the district.

How difficult is it to represent a district that is heterogeneous, with different and often conflicting interests?

It is not hard to represent this district. When it is that diverse, no single interest can kill you. You can't suit everyone—someone will be mad no matter what you do, so you can make an informed judgment. It gives you a great deal of freedom.

If you explain your vote to people, and sound well informed, and report back often to them, they will forgive a few votes that they might not agree with. I tend to get into trouble with the right-wing Republicans, but the local chairman of the party says, "Even if we don't always agree with you, at least give us reasons for your votes."

Do you have trouble with single-issue groups?

Not very much. The two toughest are the anti-gun control people and the anti-abortion people. They are very organized and they don't agree with me—I am too moderate for them. What has saved me is that in this county there is so much diversity that these small groups are swallowed up—they just are not that numerous.

How do you define the job of being a legislator—what are the most important parts of it, or the things you wish you could spend more time on?

Everyone here faces a problem: There are two competing job descriptions that are irreconcilable (at least in terms of the time available). You must choose between being an ombudsman or being a legislator or lawmaker. Everyone here makes a conscious or unconscious choice about how much time to spend on each. I tend to be oriented toward legislation. If I didn't devote so much attention to the media in my district, I would probably be hurt politically because I have not given that much attention to constituency service.

The young Massachusetts legislator is serving his third term, representing a safely Democratic, middle-income district in the suburbs of Boston. He enjoys talking about his job and seems to enjoy being a representative and a politician. How does he stay in contact with constituents?

I return every phone call I get. I answer every letter. I speak every chance I get. When I go to the market to shop, I see people who know me. Friday when I go to the law office, there will be people who want to talk to me about problems and who know that I will be available to them.

The job of representing the district on policy matters appears to be quite simple from his perspective.

I can't think of a time when I have voted contrary to what the district wants, because I vote the way they want me to. I am a *representative*—I represent my district. Partly this is because I am really typical of the district, and partly because if conflicts arose I would go along with the district. But I have never found such a conflict on issues when the constituents are well informed about them. I have never cast a vote different from what the district majority would cast if they were well informed about the issue.

How important is constituency service in your job?

About 98 percent of my job concerns casework. Mostly it is jobs that they want, sometimes food stamps or housing, but usually jobs. As long as you return the call or letter and try to do something, people will appreciate it, and it will help you politically. If I get a job for someone, sooner or later someone else in the family will call about a job. If you don't do constituency work, you don't help yourself. But if you do that work, you just create more work for yourself and the job gets too big to handle.

These legislators, like most I interviewed, come from districts that appear to be secure, but they attribute their success to hard work in the district. The Massachusetts member says, "I don't have to campaign at election time because I campaign seven days a week and twenty-four hours a day." They are conscious of the need to maintain contact with constituents, one relying heavily on press conferences, and the other stressing more informal, personal contacts. It would be difficult to stereotype either one as a delegate or a trustee in their responsiveness on policy issues, but the Ohio legislator seems to be more concerned about how to handle those constituents who disagree with him. The Ohio representative sees virtue in a heterogeneous district, while the Massachusetts member appears to enjoy a district that is homogeneous enough that he can typify its viewpoints. We will find both viewpoints common among legislators. The clearest difference between these two members concerns the priority they give to legislation or to casework.

Legislators are generally divided over this question of what aspect of their job, which component of representation, is more important.

The purpose of this study is to understand the meaning of representation in the context of American legislatures. The principal method is interviewing—some 220 members of the House in nine states. This means, of course, that representation will be defined from the perspective of the legislator, not the constituent. Although most of these interviews were carried out in the state capital, the focus of the interviews is not on the decision-making process in the legislature but on the legislator's district. The scope of my questions is well illustrated by the interviews that have beem summarized: perceptions of the district, techniques of communicating with constituents, policy responsiveness to the district, and serving the needs of groups and individuals in the district.

The study of representation in American state legislatures is a very large assignment. Ideally it would involve in-depth surveys and observations of 7,500 legislators in the legislatures and in their districts; even more ideally it would include surveys of their constituents. Although it is possible to use mail questionnaires to reach large numbers of members, I decided that the information needed for an understanding of representation could best be gained from personal interviews, and thus it was necessary to limit the study to a smaller number of states. The fact that I had an opportunity to travel for a number of months reinforced the decision to use personal interviews. The logistics of time and travel funds required that I conduct the interviews largely in state capitals and that I get information about district activities from interviews, rather than from personal observation, such as Fenno did in his study (1978). I conducted 221 interviews in nine states over a nine-month period from September 1978 to June 1979. The states were California, Massachusetts, Ohio, Colorado, Tennessee, North Carolina, Texas, Indiana, and Kentucky. The criteria used in selecting these states, and the methods used in conducting the interviews are summarized in the Appendix.

## The Research Setting: Nine State Legislatures

The goal of political scientists is to develop generalizations that are not limited to particular times and places. Most of what we know about legislative representation in the United States comes from studies of congressional representation. Within recent years the work of such scholars as Fenno (1978), Mayhew (1974), Fiorina (1974, 1977b), and Kingdon (1981) has significantly enhanced our understanding of congressional representation. We have learned more about how members evaluate input from constituents in making legislative decisions; we have become more aware of the multiple dimensions of representation and the growing importance of allocative and service functions; and we have discovered the importance of the congressman's "home style"—how he relates to his district.

This renaissance of interest in congressional representation has not been matched, however, by studies at the state or local level. Most recent research on state legislatures has been confined to a single state, and very little of it has dealt with representation or specifically tested the hypotheses being developed by students of congressional representation. (See Gove, Carlson, and Carlson, 1976; Hevesi, 1975; and Kirkpatrick, 1978.) At the local level there is one major study by Eulau and Prewitt (1973), a comparative analysis of eighty-two city councils in the San Francisco Bay area. Although the data for that study were collected in the mid-1960s, before most of the research we have mentioned on congressional representation, the authors are concerned with similar questions about representation.

One purpose of this study is to determine whether some of the recent findings about congressional representation are applicable to representation in state legislatures. There are several reasons why state legislatures provide excellent arenas for examining the process of representation. Perhaps the most obvious fact is that there are almost 7,500 members in the ninety-nine legislative bodies in American states. Although these legislatures are smaller and less professional than Congress, their organization, structure, and functions resemble those of Congress in many ways. If we are seeking to broaden our understanding of representation by looking beyond Congress, a study of state legislatures is the next logical step.

Despite their similarities to each other and their resemblance to Congress, state legislatures vary along a number of dimensions that provide us with a chance to better understand the variables affecting representation. States vary in the balance between legislative parties and in the strength of party cohesion; a number of them developed much closer two-party balance during the 1960s and 1970s. There are variations among the states in political culture and among legislative institutions in traditions and norms. Some legislatures are much more professional than others, with longer sessions, better staffs, and more nearly full-time members. The trend in recent years has been toward greater professionalism and also to enhanced resources and staffing for the state legislatures, but large variations remain from state to state.

These changes have had some interesting consequences for an

examination of representation. The state legislator today devotes more time to the job and has more staff assistance than was the case ten or fifteen years ago; at the same time the demands on him for legislative action and district and constituency service are much greater than in the past. In short, the job of being a representative is more complex and demanding than it used to be, and thus more interesting to study. And yet the state legislator's office has not yet become institutionalized, like that of a congressman. It is still possible, in studying a state legislator, to examine an individual. The state legislator has greater freedom to choose his role than a congressman, and that role is often still evolving. He is closer to his constituents and still lives among them much of the time; he has greater opportunities for firsthand contact and knowledge than most congressmen have.

A brief summary of the more important variations among state legislatures will provide some perspective for our study of representation. One of the most important dimensions along which states differ is the strength of two-party competition, although there has been a trend toward greater competition in many of the states. In our sample of nine states, Texas, North Carolina, Tennessee, and Kentucky are examples of state legislatures dominated by the Democratic party, although the Republican minority has been a significant force in all except Texas. All have had brief periods of Republican gubernatorial control during the last two decades. Democrats have dominated the legislature but not the governorship in Massachusetts. In California Democrats have held modest legislative majorities and the governorship has been closely contested. Indiana, Ohio, and Colorado are closely competitive states with Republican majorities most of the time, although Democrats in Ohio have benefited from a favorable districting plan they passed. (A table in the Appendix summarizes legislative and gubernatorial control in these states from 1961 through 1980.)

The closer the two-party competition, the greater the likelihood that party norms will be strong, but those norms vary even in states with strong competition. Party discipline is likely to be greater in states where each party represents a relatively homogeneous set of interests and where there are clear differences between the two sets. An obvious example is a state where the Democrats represent the major cities and the Republicans represent suburbs, small towns, and rural areas. (See Jewell and Patterson, 1977, pp. 381–88.)

In a state legislature with a strong norm of party regularity, the legislator must weigh this norm and the demands of his party's leaders against the interests of his district, if and when they conflict. He may find that the legislative party provides him some protection against the demands of single-issue groups in the district. There are also differences in impact of party norms on those in the majority party and in the minority party. A minority legislator may find it difficult to pass legislation or to gain benefits that will help the district—unless he is willing to make compromises or deals with the majority party.

There are a number of other norms that prevail in legislatures, which the freshman soon learns about. Some of them may have little to do with representing the district; an example would be a norm to discourage extensive participation in debate. Others may be more pertinent for representation. The new legislator must learn the norm of reciprocity; for example, he must be willing to go along with local legislation proposed by another member if he wants his own local bills to pass without difficulty. He learns how far he can go in trying to amend budget bills to help his district. He learns from other members how much importance they attach to constituency service, and how often he can miss meetings or sessions in the capitol to attend to appointments back in his district. In addition to learning norms, of course, he may learn some techniques for representing his district better: how to write a newsletter, where to get information about highway projects planned for the district, how to get the media to cover his activities. It is likely that many of the norms that are familiar in one legislature are common to most others, but there are also some significant differences. Local legislation is handled differently in different bodies, for example. It was my judgment, after evaluating constituency service in nine legislatures, that there was a much stronger consensus about the importance of such work in some legislatures than in others.

The state legislatures vary substantially in their level of professionalization: the length of sessions, frequency of turnover, salaries, the availability of staff and resources such as office space and free postage. As I explain in the Appendix, and illustrate in Table A.1, the nine states selected for this study were chosen to provide a range of legislatures from the more professional to the less. California, Massachusetts, and Ohio rank near the top; Colorado, Tennessee, and North Carolina are in the middle; Texas, Indiana, and Kentucky are among the least professionalized.

Perhaps the most important ingredient of professionalization is the length of the session. At one extreme are the legislatures that meet for several days a week during most of the year, with occasional breaks for election campaigns and vacations. At the other extreme are the legislatures that are restricted by the constitution to a regular session every two years that is limited to three months or less. In some of the latter states special sessions are frequent enough to guarantee an average of at least one session a year. Some of these states with restricted regular sessions make much use of interim committees. As a consequence of these trends there are few states where the legislators are totally inactive for twenty months out of twenty-four. Nevertheless, there are significant differences among the states in the amount of time devoted to legislative work and the demands made on legislators. During the four years from 1973 through 1976, seven states averaged fifteen to twenty-four months in regular sessions in a biennium, including Ohio, Massachusetts, and California. Twenty-four states averaged six to thirteen months in session, including Colorado, Tennessee, and North Carolina. Nineteen states averaged two to five and a half months in session, including Indiana, Texas, and Kentucky.

In those states where the legislature is in session for half or more of each year, a legislator's job is very nearly a full-time one since the demands of the constituency and the need to campaign every two years fill up most of the days when there is neither a legislative session nor a committee meeting. Most of the members whom I interviewed in California and Massachusetts were full-time legislators; in Ohio there was a continuing debate among legislators about whether the trend toward full-time service was inevitable and whether it was desirable. In most of the states, a conscientious legislator must devote at least half-time to this job.

Obviously the increase in numbers of the full-time legislators has some important implications for representation. Such legislators have a greater stake in being reelected. They have not only more time but a greater incentive to maintain constituency contacts, provide services, and build a political organization for the next election. They are more willing to vote for funds to provide more staff members, district offices, and postage for mass mailing of newsletters. We would expect a full-time legislator to be more inclined to seek and to win reelection and to develop more expertise in the legislature.

The length of legislative sessions has implications for representation beyond the trend toward full-time members. The longer the legislature is in session, the more visibility the member gains and the greater likelihood that constituent requests will be directed to him. In the legislatures that meet for a large portion of the year, the sessions usually run from Monday afternoon or evening until Thursday morning. Members then spend about half of each week in their districts attending meetings and dealing with local problems. This schedule makes them both visible and accessible through most of the year. In those states where there are relatively short sessions of three or four months every year or every other year, the legislative sessions are likely to be busier and to become frantic during the closing weeks. Members must spend most of the week in the capital, leaving little time for contacts in the district. The members can devote the remaining eight or nine months of the year to their districts, but since their visibility decreases, they may have fewer opportunities than they would like to meet with groups in the district. This is becoming less of a problem as the job of the legislator expands, even in states with brief sessions, but it remains true that the schedule of sessions has a major impact on how legislators represent their districts.

How a legislator represents his district depends to a large extent on the resources at his disposal. Obviously the legislators can make a collective decision to increase these resources, but the single legislator is limited by the services that are provided unless he is prepared to pay for them himself or unless he can borrow staff or office space from his business. However eager he may be to maintain communications with his district, the legislator with a large number of constituents cannot answer many letters without a secretary and cannot send out many newsletters with the postal frank. The legislator with professional staff members can deal more effectively with constituency service requests, especially if he can afford to locate staff members in a district office. The legislator with several staff members can also be more active in the legislative arena: using staff to attend committee hearings and meetings back in the district, to provide research on bills, and to publicize the legislator's record on issues with press releases and letters to interested groups.

Among the states that I surveyed, California legislators have by far the largest staff and the most benefits. Their offices in Sacramento resemble congressional offices, crowded with secretaries and professional staff; in addition, they have district offices. It should be noted that the Assembly districts in California have half the population of congressional districts. Despite the relative brevity of its sessions, the Texas legislature provides enough funds to members so that they can hire professional as well as secretarial staff and it authorizes district offices; members often move some staff from the capitol to the district when the session ends.

Massachusetts and Ohio are examples of states that provide minimum staff resources to individual members even though they have long sessions and heavy workloads. Massachusetts legislators were assigned one professional staff member apiece for the first time in 1979; an Ohio House member has only a secretary. Colorado is another example of a state with relatively long sessions that provides no individual professional staff and in fact provides only a secretarial pool. Colorado legislators only recently were given office space—about the size that might be assigned to a graduate student at a university. Tennessee and North Carolina provide modern office space and secretarial help, but nothing more, to the average member. Kentucy and Indiana, with their relatively short sessions, provide individual members with no professional staff and with a bare minimum of accommodations.

As we describe how legislators handle their job, particularly how they maintain contacts with and perform services for their constituents, we should keep in mind the large disparities in the resources allocated for this purpose in the various states. In a few states the job of the legislator has become institutionalized, somewhat like that of a congressman; in most states the job is very much a one-person operation.

### The Meaning of Representation

A starting point for a study of representation in the American states ought to be a review of the classic literature on representation to understand the term and to perceive the major theoretical controversies surrounding the representative function. Much of the literature on representation in the past, however, does not seem pertinent to the complex processes of representation that exist in modern society. Heinz Eulau (1978, p. 31) has asserted that "in spite of many centuries of theoretical effort, we cannot say what representation is"; "our conceptions of representation are obsolete." He argues that we have viewed representation in the terms defined by Edmund Burke but that the character and problems of representation have changed since Burke's time. We have subjected Burke's theories to empirical testing and found them lacking. "On the other hand, because we have not really addressed ourselves to problematical situations in our current reality, we have been unable to come up with relevant knowledge as to what representation means in our time" (p. 49).

The most thorough and thoughtful recent study of this topic is Hanna Pitkin's *Concept of Representation* (1967). She shares the view that the classic definitions and discussions of representation are of limited value today because each provides only a partial picture of representation. She criticizes two "formalistic" views of representation: the concept of "authorization," derived from Thomas Hobbes, and the diametrically opposed but equally formalistic concept of "accountability." She argues that both approaches are of limited utility because "neither can tell us anything about what goes on *during* representation, how a representative ought to act or what he is expected to do, how to tell whether he has represented well or badly" (p. 58). Pitkin discusses the idea of "descriptive representation"—that representatives should as nearly as possible be a cross-section of the citizenry. In reality, of course, legislators tend to be better educated, more predominantly male, and more middle aged than the majority of their constituents; and there is no consensus about which characteristics should be accurately represented in the legislature, nor which, if any, are good predictors of behavior. Pitkin points out that descriptive representation leaves a number of questions unanswered, including that of how representatives should actually act and how they should be held accountable. She also criticizes as incomplete the idea of "symbolic representation" and its concern with whether constituents feel that they are represented.

The focus of Pitkin's study is on representation as a form of activity, and on the behavioral norms concerning how a legislator should represent his constituents. She reviews the controversy associated with Burke that has for so long dominated debates on representation: "Should (must) a representative do what his constituents want, and be bound by mandates or instructions from them; or should (must) he be free to act as seems best to him in pursuit of their welfare?" (p. 145) After a brief review of the conflicting views that have been expressed on this controversy, Pitkins suggests, "What is most striking about the mandate-independence controversy is how long it has continued without coming any nearer to a solution, despite the participation of many astute thinkers" (p. 148). She argues that the conflict has remained unsolved because in a sense both sides are right, and if either position is advanced to its logical conclusion, the result is not actually representation. "The seemingly paradoxical meaning of representation is perpetuated in our requirements for the activity of representing: the represented must be both present and not present. The representative must really act, be independent; yet the represented must be in some sense acting through him. Hence there must be no serious persistent conflict between them" (p. 154).

Pitkin suggests that this principle of representation establishes certain ground rules for defining what types of activity can properly be described as representation: 1) the representative must be able to act with independence; 2) he must act in the interests of constituents and normally in accord with their wishes; 3) if he acts contrary to their wishes, he must be prepared to explain why (pp. 164-66). Within this broad framework, as she points out, "there is room for a variety of views as to what a good representative should and should not do" (p. 166). Representatives may differ in the efforts they make to determine what constituents think, in the importance they attach to organized ex-

pressions of opinion from small groups of constituents, in the importance they attach (and the methods used) to explaining their record to
constituents. Representatives may also differ in the answers they give
to questions from political scientists about their representative role, but
(if Pitkin is correct) behavior that follows a pattern of either total independence or total dependence on constituents falls outside the boundaries of true representation.

The debate over the independence of representatives is of marginal
utility for an understanding of representation not only because it poses
an unrealistic dilemma but because it is so simplistic. It focuses our attention on one small part of the complex responsibilities that modern
representatives face. When Eulau (1978, pp. 49-50) says that we have
not addressed ourselves to modern realities, he is talking about the
complexities of the modern political process:

The circumstances of modern government are such that neither responsibility
nor responsiveness can be assured through the technique of representation. Despite all the oratory of the politicians, they cannot possibly be responsive, in the
traditional sense, to individual constituents whose numbers are in the hundreds
of thousands or millions, whose interests are enormously diverse, and whose
understanding of the complexities of public policy is minimal. At the same
time, and for very much the same reasons, it is increasingly impossible to hold
the representative responsible for his decisions. As we observe the electoral process, still considered the main technique to enforce responsibility, it is evident
that the electorate is chiefly guided by rather vague and often confused moods
about the drift of public policy in general rather than by a clear perception as
to whether the individual representative has acted responsibly or not within his
discretionary capabilities.

John Wahlke (1978, pp. 74-75) has argued forcefully that our concept of representation, focused on what he describes as a "simple
demand-input model," is almost entirely inconsistent with what we
know about the behavior of citizens. His description of the empirical
realities undermining this model is vivid enough that it deserves to be
quoted in full:

1. Few citizens entertain interests that clearly represent "policy demands" or "policy expectations," or wishes and desires that are readily convert-
ible into them.
2. Few people have thought-out, consistent, and firmly held positions on
most matters of public policy.
3. It is highly doubtful that policy demands are entertained even in the
form of broad orientations, outlooks, or belief systems.
4. Large proportions of citizens lack the instrumental knowledge about

political structures, processes, and actors that they would need to communicate policy demands or expectations if they had any.

5. Relatively few citizens communicate with their representatives.

6. Citizens are not especially interested or informed about the policy making activities of their representatives as such.

7. Nor are citizens much interested in other day-to-day aspects of parliamentary functioning.

8. Relatively few citizens have any clear notion that they are making policy demands or policy choices when they vote.

It may be useful to spell out more specifically some of the basic reasons why the modern representative finds it difficult to act "in the interest of the represented, in a manner responsive to them," in Pitkin's words (1967, p. 209).

1) In many state legislative districts and all congressional and senatorial districts there are large numbers of constituents.

2) In most districts the constituents' interests are diverse and perhaps contradictory. When constituents have conflicting interests or when they are sharply divided in viewpoint, it is impossible to act in the interest of, or to be responsive to, all of them. The larger and more diverse the district, the more frequently a legislator will face this dilemma.

3) In Pitkin's words (1967, p. 220), "the representative knows of the voters' ignorance and apathy and irrationality, the diversity of their views and interests. Further, he seldom has access to accurate information about what views and interests they do have." Most voters have little interest in most issues, and when they do voice their opinions, they may display little accurate information about the topic.

4) Most of the policy demands on legislators come from organized groups; often they represent relatively small numbers of constituents, and their views may be in conflict with those of the vast majority of constituents—or at least the views that vast majority would express if they became aware of the issue. Should the legislator respond to the articulated demands of the few or the views that he believes a much larger number probably hold?

5) On some issues the legislator has much greater knowledge than most constituents or even organized groups in his district; on some issues he disagrees with the majority views expressed in his district. Under these circumstances, given the facts outlined above, legislators find it tempting to follow their own judgment.

6) On many issues, the interests and demands of constituents are so weak and unclear that they are overshadowed by those forces in the legislative environment that are much closer, more demanding, and

better informed: fellow legislators, members of committees, legislative party leaders, the chief executive, experts in administrative agencies, and lobbyists. If the legislator chooses to follow the lead or take the advice of one or more of these cue-givers, he is not necessarily ignoring or betraying the interests of his constituents. He may accurately perceive that the issue does not affect his constituents, or does so only marginally. He is likely to turn for advice to legislators who represent districts similar to hs or to other cue-givers who share his general philosophy. Moreover, by agreeing to vote for certain positions on issues of little interest to his district, he may gain a bargaining advantage that can be used when another issue arises that is of greater interest to this district.

We can also be more specific in describing the weaknesses in the electoral system that Eulau asserts have undermined the concept of responsibility. Some of these weaknesses may be long-standing ones, but political scientists have become more aware of them since the development of survey research on elections.

1) Sometimes voters cannot hold the incumbent responsible because he does not run again; when he runs he may have no serious opposition in the primary election, and the outcome of the general election may be largely determined by traditional party patterns of allegiance in the district.

2) Voters often make choices based on party loyalty or the personality of the candidates rather than the issues.

3) Voters are often poorly informed about issues and are rarely well informed about the voting record of incumbents. The campaigns of the incumbent and his opponents often fail to clarify the issues, inform the voters, and enhance their opportunity to hold the incumbent responsible for his record.

If the "simple demand-input model" of representation is unrealistic, and if representation in our complex society can assure "neither responsibility nor responsiveness," it is tempting to conclude that a study of how legislators represent their constituents is a waste of time. Wahlke (1978, pp. 81-89) has concluded that it is more productive to shift our attention from the demands of constituents to their support for the system as the key to understanding representative democracy. My own efforts to grapple with the concept of support and to operationalize it in empirical studies have made me less sanguine about its utility.

Pitkin (1967, pp. 221-22) has suggested that it may be helpful to shift the level of analysis of representation from the individual to the institution:

But perhaps it is a mistake to approach political representation too directly from the various individual-representation analogies—agent and trustee and deputy. . . . Perhaps when we conventionally speak of representation, representative government, and the like, we do not mean or require that the representative stand in the kind of one-to-one, person-to-person relationship to his constituency or to each constituent in which a private representative stands to his principal. . . .

Political representation is primarily a public, institutionalized arrangement involving many people and groups, and operating in the complex ways of large-scale social arrangements. What makes it representation is not any single action by any one participant, but the over-all structure and functioning of the system, the patterns emerging from the multiple activities of many people.

I would agree with Pitkin on the importance of institutional representation, for a number of reasons. The institution is more durable and stable than the individual legislators. If a legislative institution can be accurately described as representative, an individual citizen may be thought of as benefiting from virtual or collective representation, even though his own representative is ineffective or unresponsive. Weissberg (1978) has suggested that citizens are probably better represented by legislative bodies in a collective sense than they are by their elected legislator and has argued that electoral control of a legislator is not a prerequisite for representation. In fact, he says, it is likely that the legislator whose views are closest to that of a citizen is not the one who represents his district.

If the legislative institution is characterized by representation, the norms of that body may influence the role perceptions and behavior of its members, however unresponsive they may have been when first elected. The concept of representation as an institutional characteristic is an important one, and empirical efforts to measure legislatures according to their representative character are clearly worthwhile. Note, for example, the efforts by the Citizens Conference on State Legislatures (1971) to evaluate the fifty state legislatures in terms of how representative each was, among other criteria. A more scholarly example is the study by Eulau and Prewitt (1973) of the representative character of eighty-two city councils, which is based explicitly on Pitkin's proposal that representation be studied as an institutional phenomenon.

A recognition of the utility of studying representation as a characteristic of the institution need not lead us to abandon the effort to understand representation as it is practiced by individual legislators. That is the central focus of this study: the legislator's perspective on representation. How does the legislator define his constituency and represent his constituents? Is representation affected by differences in the experience and attitudes of legislators, the types of districts they represent, or the legislative institutions that they belong to?

Although many issues are not salient to constituents, we want to know what types of issues are perceived by legislators as being salient to their constituents, or to significant numbers of them. Although it is often difficult for legislators to judge constituent opinion, we want to know what efforts they make and how successful they think they are in making these judgments. Do they perceive constituent interests and demands to be as diverse and contradictory in fact as they would seem to be on paper? Under what conditions do they believe that issues become salient during election campaigns? What kinds of choices do they have to make on policy issues, and how do they make these choices? What kinds of needs and demands arise in their districts in addition to legislative issues, and how much priority do they give to dealing with these kinds of problems?

Modern legislative representation is more complicated than the simple demand-input model would suggest, and the choices faced by legislators are much more complicated than the simple choice between being delegates or trustees. Representation is made more difficult by both the fact that constituent opinion is unformed or unclear on some issues and that it is conflictual on others. These realities of the modern political process make representation difficult; they do not make it impossible. The job of being an effective representative is a demanding one, requiring time and effort, judgment, and skill in communications and in political negotiations. Political circumstances, such as the character of the district, make it much more difficult for some legislators than for others. After talking to more than two hundred legislators, I am convinced that many of them have become skilled at the job, some have found ways of minimizing or at least controlling the difficulties inherent in it, and most of them believe that they are representing their constituents effectively.

The fact that representation has become a complex process does not make it either useless or impossible to study. I would argue that these trends make it more important and more fascinating to study. There may be little point in classifying legislators as delegates and trustees or counting the number in each category. But it is still important to understand how they make choices when conflicts arise on policy questions. If previous approaches to the study of representation have exaggerated the extent of policy inputs from constituents, we can try not only to describe policy inputs in more realistic terms but also to determine what other kinds of demands are made on legislators.

We must begin with a clear understanding of what we mean by representation, and like most writers I will accept as a starting point the definition used by Hanna Pitkin (1967, pp. 209-10):

Representing here means acting in the interest of the represented, in a manner responsive to them. The representative must act independently; his action must involve discretion and judgment; he must be the one who acts. The represented must also be (conceived as) capable of independent action and judgment, not merely being taken care of. And, despite the resulting potential for conflict between representative and represented about what is to be done, that conflict must not normally take place. The representative must act in such a way that there is no conflict, or if it occurs an explanation is called for. He must not be found persistently at odds with the wishes of the represented without good reason in terms of their interest, without a good explanation of why their wishes are not in accord with their interest.

We must also recognize the point made by Heinz Eulau (1978, p. 50) that "the core problem involved in representation is the relationship that exists between representative and represented." He suggests (pp. 50-51) that we must therefore pay attention to the question of status and recognize that there are differences between the status of the representative and the represented. From this it follows, according to Eulau (p. 69), that—in order to be responsive—legislators do not simply have to react to the demands of constituents. In other words, to study representation it is not enough to find out whether legislators vote in accord with the wishes of constituents (a question that is very difficult to answer empirically). It is more important to determine *how* legislators respond to constituents. The study of representation involves the study of how legislators measure and evaluate constituent wishes; how they become familiar with the needs and interests of the constituency; how they weigh conflicting demands and interests, some of which are articulated much more strongly than others; and how they explain their decisions to constituents.

One other point needs to be made about the way representation is defined in this study. Eulau and Prewitt (1973, p. 426), in their study of city councils, define representativeness as a characteristic of "the relationship between the council and the community when the former governs in a manner responsive to the expressed interests of the latter." By limiting their definition to situations where the interests of the community are "expressed," they deviate from Pitkin's definition of representation. They acknowledge this difference, but assert that their definition "is more viable in empirical research with the data at hand" (p. 426). For our purposes, however, it is essential to stick with Pitkin's definition. We are interested in how representatives respond to both the articulated demands and the unarticulated interests of their constituents. The reality faced by the legislator is that the needs and interests of constituents are often not articulated clearly as demands. One of his major tasks is to determine what these interests are and what his constituents think. And one of his most important responsibilities is to weigh the often loudly articulated demands of a few against the unarticulated wishes of the many, to determine if these involve a conflict and to decide what choices to make if there is a conflict.

## The Components of Representation

This study is organized around four major components of representation: communications with constituents, policy responsiveness, the allocation of resources for the district, and service to constituents. I shall define what is meant by each of these and why each is an important component of representation, that is, the relationship between the representative and the represented.

Communication is not usually described as a component of representation; others might consider it to be a prerequisite for, or a technique of, representation. I believe that we can arrive at a better understanding and evaluation of representation if we incorporate communication as an essential part of the process. One of the most common demands made by constituents is that their representatives be accessible, that they stay in touch. For the legislator to find out and evaluate what his constituents are demanding, he must develop an effective system of communications. To explain to constituents what he has done, and why, he must also develop a communication system. I would suggest that the communication component of representation has at least three aspects:

1) The legislator must be accessible to constituents. He must spend time in the district, answer his mail and phone calls, and use his staff to maintain contact when he cannot do it personally. He must publicize his accessibility—visits to the district, office hours, phone numbers. If the legislator is inaccessible or constituents do not know how to contact him, they are less likely to make their views known or to bring their problems to him.

2) The legislator must actively seek to learn about the needs and

views of his constituents. This would include becoming familiar with the district and its needs and problems: roads in disrepair, inadequate housing, unemployment, racial tensions, for example. It would include becoming familiar with groups in the district and their leaders, attending meetings, developing contacts, so that he can learn and evaluate their demands. The member must read his mail, listen to the phone calls, read the newspapers. He may go beyond this and actively solicit views by polling groups and individuals either formally or informally.

3) The legislator must exercise leadership, educating his constituents and explaining his activities. The legislator explains the problems confronting the state and district and describes bills that are pending in the legislature. He explains his actions and votes on issues. He informs groups and individuals about governmental programs that might be useful to them. He does these things in newsletters, or radio and television appearances, or speeches to groups and one-on-one contacts with constituents.

The techniques will vary from member to member, and one of our purposes in this study is to determine what techniques are used and with what effectiveness. It is important to remember that communication is a two-way process. It is equally important for representation that legislators be accessible and listen to constituents, and that they explain their views and actions to them.

The next three components of representation are the familiar ones outlined by Eulau and Karps (1978, pp. 62-66). Although the lines between them are not always sharply drawn, the distinctions are generally useful. Policy responsiveness pertains to the making of public policy and the views espoused and activities undertaken by the legislator on legislation, the appropriation of funds, and (in some cases) the oversight of the executive. This is the central focus of most studies of legislatures, as well as the focus of the classic literature on representation.

A starting point for the study of policy is to determine what types of issues affect the district or lead to demands from constituents. I will examine constituency demands as they are perceived by legislators and then analyze differences in both the focus and the style of representation to provide a realistic picture of how legislators make choices. I will seek to determine what factors affect variations in the way legislators represent their districts on policy matters. Throughout this analysis, I will attempt to compare the findings from my survey of state legislators with the theories and empirical findings of other studies.

Allocation responsiveness concerns the legislator's efforts to gain governmental goods and services for his district. These are general rather than individual benefits, but they frequently benefit one part of the district or one group more than others. Examples might be a traffic light or a park or better police protection in some neighborhood. For the most part, we would expect that benefits for groups or areas in the district will not be controversial or cause conflicts among constituents (except conflicts over priorities in the allocation of resources). There may be occasions when this is not true, and when the legislator risks losses as well as gains from getting resources for his district. (For example, a new state facility—such as a vocational education center— might stir opposition from those in the neighborhood where it would be located.) For the most part, however, legislators do not run the risks in gaining resources for their district that they often run when voting on legislation. State legislators are often asked to help get resources from local government or even the national government.

Service responsiveness pertains to the needs of individuals or groups. They often want help in dealing with governmental agencies: assistance in finding the right agency, faster decisions from bureaucrats, exception to rules, special benefits, or jobs with government. Businessmen need help in dealing with agencies and may also want advice on how to do business and get contracts with government. State legislators are often asked to provide help in dealing with either local or national agencies. Not infrequently legislators are asked to help constituents who are having trouble with private business or individuals: the landlord who will not repair a building, the utility that has turned off the gas or electricity, or the repairman who has done a poor job. Legislators are even asked to intervene in personal and family disputes. Legislators differ in the importance they attach and the amount of time they spend on these types of activities, and I am interested in explaining these variations.

Eulau and Karps (1978, pp. 66-67) identified one other component of representation, called symbolic responsiveness, which they described as more psychological than behavioral. They relate this concept not only to the question of public support but also to the legislator's home style (in Fenno's terms)—how he behaves in the constituency to generate trust and support. I would argue that the way in which a legislator behaves in his district—described by Fenno (1978), for example—is one aspect of the communication component of representation, described above. The question of whether such activities are successful in generating trust and support is a much more difficult one—and I do not have any data on the attitudes of constituents in the districts represented by the legislators whom I interviewed. The final chapter of this study does, however, deal with this question by trying to evaluate what constituents expect from their legislators and how well the latter are perceived to be fulfilling these expectations.

## Outline of Study

The purpose of this study is not only to describe the various ways in which American state legislators represent their constituents but also to explain as fully as possible the variations in their approaches to representation. Throughout the study we will be looking for three broad sources of variation based on the characteristics of individual legislators, the nature of districts, and differences among the states.

The pertinent characteristics of individual legislators include their background, experience, goals, and attitudes. Anyone who interviews legislators about their work soon learns that their perceptions and the choices that they make are highly individualistic, reflecting differences in personality and experience. Legislators cannot be easily or accurately stereotyped, and explanations of their behavior as representatives must take into account these individual characteristics.

The important characteristics of the district include its electoral structure, heterogeneity or homogeneity, socioeconomic and geographic character, the political nature of the district, and the electoral experience of the legislator. There is tremendous variety among the states, and within them, in these characteristics. Differences in the size and geographic character of a district obviously determine which techniques of communication are feasible. Differences in the level of homogeneity and in electoral margins affect constituent demands and member responsiveness in policy matters.

The third category of variables pertains to differences among the states in the political and legislative system. The political culture in a state may shape constituent expectations of legislators, regarding service responsiveness for example. The length of legislative sessions, the availability of resources for members, and the norms of a particular legislature all affect how legislators spend their time in the capital and in the district, and the priorities that they assign to various aspects of representation.

In Chapter 2 I will describe the electoral environment in which legislators operate, including the nature of campaigns and the level of competition in primaries and elections, and will try to show the implications this has for representation. In Chapter 3 I will describe the varied methods of communication legislators employ, noting in particular how these are affected by district characteristics. Chapters 4 and 5 deal with the second component of representation, policy responsiveness, considering which issues are salient to constituents, how demands are organized and perceived by the legislator, and how the legislator makes choices on policy questions. Chapter 6 includes the components of allocation and service responsiveness, concentrating on the reasons why legislators vary in the priority they assign to the service role. Chapter 7 concerns public perspectives on representation. I will also seek to draw conclusions from the study of representation for our understanding of the modern state legislature.

# 2. Legislative Elections

Every two years several thousand primary and general elections are held to fill seats in the state legislature. From the viewpoint of the voter, they are overshadowed by presidential, gubernatorial, and congressional races and often by other contests at the local level. From the viewpoint of political scientists, they are equally obscure. With few exceptions, we lack both comprehensive statistical analyses and detailed case studies, and we also lack survey data on voting behavior in state legislative contests. Most legislative districts are smaller and more homogeneous than congressional districts. This should make legislative races less competitive, lower keyed, and less expensive; it should also make legislative candidates less visible except in districts small enough that voters are likely to know them personally. These assumptions remain largely untested because of the shortage of research. One other characteristic of legislative districts—the wide variation in their size and character—should make us cautious about generalizing from a few examples.

The study of legislative elections is pertinent to a study of representation for several reasons. There is a widespread assumption that there is some relationship between the size of electoral margins (and the frequency of defeat for incumbents) and the representational behavior of legislators. It is probably too simple to assume that legislators elected by narrow margins are more sensitive to constituent opinion than those from safe districts. But it is clear from interviewing legislators that they are highly conscious of their electoral environment and that this awareness permeates the process of representation.

David Mayhew (1974, pp. 13-19) has argued that the best way to understand Congress is to assume that congressmen are "single-mindedly interested in reelection" to the exclusion of all other goals. One may have doubts about whether that is either a useful analytical assumption or an accurate description of reality. But state legislators are very articulate in interviews about electoral matters. They usually know (or think they know) the dimensions of their political environment. Whenever they make decisions about allocating their time and their staff resources, maintaining contacts and lines of communications, and making choices between groups with conflicting political demands, they do so with an awareness of—and particular expectations about—the political benefits, costs, and sometimes the uncertain consequences of those actions.

If the political environment of state legislators is so important to them and has such an impact on representation, it should be possible to describe at least the outlines of that environment. I will begin by making a distinction between single-member and multimember districts. In 1979 twenty-nine states elected all members of the lower house from single-member districts, eight states elected all from multimember districts, and thirteen states used a combination of the two. Several of the states had multimember districts with as many as ten to thirteen members each, normally in the largest metropolitan counties (Council of State Governments, 1980, p. 87). This study includes only two states— North Carolina and Indiana—using multimember districts. In North Carolina no metropolitan county is divided into legislative districts; members are elected at-large with as many as eight members from a district. In Indiana, Marion County (Indianapolis) is divided into five three-member districts, and a number of other urban counties use one or more districts with three or two members. Districting patterns can be expected to affect the campaign techniques used—and therefore the cost of campaigning for office. Districting patterns may also affect the degree of competition in legislative elections and the likelihood of success for the incumbent.

The first question to ask about legislative elections concerns the rate of turnover and its causes in the legislature. Where incumbents are frequently defeated, we might expect to find legislators being forced to pay greater attention to their constituents—to be more responsive in terms of communications, policy, and service; alternatively, the frequent defeat of incumbents might be a sign that legislators were failing to be responsive.

The second question to ask is how legislative candidates campaign for office. To what extent are legislative candidates dependent on assistance from political parties or other organized groups for campaign assistance—endorsements, manpower, funds? The greater their dependence, in either the primary or the general election, the more attention they must pay to these groups in the process of representation.

The third question concerns the frequency and closeness of competition in primaries and general elections. From the perspective of the legislator, a pattern of close competition in the district means that the next election is likely to be close, and this may suggest the need to devote more time and resources to the district and more attention to policy issues that may be salient to voters. A low level of competition suggests that voters may seldom have meaningful choices among legislative candidates, that incumbents may be almost unbeatable, and that the legislature as a whole may not be particularly responsive to changes in public preferences.

Information on incumbency and competition is based on data collected for three or four elections (beginning in 1972 or 1974 and concluding in 1978) for eight of the states in this study.[1] Because of the special characteristics of individual elections (such as the 1974 Democratic landslide), we can get a more accurate picture of competition by examining more than a single election year. In some states the 1972 election (in California, 1974) was excluded because the reapportionment preceding that election obscured the effects of incumbency. Electoral data are not presented on Massachusetts because the size of the House was cut from 240 to 160 before the 1978 elections, making them atypical because there was a surplus of incumbents. (In a few cases data are not available, including primary election data in North Carolina and Republican primary data in Texas.)

### Turnover of Incumbents

One of the most significant recent trends in American legislatures is the declining rate of turnover. The average proportion of freshmen legislators in the lower houses of the fifty states has declined from 44.8 percent in the 1950s to 37.3 percent in the 1971-1976 period; comparable figures for senates are 40.2 and 32.3 percent (Shin and Jackson, 1979, pp. 97-99). There are substantial differences among the states, and the longitudinal data clearly show a decline in turnover in recent years for nearly all the states (except those that already had low turnover), but we do not have comparable longitudinal data on the proportion serving relatively long terms—more than ten years, for example.

The nine states in our study were chosen to have a range in professionalism, one measure of which was turnover. In the 1971-1976 period (and generally in the 1960s), California, Massachusetts, and Ohio were low in turnover; Colorado, Tennessee, and Texas, medium; and North Carolina, Indiana, and Kentucky, slightly higher. In the sessions during which the interviews took place (as shown in Table 1), Massachusetts and Ohio had even lower proportions of freshmen than in the past, and both states had substantially higher proportions of long-term members (more than five terms) than did the other states. The reduction in the size of the Massachusetts House, of course, contributed to the small numbers of freshmen in the 1979 session. In the 1976 Ohio

TABLE 1. Distribution of All House Members According to Number of Terms
Served (including present term; percentage)

| State | Year | \multicolumn{7}{c}{Number of Terms Served} | % Freshmen Members | |
|-------|------|----|----|----|----|----|----|-------|---------|---------|
| | | 1 | 2 | 3 | 4 | 5 | 6 | 1 & 2 | 1971–76 | 1961–70 |
| CA | 1979 | 29 | 23 | 19 | 10 | 5 | 15 | 51 | 24 | 25 |
| MA | 1979 | 14 | 19 | 21 | 10 | 9 | 27 | 33 | 26 | 25 |
| OH | 1978 | 9 | 22 | 25 | 12 | 9 | 22 | 31 | 27 | 35 |
| CO | 1979 | 35 | 20 | 15 | 12 | 5 | 12 | 55 | 38 | 46 |
| TN | 1979 | 23 | 20 | 14 | 14 | 15 | 13 | 43 | 38 | 55 |
| NC | 1979 | 30 | 21 | 21 | 10 | 6 | 13 | 51 | 41 | 44 |
| TX | 1979 | 17 | 27 | 17 | 23 | 4 | 13 | 44 | 33 | 35 |
| IN | 1979 | 20 | 14 | 22 | 19 | 11 | 14 | 34 | 41 | 53 |
| KY | 1978 | 27 | 19 | 21 | 10 | 9 | 14 | 46 | 41 | 51 |

## Summary of Fate of Incumbents in Elections in Eight States*

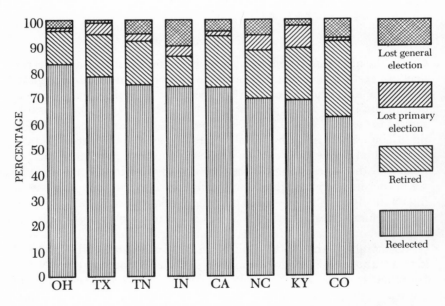

*The following election years are included: Ohio: 1974-78, Texas: 1974-78, Tennessee:
1974-78, Indiana: 1974-78, California: 1972-78, North Carolina: 1974-78, Kentucky:
1973-77, Colorado: 1972-78.

elections the proportions of incumbent defeats and retirements were both unusually low. California, by contrast, shows an increase in the proportion of freshmen. Except for Colorado, which remains stable, the states that have had medium or higher rates of turnover had substantially lower turnover in the 1978 election (1977 in Kentucky) than in the recent past. Kentucky and Tennessee have both had a steady decline in turnover since the 1960s and during the 1970s; the low turnover in the 1977 and 1978 elections was due to fewer retirements and in Tennessee fewer defeats than usual. The decline in turnover in Texas is very recent; the drop in turnover in Indiana is more gradual.

The figure (page 26) summarizes the basic information about the electoral fate of incumbents in the eight states (excluding Massachusetts) over a period of several elections. The rates of turnover shown in the figure for the eight states are generally lower than the 1971-1976 figures shown in Table 1 because the figures include 1978, when turnover rates were unusually low in several states, and excludes for most states the 1972 election, in which reapportionment led to higher turnover than usual.

It is clear from the figure that in most of the states retirement is a more common cause of turnover than is defeat at the polls. The proportion of legislators retiring is lowest in Ohio and Indiana, states with strong party systems; it is highest in Colorado. The proportion of incumbents who get beaten in party primaries is very low. In Ohio and Colorado the extremely low level of primary defeats can be explained by strong party organizations and informal or formal party endorsements in primaries, which lead to a very low level of primary competition. The reasons for few primary defeats are less obvious in other states such as California, with a weak party system. We would expect more primary competition and more defeats of incumbents in primaries of southern states, where there is less two-party competition. Primary defeats are slightly higher in Kentucky and North Carolina (8 and 6 percent), but in Tennessee and Texas they are not much more frequent than in stronger two-party states.

Incumbent defeats in general elections are usually not more than 5 percent (a slightly higher percentage of those who seek reelection). The few exceptions can usually be explained by particular circumstances. The Republican party in North Carolina suffered a major defeat in 1974 when a Republican governor was swept out of office and the Republican membership in the House was cut from thirty-five to nine. Most of the defeats of Republican incumbents in Indiana occurred in the same year. If we look at the combined effects of primary and general election losses, they are highest in Indiana, North Carolina, and

Kentucky during this period. Except in Indiana, however, it remains true that a majority and usually at least two-thirds, of the incumbents who do not return, retire. Some of the retirees, of course, run for other offices.

One obvious conclusion to draw from this summary is that the chances of electoral defeat for most incumbents are not large. To understand the consequences of that for representation, we need to know more about the reasons why incumbents usually are reelected. It may be because they are relatively insulated from national political trends. In many cases success in general elections can be attributed to lopsided partisan margins in the district. It may be because legislative incumbents have substantial advantages in the campaign or seldom face strong challengers.

## Primary Elections

*Campaigning.* It is difficult to generalize about election campaigns because they vary along a number of dimensions. House candidates who campaign in Kentucky have less than 35,000 constituents, while Assembly candidates in California have over a quarter of a million persons to contact. Organizing a campaign in a compact urban district is much different from organizing one in a rural district that sprawls over several counties. Moreover, in the multimember districts of North Carolina a candidate must campaign in an entire county (including metropolitan counties); the situation is similar in Indiana, though the multimember districts are smaller and not usually countywide. Campaign tactics may also be affected by traditional practices, or by the tactics of opponents. If other candidates campaign door to door, or rent a number of billboards, or advertise in a local newspaper, an individual may have to follow the same practice.

In most of the states more than half of the incumbents face no opposition at all in the primaries (the data for each state are in Table 2). Legislative incumbents are seldom seriously challenged and rarely beaten in the primary, but these statistics do not produce the sense of security that we might expect. Even legislators who seldom have opposition are acutely conscious of the possibility of being challenged; they watch closely for signs that potential opponents are planning to run. One veteran legislator in Kentucky told me that if you are elected once or twice without opposition you not only run the risk of getting lazy but you may soon have opponents because your electoral strength has not recently been tested. Most successful legislators campaign hard, no matter how weak the opposition, because they believe that a large electoral margin is the best way to discourage strong opponents in the future.

Most legislators run on their own in primary elections. They build their own organizations, often relatively small ones, and raise their own funds. They spend a great deal of time in personal campaigning, going door to door if the size and geography of the district make that possible. Many of them won their first election by door-to-door campaigning, and they are convinced that this is the most effective way to maintain contacts and visibility. They find that constituents are impressed if their legislator takes the time to make "house calls," even after he is elected. Some legislators have found it particularly effective to visit the precincts between election campaigns.

Precinct visits between elections are part of a broader strategy: using all the resources of office to build a political base. Incumbent legislators frequently receive invitations to speak to groups; they are asked by groups and individuals to perform services; they can publicize their activities in newsletters, press releases, and speeches. The campaign for renomination and reelection does not begin on the filing date. The campaign never stops. Every aspect of a legislator's activities can contribute to his reelection, and the legislator who does his job most effectively is least likely to find that he has strong opposition in the primary or the general election.

Although legislators often believe that strong primary opposition is a sign that they are doing something wrong, several other factors may make primary competition likely. In some multicounty rural districts it is difficult even for an incumbent to build a political base outside his own county, and challenges are likely to come from other counties in the district. Primary voting patterns in such districts, particularly when there is no incumbent, are likely to follow county lines, and the winner may be the candidate from the largest county, or the only candidate from one county to run against multiple candidates from other counties. In urban districts that are racially mixed, a white incumbent is likely to have a black opponent in the primary, or a black incumbent may have a white opponent. Several white legislators mentioned the problems they face in districts where the racial balance is shifting from white to black; black political leaders are becoming less willing to support a white incumbent.

Primary campaigns are not often focused on issues. Incumbents try to build an image of being competent and accessible and serving their constituents. Challengers try to prove that they will work harder and be more accessible; they try to campaign harder and ring more doorbells, attempting to prove that they can do more for the district. Occasionally a challenger will attack the incumbent's vote on abortion, capital punishment, or some other emotional issue, but it is relatively rare for issues to play a dominant part in a legislative primary.

Most legislators do not believe it is essential to gain the endorsement of organized groups to win renomination. It is likely to be more important, of course, in primaries where there is no incumbent candidate. This is not to say that incumbents are scornful of groups or make no efforts to win their support. But if a legislator has originally been nominated and elected without the endorsement of a group (or despite its endorsement of someone else), he is not likely to be particularly concerned about trying to get such an endorsement in the next race. Obviously in a district where a particular group, such as a labor union, is strong, a legislator will try to avoid antagonizing the group, hoping that it will not recruit or support an opponent. Members who have been elected initially with the support of a group will want to keep that support, but they often feel that they have enough advantage as incumbents that they are not so heavily dependent on endorsements as they were in the first election. Legislators in states like Texas, which have shifted from multimember to single-member districts, believe that endorsements are less important in single-member districts, where their own political strength is greater, than they are in a large district.

This picture of the independent legislator—who raises his own funds, runs his own campaign, and seeks renomination on his record of service to constituents—is accurate in most districts of most states. But there are some examples of legislators who must pay more attention to the party organization—or other political groups—if they are to be renominated. As we would expect, neither the state party nor the local party plays a significant role in the southern states being studied, though the support of individual political leaders may be valuable in a primary campaign. In Louisville, for example, precinct leaders are often active in primaries. In the absence of a strong party organization, other groups may try to fill the vacuum. During the 1950s and 1960s, for example, Kentucky governors sometimes endorsed legislative candidates in Democratic primaries during the mid-term election. These endorsements resulted not only from the traditional Democratic factionalism but also from the governor's desire to elect legislators who would support his program; occasionally an effort was made to defeat an incumbent in the primary. In recent years, however, there has been little evidence of this strategy. In Texas there are reports that the Speaker channels campaign funds from interest groups to those legislators who are committed to support him, but the extent and effect of this practice is not well documented.

In the northern states in this study we do find some examples of party organizations taking sides in legislative primaries. In California the party organizations are not well enough organized or disciplined to make such efforts. In Massachusetts some local parties make such endorsements, but (particularly among Democrats) the party organizations are too fragmented to have much effect. Ohio is one of the states in which many local party organizations make endorsements in primaries, which is probably one reason why less than 30 percent of the primaries are contested. It is not clear how often the endorsed candidate wins or how important the endorsement is to a candidate. Most incumbents apparently win endorsements with little difficulty. There is a feeling that the shift from at-large to single-member districts in the urban counties, which took effect in 1966, reduced the influence of party organizations over incumbents. Because the voters were not faced with a long list of legislative candidates, they were not so dependent on party slates; moreover, legislative incumbents established their own political organizations within districts.

The local party organizations are traditionally strong in Indiana, and they make endorsements in many counties; this is certainly the case in Marion County (Indianapolis) and some of the other larger ones. It is clear from interviews with Indiana legislators, particularly Republicans from Marion County, that they pay an unusual amount of attention to local party organizations. They send out newsletters to them, meet with them regularly, and play an active role in the local organization. Party endorsement of incumbent legislators is not automatic; although the organizations do not apparently demand ideological purity or a perfect voting record, they expect to be contacted and cultivated. At the same time it is clear that party endorsement does not guarantee success in the primary. In recent years a number of candidates, including some I interviewed, have been nominated over the opposition of the organization. Some legislators believe that the organization has less influence in Marion County since the county was split into three-member districts. Legislators carry more weight in their own districts where the endorsements are made.

Colorado is the state where we find party endorsements to be most important in primary elections. One reason for this is that the primary law provides that the endorsed candidate gets the top position on the ballot and only candidates with at least 20 percent of the endorsing-convention vote can be on the primary ballot. This is one reason why only 18 percent of primaries were contested. Legislators indicated that they worked very hard to get primary endorsement and to keep it. Incumbents are not automatically endorsed. Although there have been examples of incumbents being denied endorsement because they were mavericks, endorsement seems to depend more on the political skills of the candidates who seek it. In Colorado, as in Ohio and Indiana, party endorsements now seem to be somewhat less important because of changes in districting; Colorado shifted from at-large to single-member districts in the mid-1960s.

In those states where the party organization influences the primary nomination there is an effect on the process of representation. The legislator must be sensitive to a partisan constituency—specifically the precinct leaders and others who are active in party affairs. In those districts where party organizations are strong and active, and influence nominations, we find legislators paying close attention to party activists as they develop patterns of communications. But we do not find strong evidence that the party activists make many policy demands on legislators or try to defeat incumbents because of disagreements with them on legislative issues.

What can we learn from primary election campaigns about representation? Most legislative candidates campaign independently, without much reliance on party organizations or other organized groups for endorsements, manpower, or money. Such candidates are not forced to make commitments that will affect their behavior as representatives. Issues seldom play an important part in primary campaigns, and consequently few successful candidates are constrained by the stand they took on issues during the primary. Incumbents have an inherent advantage in mobilizing the resources necessary to win renomination, which helps to explain why relatively few face a serious challenge in the primary. Despite this fact, most legislators do not feel very secure or overconfident about their electoral prospects, and consequently they tend to be sensitive to criticism or potential opposition in the district. We have also noted that there are some states where strong party organizations affect primaries. In these states legislators must be sensitive to party activists not only during campaigns but throughout their term as representatives. Finally, there are states like California where the cost of campaigning in a seriously contested primary is high enough to force reliance on organized groups for financial aid.

*Competition.* Few incumbents are defeated in primaries, although this is less rare in some southern states (see Figure). But how many incumbents face close competition, or any competition at all; and how much competition occurs in races without incumbents? To measure primary competition, I have compiled data on margins in primaries for the party of the incumbent. Data are not included for primaries in the

TABLE 2. Summary of Electoral Margins of Winning Candidate
in Primary of Incumbent's Party (percentage)*

| Range of Electoral Margins (%) | IN | CO | CA | OH | TN | KY | TX |
|---|---|---|---|---|---|---|---|
| Under 50 | 6 | 3 | 13 | 6 | 7 | 17 | 14 |
| 50–60 | 15 | 9 | 7 | 6 | 12 | 18 | 15 |
| 61–70 | 16 | 5 | 6 | 6 | 16 | 14 | 7 |
| 71+ | 15 | 2 | 19 | 11 | 15 | 9 | 13 |
| 100 | 48 | 82 | 55 | 71 | 50 | 43 | 51 |
| Total | 100 | 101 | 100 | 100 | 100 | 101 | 100 |
| (N) | 300 | 195 | 240 | 297 | 297 | 300 | 268 |

*Data in Texas cover only Democratic primaries and pertain only
to the first primary election, not the runoff. The following
election years are included: Indiana: 1974–78, Colorado: 1974–78,
California: 1972, 1976, 1978, Ohio: 1974–78, Tennessee: 1974–78,
Kentucky: 1973–77, Texas: 1974–76.

party out of power, even when there is turnover in party control of the
district, since other studies indicate that such primaries usually have a
low level of competition.[2]

Table 2 compares electoral margins for the primary of the party
holding the seat for seven of the states. Data on margins were not available for North Carolina; but during the three elections (1974-1978) the
proportion of uncontested primaries in that state was 28 percent, lower
than in any of the others. Generally, Table 2 shows a low level of competition. In Indiana and California, the northern states with the most
competition, only about half of the seats are contested and only one-
fifth are won by margins of 60 percent or less. There is much less competition in Colorado and Ohio, states with strong party organizations
that have some influence on legislative recruitment. We would expect
more primary competition in the South, particularly in areas lacking
two-party competition. But only in Kentucky and North Carolina are
more than half of the primaries contested; only in Kentucky and in the
Texas Democratic primary are close to one-third of the seats won by
margins of 60 percent or less. (The Texas data on margins refer to the
first primary, and not the run-off.)

Table 3 enables us to distinguish between Democratic and Republican primaries, and between incumbents and nonincumbents. We can
begin with a generalization that applies to both parties in each of the
states: the winning margins are much higher and the proportion of uncontested races is much higher in races with incumbents than in those

TABLE 3. Margin of Winning Candidate in Primary of the Party Holding Seat Prior to Election, by Party, Incumbency, and Success of Incumbent (percentage)*

**Democratic Seats**

| Margin (%) | CO Won | CO Lost | CO No | OH Won | OH Lost | OH No | CA Won | CA Lost | CA No | IN Won | IN Lost | IN No | TX Won | TX Lost | TX No | TN Won | TN Lost | TN No | KY Won | KY Lost | KY No |
|---|---|---|---|---|---|---|---|---|---|---|---|---|---|---|---|---|---|---|---|---|---|
| Under 50 | 3 | – | 8 | 2 | 0 | 59 | 0 | 0 | 64 | 3 | 33 | 33 | 3 | 40 | 50 | 3 | 17 | 17 | 5 | 38 | 47 |
| 50–60 | 3 | – | 21 | 4 | 100 | 12 | 5 | 0 | 14 | 14 | 67 | 33 | 10 | 33 | 28 | 6 | 67 | 35 | 14 | 43 | 20 |
| 61–70 | 7 | – | 4 | 4 | 0 | 18 | 0 | 0 | 0 | 14 | 0 | 25 | 4 | 27 | 12 | 20 | 17 | 22 | 14 | 19 | 11 |
| 71–99 | 0 | – | 4 | 16 | 0 | 0 | 26 | 0 | 5 | 22 | 0 | 0 | 17 | 0 | 2 | 18 | 0 | 4 | 13 | 0 | 4 |
| 100 | 88 | – | 63 | 74 | 0 | 12 | 69 | 100 | 18 | 48 | 0 | 8 | 65 | 0 | 8 | 53 | 0 | 22 | 53 | 0 | 18 |
| Total | 101 | 0 | 100 | 100 | 100 | 101 | 100 | 100 | 101 | 101 | 100 | 99 | 99 | 100 | 100 | 100 | 101 | 100 | 99 | 100 | 100 |
| (N) | 74 | 0 | 24 | 160 | 2 | 17 | 131 | 2 | 22 | 116 | 3 | 12 | 203 | 15 | 50 | 153 | 6 | 23 | 166 | 21 | 45 |

**Republican Seats**

| Margin (%) | CO Won | CO Lost | CO No | OH Won | OH Lost | OH No | CA Won | CA Lost | CA No | IN Won | IN Lost | IN No | TX Won | TX Lost | TX No | TN Won | TN Lost | TN No | KY Won | KY Lost | KY No |
|---|---|---|---|---|---|---|---|---|---|---|---|---|---|---|---|---|---|---|---|---|---|
| Under 50 | 0 | – | 3 | 1 | 0 | 14 | 0 | 100 | 58 | 1 | 0 | 38 | 2 | 0 | 26 | | | | 9 | 100 | 17 |
| 50–60 | 3 | – | 27 | 3 | 50 | 22 | 2 | 0 | 25 | 8 | 78 | 29 | 9 | 0 | 23 | | | | 11 | 0 | 33 |
| 61–70 | 0 | – | 13 | 2 | 50 | 18 | 2 | 0 | 8 | 17 | 11 | 14 | 6 | 100 | 13 | | | | 16 | 0 | 6 |
| 71–99 | 1 | – | 7 | 5 | 0 | 5 | 17 | 0 | 0 | 13 | 11 | 0 | 16 | 0 | 16 | | | | 7 | 0 | 6 |
| 100 | 96 | – | 50 | 88 | 0 | 41 | 80 | 0 | 8 | 60 | 0 | 19 | 67 | 0 | 23 | | | | 57 | 0 | 39 |
| Total | 100 | 0 | 100 | 99 | 100 | 100 | 101 | 100 | 99 | 99 | 100 | 100 | 100 | 100 | 101 | | | | 100 | 100 | 101 |
| (N) | 67 | 0 | 30 | 94 | 2 | 22 | 60 | 1 | 24 | 139 | 9 | 21 | 82 | 1 | 31 | | | | 44 | 6 | 18 |

*The following election years are included: Colorado: 1974–78, Ohio: 1974–78, California: 1972, 1976, 1978, Indiana: 1974–78, Texas: 1974–76, Tennessee: 1974–78, Kentucky: 1973–77. The data include the first primary, not the runoff.

without. This is not a surprising finding, but it is an important one. Not only are incumbents rarely defeated in primaries but they seldom face serious challenges. In the North the Indiana Democratic primary was the only one in which more than 10 percent of incumbents had winning margins of 60 percent or less. Among southern parties included in the table, from 9 to 20 percent of incumbents won by 60 percent or less.

Colorado uses preprimary endorsements by party organizations, and incumbents rarely lose; none lost during the three elections under study. The strong party organizations in Ohio and the long tenure of members there both contribute to limited opposition and lopsided majorities for incumbents. In Colorado and Ohio the Republican primary has even less competition than the Democratic one. The low level of competition in California primaries, particularly among Republicans, cannot be attributed to strong party organizations, but may be due to the resources available to incumbents and the high cost of running for the legislature in that state. It is noteworthy that primaries without incumbents are unusually competitive in that state; 60 percent are won by less than a majority. Although Indiana political parties are generally classified as strong, there is a moderate level of competition with incumbents in the race, particularly among Democrats; there is a high proportion of closely contested primaries without incumbents in both parties (though the total numbers are small). Indiana is one of the states using multimember districts; this requires a different method of calculating electoral margins (cited in an earlier note) that makes it difficult to compare Indiana to other states. In 16 percent of the cases in Indiana there were contested primaries but the number of candidates was less than twice the number of seats in the district.

In the Texas Democratic primary, there are dramatic differences in the level of competition between those districts with and without incumbents running. In Tennessee both party primaries have few close races with incumbents and much more competition without. The pattern is similar in Kentucky except that the Democrats have more incumbents defeated and more close races without incumbents, while the Republicans have fewer contested races without incumbents. Although data on electoral margins in North Carolina are not readily available, the existence of a large number of seats in multimember districts makes it possible to measure competition in a different way. While only 28 percent of seats were uncontested, another 41 percent were partly contested. This latter category refers to races in multimember districts having a number of candidates fewer than twice the number of seats.

In such districts, all the candidates have opposition, but less than half of them can lose. About one-third of the Democratic primaries with an incumbent running were fully contested, and about half of those without an incumbent; only 12 percent of Republican primaries were fully contested. One reason why incumbency seems to have less impact in North Carolina than in most states is that in multimember districts when some but not all incumbents seek renomination there is no way for a candidate to avoid challenging the incumbent.

Tennessee, Kentucky, and Texas are states in which only about half (or less in Texas) of the general elections are contested and only about half of the primaries of the incumbent's party are contested. We would expect more competition in the majority party's primary in districts where that party faces little or no opposition in the general election. This is not only because there is more incentive to enter the primary but also because whatever opposition there may be to an incumbent is likely to be channeled into the primary election only. This pattern generally prevails, but there are more than a few cases of incumbents winning renomination and reelection without opposition and occasionally even a nonincumbent wins both races unopposed. The proportion of incumbents unopposed in both races is: Kentucky—Democrats 28 percent, Republicans 14 percent; Tennessee—Democrats 30 percent, Republicans 24 percent; Texas—Democrats 46 percent. In North Carolina only 7 percent of Democratic incumbents and no Republican incumbents had such good fortune, but many others ran in multimember districts that were only partially contested in both races.

## General Elections

*Campaigning.* The pattern of general election campaigns for legislators is similar to that for primaries, although there are more contested, and more closely contested, races. Most state legislators run their own campaign, with little assistance from or dependence on the local and state party organizations. In those states and districts where the party is strong, however, party support may be important for reelection. As a general rule, we can say that legislators put together their own organizations, raise funds, and engage in personal campaigning; they do not sit back and wait for the party organization to provide help or for the coattails of statewide candidates to sweep them into office. For those who have already run a primary race, the fall campaign is simply an extension, using the same techniques and organization. Even in those states where the party organization is relatively strong, its members are likely to concentrate their attention on statewide races and/or county or city level elections. The experienced legislator is likely to develop and maintain his own organization, including persons who may or may not be active in party politics and in other elections but who can be counted on to work for him. In districts where the local party organization is weak, it is not unusual for the legislator's organization to be the core of the party organization.

Obviously, where the party is well organized, it provides common services to legislative candidates: maintaining a headquarters, registering voters, manning the polls, and getting out the vote. Legislative candidates may get their names on billboards and get introduced at political rallies; but these are fringe benefits, peripheral to their own campaigns. Even those legislators who acknowledge the assistance of the party organization stress the importance of their own campaign efforts and organization. It is also obvious that many legislators represent districts that are safe for their party; this is a familiar pattern not only in the South but in many northern states. But legislators believe that party identification is becoming less important as a voting cue—that  more voters are independents—and therefore their personal campaign efforts make a difference. This view is shared not only by legislators who hold seats in districts where their party appears to be in a minority but by others whose comfortable margins appear to be based on their party's dominant position in the district. The latter often suggest that their margins are deceptively large and could be reduced by a strong opponent.

Two states provide an exception to this pattern. In North Carolina the use of county-level at-large elections encourages legislative candidates in each party to campaign as a team. In the metropolitan counties it is not practical to campaign door to door. Candidates not only run as a team and combine resources for advertising, but they divide up the speaking engagements. These candidates also rely more heavily on group endorsements than seems to be the case elsewhere. The fact that all the candidates are, theoretically, running against one another in at-large elections seems to provide another incentive for team effort. Even in these cases, however, most candidates do some campaigning on their own, and there are examples of elections in which candidates have failed entirely to campaign as a team.

In Indiana it is also common for legislative candidates in multi-member districts to run as a team. This is particularly common in Marion County, where the Republican party organization is unusually strong. Candidates work closely with one another and with the party organization. One factor conducive to party teamwork in Indiana is an unusually high level of straight-ticket voting. In multimember districts in Indiana (both in Marion County and elsewhere) it is common for the legislative candidates in one party to run within one or two percentage points of one another even in cases where some in the district are veteran legislators and others are not incumbents. This extraordinary level of straight-party voting, of course, reduces the importance of individual campaign efforts and makes the legislator more dependent on the party, not only for campaign assistance but for votes.

*Financing.* Even though a legislative candidate may not be dependent on the political party in most districts for endorsements, campaign help, or straight-ticket voting, his independence may be jeopardized if he has to raise large sums of money for his campaign. The question to be answered is two-fold: how much does it cost to run for election, and where do candidates get the money? Obviously if a candidate can run a successful campaign for a few hundred or a couple of thousand dollars, he can finance it himself or through help from friends or small contributors who will make few demands on him. If the costs are heavy, the legislative candidate becomes dependent on the party organization to help raise money and/or on groups and individuals that expect some consideration in return. These questions are not easy to answer because data on campaign financing are not readily available in some states, and because this topic was not a major focus of the present study. We do have some data, however, from Kentucky, Tennessee, and North Carolina, states where campaign costs are generally low, and from California, where they are unusually high. We also have some evidence from California, and scattered examples from other states, about the sources of funding.[3]

The same variables that affect the character of legislative campaigns affect costs: the level of competition, population of district, urban-rural character, nature of available communications, traditional campaign practices. Obviously it costs less to campaign door to door than to purchase media advertising. In urban areas the costs of television advertising are prohibitively expensive for most candidates because only a small proportion of the viewing audience lives in a single-member district. It is also possible, of course, that more money is spent in races where parties, interest groups, or others are willing to invest more funds.

Perhaps the best single measure of campaign costs is the average or median cost of campaigning for winners in contested races. (Generally uncontested winners spend much less and distort the average. If losers are included, the results can be misleading because some pro forma candidates make little investment in time, energy, or money.)

North Carolina is a good example of low spending in the 1974 election. The median spent in the general election by winners was only $1,500 in 100 contested races; the highest was $15,500, but only one other candidate spent over $6,000. This is even more remarkable considering that many of these candidates were running at-large in metropolitan areas; most winners in those areas did spend above the median—often $3,000 to $5,000. Of course the fact that party candidates ran as a team made possible some economies in advertising. Among the twenty candidates running unopposed, fourteen spent nothing and the others spent no more than a few hundred dollars.

Data are available for the Kentucky House for 1977 and 1975, data that combine primary and general election spending. In 1977 the median for contested winners was $3,600; the highest figure was $19,800, but only five candidates spent over $10,000. Only fifteen of twenty-four winners with no primary or election opposition spent anything, most of them a few hundred dollars. In 1975 the median figure for contested winners was $2,300; the largest figure was $13,400, which was the only total over $10,000. Most of the twenty-one unopposed candidates spent little or nothing. In Tennessee data are available on 1976 primary and general election spending for twenty of the legislators who were interviewed. The median in contested races was $5,800; the median in four cases with neither primary nor election opposition was $3,400.

In Kentucky and North Carolina, and less likely in Tennessee, a candidate can run an extensive enough campaign to win if he can raise a few thousand dollars from himself and others—and if he has the other characteristics needed by a winner. Of course, these states are less urban than most, and ones in which a substantial proportion of areas is dominated by one party. Ordinarily winning candidates are likely to spend more money than losers; those who are incumbents are more experienced in raising funds; those who are perceived as probable winners are more likely to get funds from those groups that want to make demands on legislators. In Kentucky we have data that show this is generally true but that there are exceptions. Combining data for the House in 1975 and 1977, we find twenty-eight cases where the winner in the general elections spent less money than the loser (excluding primary spending); nineteen of these winners were incumbents, and eight winners were in races with no incumbents. There were forty-nine primary winners who spent less than losers; twenty-two were incumbents, nineteen were in races with no incumbent, and eight defeated incumbents.

In contrast to the spending in the three southern states, campaign costs in California are among the highest, if not the highest, in the nation. Data for 1978, which cover only general election costs, show that the median spent by contested winners was $43,900; the few unopposed winners spent $18,000; and losers spent $13,000. The highest spending by a winner was $162,500; fourteen spent over $100,000. The highest spending by a loser was $176,600; nine spent more than $100,000. There were ten races in which a total of over $200,000 was spent. (These figures do not include funds spent by candidates as donations to other candidates.) In eleven cases the losing candidate spent more than the winner, including three of the six cases where incumbents were defeated. Spending levels were highest for both winners and losers in the nine races where there was a partisan turnover of the seat; in many of these races there was a rough balance of spending by the two parties. There was also a high median level of spending by both parties in several close races without incumbents and in the closest races with incumbents; in most of these races there was a close two-party balance of spending. In the remaining races with and without incumbents, the spending by the winning party declines gradually, and spending by the losing party declines rapidly, as the size of the electoral margin increases. In almost one-fourth of the districts there was either no opposition or the winning margin was over 70 percent, and the losing party, where it had a candidate, spent a median of only about a thousand dollars.

The topic of campaign fund-raising was not an important focus of interviews with legislators, but when it came up there were seldom any references to assistance in fund-raising from state or local party sources. It seems likely that the strong local party organizations in states like Indiana and Ohio assist in raising funds, but no data are available on that. Data for Kentucky show that in 1977 the state Democratic party gave an average of $200 to $500 to some thirty House candidates, and the state and national Republican parties gave from $250 to $1,000 to about fifteen of them. In California the state Democratic party organization in 1978 gave some $24,000 to twenty-four Assembly candidates; most received less than $1,000, but a few got between $3,500 and $5,000. Much more was raised by the Assembly leadership. The Republican state party organization gave $328,000 to Assembly candidates; most of it (three-fourths) went to sixteen who each got from $10,000 to $34,000; ten got from $1,000 to $8,100; and fifty-eight got under $1,000—most of them just a token amount.

There is also scattered evidence in a few states of fund-raising efforts by the legislative caucus of leadership. In Tennessee the House Democratic caucus raised funds for legislative candidates, but the total amount and distribution data are not available. I noted earlier rumors that the Texas Speaker channeled campaign funds to legislators who supported him. In Ohio the Republican House caucus put some $70,000 into 1978 races, concentrating on districts that were believed to be marginal.

The best example of legislative campaign funding organized by the legislative leadership is in California—a system used primarily by Democrats. The system was originated by Jesse Unruh when he was Speaker of the Assembly (1961-1969). Unruh encouraged the interest groups and individuals who were willing to contribute to Democratic legislative candidates to make the contributions to him; then he allocated the funds to those incumbents and legislative candidates whose need for campaign funding he considered most important. This was obviously an important tool of his strong leadership as Speaker.

In the years since then an elaborate system of legislative fundraising has developed, primarily among Democratic leaders of the Assembly, although Democratic Senate leaders and Republican Assembly leaders have followed the pattern on a smaller scale. In the Assembly, Republican leaders contributed about $93,000 to individual Republican candidates or to a general fund for Republican candidates for the 1978 election. Meanwhile the Democratic leadership in the Assembly was raising about $520,000 to distribute to Democratic candidates for the Assembly.

The record shows that more than half of the Democratic Assembly total was raised and distributed by the Speaker and the majority leader, but a total of thirty-eight Democrats in the Assembly made some contributions to other legislative candidates. Most of those participating in the process were party or committee leaders. It is not evident from the record how this process of legislative campaign funding is coordinated, but it appears that the party leadership expects Democratic legislators who hold legislative office and/or who hold relatively safe seats to raise funds for their colleagues. The leadership also apparently decides how these funds will be allocated.

These funds that are raised by the legislative leadership are allocated to relatively few races where they are most needed. Almost 90 percent of the funds allocated by the leadership to Democratic Assembly candidates in 1978 went to just fifteen races, with contributions ranging from $14,000 to $69,000. In most cases the contribution from legislative leadership in these races represented between 15 and 35 percent of the total spending in those races, but in a couple of cases it was 60 percent or more. Seven of these fifteen Assembly races involved incumbents, including two who were beaten and five who won by relatively narrow margins (under 60 percent). The eight nonincumbents included two who were trying, unsuccessfully, to challenge incumbents and six running for open seats, half of them successfully.

Obviously the range of costs for legislative campaign varies widely among the states. In several of our southern states, costs are generally moderate, and although there is some evidence of support from the state or legislative party, it seems unlikely that these contributions are large enough to have much effect on legislative independence. At the other extreme is California, where districts are large and communications are often expensive. In some of the closely contested Assembly races, spending by one or both candidates passes the $100,000 mark; in these and many other districts the candidates are dependent on large contributions. It is significant that both parties have stepped into the breach, contributing substantial proportions of these costs. It is particularly intriguing that the Democratic Assembly leadership, and to a lesser extent Republican leaders, play a major role in this fund-raising and distribution. It provides an ingenious way of insulatng legislators from the interest-contributing funds. We can only speculate on the extent to which it makes legislators indebted to their legislative leaders— particularly on the Democratic side.

*Campaigns and Representation.* The impact of general election campaigns on the process of representation is similar to the impact of primary campaigns. Most legislative candidates run both campaigns with a high degree of independence from political party and other organizations. The contribution of party organizations to the general election campaign is greater, but most legislators do not believe it is vital to their success. Those states where the party influences the primary election are generally ones where it is well-enough organized to contribute significantly to the general election campaign. Ohio and Indiana would be the best examples of this. In Indiana the tradition of straight-ticket voting and the use of multimember districts make the candidates more dependent on the party organization than is true in other states.

Indiana and Ohio, as well as Colorado, are states in which the legislative process seems to be more permeated by partisanship than is the case in most other states in this study. (Massachusetts also fits this category, but I have not analyzed electoral data there.) It is difficult to prove what kind of a linkage there may be between the electoral process in those states and the sensitivity of legislators to partisan considerations in making policy decisions.

In a sense California is a special case because the size of the districts and the scale of campaigning have escalated the costs of running for office so that those who are elected are indebted to their contributors to a degree not found in the other states. Our interviews in California did not reveal that legislators feel bound to heed the demands of those groups who contributed to campaigns, but this is not the kind of information we would expect legislators to volunteer (and it was not a question regularly asked). What is most interesting in California is the extent to which the Democratic legislative leadership and the Republican state party organization have raised funds for legislative candidates who are most in need—thus reducing their dependence on interest groups but making them more dependent on, and perhaps more responsive to, party leadership.

*Competition.* We turn to an examination of competition in general elections with several purposes in mind. In order to understand the electoral pressures on legislators, we want to know what proportion of them usually face close competition in November races and how much this varies from state to state. In order to understand the political advantages or disadvantages of incumbency, we want to know how much partisan turnover occurs, and how close the races are, in the absence of incumbents in the race. Earlier we noted that the proportion of incumbents losing general election races was generally less than 10 percent, and in some states much less. Obviously some incumbents enter the general election campaign with a great advantage over others because of the normal partisan distribution of vote in the district. Legislators are also vulnerable to national and state political trends that may be an asset in one election and a liability in the next. To the extent that we find legislative incumbents winning by large margins, there may be at least three important factors: a high proportion of safe districts, the personal political strength developed by incumbents, and the reluctance of opposition party candidates to run where either of the first two conditions prevail.

Table 4 summarizes the data for each party in each state on the proportion of seats won by various margins, and Table 5 summarizes the relationships between incumbency and turnover and electoral margins.[4] Party competition is obviously closest in Indiana; more than two-thirds of the seats are won by 60 percent or less. In Colorado half the seats are won by 60 percent or less. California and Ohio have fewer closely contested districts but most seats are contested. In border and southern states, the level of competition drops; most Democratic candidates win easily, but the fewer Republican winners have smaller margins.

If we compare the margins of Democratic and Republican winners

TABLE 4. Summary of Electoral Margins of Winning Party in General Elections (percentage)*

| Range of Electoral Margins (%) | IN | | CO | | CA | | OH | | NC | | TN | | KY | | TX | |
|---|---|---|---|---|---|---|---|---|---|---|---|---|---|---|---|---|
| | D | R | D | R | D | R | D | R | D | R | D | R | D | R | D | R |
| Under 50 | 0 | 1 | 1 | 3 | 1 | 2 | 1 | 3 | 0 | 0 | 0 | 0 | 0 | 0 | 1 | 0 |
| 50–55 | 30 | 40 | 25 | 27 | 15 | 30 | 9 | 21 | 11 | 60 | 9 | 27 | 7 | 24 | 5 | 16 |
| 56–60 | 19 | 40 | 14 | 30 | 15 | 18 | 12 | 23 | 13 | 30 | 6 | 16 | 8 | 25 | 5 | 13 |
| 61–65 | 15 | 11 | 13 | 17 | 15 | 17 | 12 | 24 | 18 | 7 | 8 | 9 | 8 | 2 | 5 | 13 |
| 66–70 | 13 | 4 | 14 | 9 | 23 | 17 | 24 | 16 | 11 | 0 | 6 | 7 | 8 | 11 | 6 | 16 |
| 71–99 | 15 | 0 | 11 | 7 | 24 | 13 | 34 | 10 | 16 | 3 | 14 | 11 | 16 | 0 | 15 | 25 |
| 100 | 8 | 3 | 23 | 7 | 6 | 4 | 9 | 3 | 31 | 0 | 57 | 31 | 52 | 38 | 64 | 18 |
| Total | 100 | 99 | 101 | 100 | 99 | 101 | 101 | 100 | 100 | 100 | 100 | 101 | 99 | 100 | 101 | 101 |
| (N) | 151 | 149 | 125 | 135 | 213 | 107 | 182 | 115 | 330 | 30 | 190 | 105 | 237 | 63 | 394 | 56 |

*The following election years are included: Indiana: 1974–78, Colorado: 1972–78, California: 1972–78, Ohio: 1974–78, North Carolina: 1974–78, Tennessee, 1974–78, Kentucky: 1973–77, Texas: 1974–78.

we find that in every state, the Democratic winners have more safe and more uncontested seats, and Republican winners have more marginal seats. We would expect that in the South, but it is also true in the four northern states. This is partly the result of including the 1974 election, in which the Democratic vote was unusually strong. A closer examination of individual states will provide more clues. In Indiana the 1974 and 1976 elections produced many narrow Republican margins in normally Republican districts. The use of two- and three-member districts in the major metropolitan counties may reduce the number of lopsided electoral margins, particularly for Democrats, who are also weaker in Indianapolis than in most large cities. In California the Democrats win lopsided margins in some of the largest cities, particularly Los Angeles. The fact that the California districts have such large populations probably reduces the number of uncontested districts. The large size of districts may also give incumbents a bigger advantage, because the costs of challenging an incumbent are greater. In Ohio, the Democrats benefit from lopsided margins in the large cities, particularly Cleveland. The fact that Ohio legislators have more seniority than in most states may account for the particularly large advantage enjoyed by incumbents.

The North Carolina Republicans have not recovered from the 1974 Democratic landslide, and this is reflected in low margins even in normally Republican districts. Kentucky and Tennessee are quite similar in the distribution of partisan margins. In both states the Republican party, despite its minority status in the legislature, wins a number of seats without any Democratic opposition in the traditional mountain Republican counties in the eastern part of each state. Most of the other Republican victories are won by relatively narrow margins, many of them in suburban parts of metropolitan areas. Even in Texas we find that the Republican party wins almost half of its seats with little or no opposition, generally in the suburban parts of metropolitan areas. A large proportion of Democratic seats are won unanimously or with little opposition.

The political strength of incumbent legislators is evident from Table 5. Incumbents ran in 78 percent of the elections; 94 percent won reelection. This is close to the proportion of victories in the general election for U.S. House members who run. When there is no incumbent in the race, partisan turnover occurs 16 percent of the time, compared to 6 percent for incumbents. These figures demonstrate not only the strength of incumbency but also the large proportion of relatively safe seats.

If we look at the range of electoral margins we find, as anticipated,

TABLE 5. Summary of Electoral Margins of Winning Party in General
Elections by Incumbency and by Turnover in Eight States
(percentage)*

| Range of Electoral Margins (%) | All Races | Incumbent Running | | No Incumbent | |
|---|---|---|---|---|---|
| | | Won | Lost | No Turnover | Partisan Turnover |
| Under 50 | 1 | 0 | 2 | 2 | 3 |
| 50–55 | 17 | 11 | 67 | 19 | 58 |
| 56–60 | 15 | 14 | 25 | 16 | 23 |
| 61–65 | 12 | 12 | 6 | 13 | 8 |
| 66–70 | 11 | 13 | 0 | 10 | 4 |
| 71–99 | 15 | 16 | 0 | 16 | 2 |
| 100 | 29 | 33 | 0 | 24 | 2 |
| Total | 100 | 99 | 100 | 100 | 100 |
| (N) | 2,584 | 1,894 | 116 | 481 | 93 |

*The election years included for each state are the same as in
Table 3.

that when there is partisan turnover the margin is usually a narrow
one; this is particularly true when an incumbent is beaten. When there
is no turnover, incumbents generally win by larger margins and are
more likely to be unopposed than those nonincumbents who are running in districts previously controlled by their party. A few states do
not fit this pattern closely. In Indiana there is little difference in margins between incumbents and nonincumbents, presumably because of
the strong pattern of straight-ticket voting. Although incumbency is a
major advantage in Tennessee and Texas, it has less effect in Kentucky
and North Carolina, perhaps because so many districts are safe for one
party and (in North Carolina) because the multimember district system
forces all candidates to run against each other without regard to incumbency.

## Conclusions

One conclusion to be drawn from this description of primary and election campaigns is that most legislative candidates campaign independently, without heavy reliance on parties and other organized groups,
but there are variations from state to state. Where party organizations
are strong or where the costs of campaigning are high, legislators may
make commitments and incur political debts that affect their freedom
in making decisions as representatives.

The competitive pattern in both primaries and general elections
shows that few incumbents are beaten, only a minority have strong

competition in either race, and many are unopposed in the primary (or in general elections in southern and border states). Undoubtedly a major reason why many incumbents win handily in general elections is that their party dominates the district. Where that is the case the weakness of opposition party organizations prevents effective recruiting of viable challengers. The more closely one looks at legislative election returns in individual districts, however, the more examples he finds of politically strong legislators. This is evident from the number who increase their margin as their seniority increases and who win reelection in the face of threatening national or state political trends. This is particularly evident in the more professional legislatures; California is a prime example.

It is often assumed that legislators who have achieved electoral security have greater freedom from the pressure of constituents—particularly organized interests in the district. It is difficult to support this assumption from clear evidence in the scholarly literature, and it is equally difficult to support it from interviews with legislators. In fact most legislators do not feel politically secure, even when they have won by comfortable margins or without opposition. They are always wary of potentially strong opponents and work hard to build a record at the polls and in office that will discourage such persons from running. Those who have a strong record of electoral success appear to be just as interested in the constituency and just as attentive to its interests as those who have won by narrow margins—if you can believe what they say in interviews.

This suggests an important conclusion about the relationship between electoral security and representation. It may not be the case that electoral security makes legislators less dedicated representatives; rather, those members who work most effectively at the job are likely to achieve the strongest measure of electoral security. That is the relationship that legislators believe prevails, and there is no reason to dispute their analysis.

Incumbents have many advantages in campaigns, including name visibility, experience, knowledge of the district, and the ability to raise campaign funds. But the best campaigns begin early—just as soon as the legislator takes office. The legislator with a good head start in the campaign is the one who has developed contacts and attended meetings throughout the district; has answered his mail and advertised his willingness to serve constituents; has learned what issues are salient and how strongly constituent groups hold views on those issues, and has been responsive to his constituents. If legislators have become stronger, less vulnerable political figures in the last ten or fifteen years—as I believe they have—it is probably less a result of more skillful or expensive campaigns than of greater visibility and effectiveness in office.

Students of congressional elections have paid considerable attention to what some have called the "case of the vanishing marginals." In recent years, an increasing proportion of congressmen have been elected by comfortable margins. This has been attributed by some to changing partisan distribution in districts, perhaps facilitated by gerrymandering. But the most commonly accepted explanation is that advanced by Fiorina (1977a, 1977b): congressional incumbents are becoming better known to constituents, because of their increasing opportunities to provide benefits for their districts and for individual constituents. Constituents usually evaluate congressmen in terms of personal qualities and their service roles, rather than their record on policy questions (Parker and Davidson, 1979). Consequently, the hardworking congressman who takes advantage of opportunities to communicate with constituents and answers their requests as promptly and fully as possible is likely to get reelected even when the party balance in the district or national political tides are unfavorable.

Throughout this study we will be paying attention to the efforts made by state legislators to communicate with constituents and to provide benefits for the districts and services for constituents. These are not as extensive as they are in Congress, nor do legislators uniformly accept these as important responsibilities. But it appears that an increasing proportion of legislators are engaging in the kinds of activities that might give them visibility and a favorable image in the district. Because rates of turnover are dropping—quite rapidly in some states—more state legislators are gaining the advantages of seniority that might not only help them win reelection by comfortable margins but also discourage serious opposition in either the primary or the general election.

It is risky to examine aggregate election data (I have no survey data) and to draw conclusions about its meaning. But I believe one reasonable conclusion from recent elections in these states is that incumbency makes a significant difference in state legislative races. Just as congressional scholars are trying to explain why congressional incumbents are so strong, we need to examine what legislators are doing that gives them visibility and electoral success. As we examine how legislators represent their district, we should not lose sight of the political implications of their activities, implications well understood by the members. We will begin with the component of representation that may have the most direct political payoff: communicating with constituents.

# 3. Communicating with Constituents

For a legislator to communicate effectively with his constituents, he must be accessible, he must learn the needs and views of his constituents, and he must make his views and actions known to them. A prerequisite for successful communication is that the legislator must recognize its importance. He must want to play the role of leader and educator in his constituency. The legislator who fails to recognize the importance of communication will not devote the time and resources that are necessary to the task.

Effective communication, however, is more than a matter of recognizing priorities and having good intentions. It requires skill, imagination, and good judgment; this is an aspect of the legislator's job where experience counts. It takes skill to produce a good newsletter or devise a questionnaire that will accurately measure constituent opinions. Capturing the attention of constituents often requires imaginative techniques. Evaluating the mail received on an issue or deciding how to explain an unpopular vote to angry constituents requires a high level of political judgment.

The job of communicating effectively to constituents is more difficult for some legislators than for others. There are two major reasons for these differences: variations in the size and character of districts and varied levels of resources available for communication. In this chapter I will describe the problems of communicating in various types of urban and rural districts and will look at the types of resources that are available for communication in different states. I will then examine specific techniques of communication that are being used, including the use of the media, newsletters, and opinion surveys, letters to and from the legislator, and personal contacts with organized groups, the district office, and individual constituents.

## District Variations

Communicating with constituents is a practical matter, requiring particular resources and skills as well as imagination and enthusiasm. The legislator must learn how to use the existing organizations and media and how to cope with the geographic limitations of the district. Communication patterns and opportunities are affected by the character of the district and by varied methods of districting, whether metropolitan or nonmetropolitan, whether single-member or multimember.

Some districts in metropolitan areas are so concentrated that the representative can walk across the district in an evening. Many rural districts, on the other hand, cover hundreds and even thousands of square miles. One House district in southwestern Texas contains more than 22,000 square miles; the distance between towns in the southwest and northeast corners of the district is over 300 miles. In some districts mountain ranges, poor roads, or other features make it difficult to get from one populated center to another.

The reapportionment revolution produced equality in the population of districts within states, but from state to state there are large variations in the average population of districts. In the twenty-eight states that use only single-member districts, the average (1970) population of lower house districts ranged from 250,000 in California to 7,000 in Montana; the median state was 31,000 and sixteen of the twenty-eight fell in the range of 20,000 to 44,000. (The Nebraska unicameral is included.) The seven states included in our study (with single-member districts) are considerably above the average in district population, ranging from 32,000 in Kentucky to California's 250,000. It is more difficult and perhaps misleading to summarize the average population in states making some use of multimember districts. It is not clear whether a one-member district with 30,000 people is comparable to a three-member district with 90,000 people. The average population per House member (not per district) in the twenty-two states with some multimember districts ranged from 1,800 in New Hampshire to 90,000 in New Jersey; the median state was 18,500. The two states in our study had averages per member of 52,000 in Indiana and 42,000 in North Carolina, well above the average.

Obviously we would expect members who serve a large number of constituents to get more mail and visits and more demands for assistance; they would need more staff; it would be more time-consuming and expensive to campaign, send out newletters, develop and maintain personal contacts with a significant proportion of the constituents. Not only the absolute number of constituents but the geographic character of the district has an important effect on communication. The most obvious difference is that to be found between metropolitan and nonmetropolitan districts.

*Metropolitan Districts.* Legislators representing single-member districts in a metropolitan area face a common problem. The major newspapers, radio, and television stations cover the entire metropolitan area; the legislator's district covers only a fraction of that area. All the legislators in the area compete for media coverage with one another and with other officials. To get much attention from the media, the legislator must do or say something of interest to the whole community or state. A press release dealing with some problem that primarily concerns one district is not likely to get printed in the metropolitan newspaper.

Most legislators in metropolitan areas agree that it is very difficult to get coverage in the major newspapers or on radio or television. A Memphis legislator says that the newspaper of that city treats the legislature "like stepchildren." A Dallas legislator asserts that the newspapers of that city cover the governor, the Speaker of the House, and the legislature as a whole, but pay little attention to the legislators from Dallas. Similar complaints come from legislators in cities like Boston, Cincinnati, Denver, and Louisville. Some legislators believe that the poor coverage they receive is part of a broader problem of limited media attention to the legislature. Some complain that the press is primarily interested in stories that will show the legislators in a bad light: "They ridicule us instead of covering us." Whether the media coverage of the legislature as a whole is adequate or fair, the basic problem in metropolitan areas is that there are too many legislators representing small districts in the area for any single legislator to get much attention from the media.

There is a consensus that the best way to get the attention of the media is to be involved in controversial legislation. By definition, of course, controversial issues can hurt a legislator as well as helping, and publicity on such an issue may be a mixed blessing. Some legislators deliberately become involved in controversies. They may be highly issue-oriented, or liberal or conservative ideologues, or they may simply use such issues as a vehicle for publicity. These legislators do not complain about the difficulty of getting attention and a few admit they are perceived by colleagues as getting too much attention.

Controversial issues are not the only route to media coverage. One legislator suggested that it helps to have an interesting personality. The entry of more women, blacks, and other minorities to the legislature has focused media attention, at least temporarily, on some of these members. Being an "interesting personality," though, may be a matter of technique and not just an inherent characteristic. One legislator who is in the advertising business claims that he can get any news release printed in the paper because he has personal contacts and knows how to prepare a release for publication. A Boston legislator who appears frequently on television says, "I get lots of media publicity because I am a media person, and the media like it and cover me."

Those legislators who work hardest to gain attention in the metropolitan media sometimes are aiming at broader audiences. They may be planning to run for the state senate, a city or county office, or statewide or congressional office. (The Boston legislator just quoted has now become a congressman.) The legislator with broader ambitions, particularly statewide ones, has an advantage if he lives in a metropolitan area, because the media in that area—if they pay some attention to him—will reach a larger constituency than most rural legislators can claim.

Metropolitan legislators often find that they can get attention in local weekly newspapers, which cover all or parts of their districts. A Cincinnati legislator has eight weekly papers in his district; another in a suburb of Cleveland has four. These newspapers are often found in suburban areas, but legislators representing central city districts in Cleveland and Denver also mentioned their utility. Black legislators can take advantage of black newspapers, and there are also Spanish-language papers in cities like Denver and San Antonio.

Legislators differ in their judgment about how useful these papers are. Some local papers have small circulations; others are little more than advertising sheets; some pay scant attention to political news. But many metropolitan legislators have found local weekly newspapers to be an effective way of communicating with constituents. Because of their local orientation, the papers will cover a legislator's statements, meetings, and activities that are directly related to the district. Since these newspapers do not have large staffs of reporters, they must rely more heavily on press releases. Some legislators write a weekly column and find that most of the local papers will publish it. A San Antonio legislator showed me a local newspaper that had given front-page coverage and a picture to the routine news of his committee assignment. While relatively few metropolitan legislators may be able to get such coverage from local papers, those who have newspapers in their district recognize them as a significant asset.

One of the most important means of communicating to constituents is through meetings of groups. The better organized a community is, the easier it is for a legislator to develop and maintain contacts. Legislators find it difficult to attract an audience when they schedule a meeting on their own. It is much more effective to gain invitations to

speak before regularly scheduled meetings of groups. Many groups
have an interest in legislative issues, but even groups with less specific
legislative interests are often happy to schedule a legislator because of
their need to fill up a program.

Many groups in metropolitan areas are organized at the city or
county level: the Chamber of Commerce, Rotary Club, League of
Women Voters, county medical organization, city or county school-
teachers or firemen. In addition, there are organizations with narrower geographic boundaries: neighborhood associations, churches,
parent-teacher organizations in individual schools, and sometimes business and professional associations in smaller communities within the
metropolis. Neither of these organizational patterns is ideal from the
viewpoint of the legislator who represents a single district and who
would prefer groups to be organized at the district level. Legislators
seek the opportunity to speak to citywide or county-level groups for a
variety of reasons. Although most of those attending such meetings will
not be constituents, some of them will be. A speech to such a meeting
may be reported in the press or on television and read or heard by constituents. Moreover, this may be the best way to maintain communication with organized interests that share his legislative interests or that
have membership in his district. In a large metropolitan area, however, the average legislator may find it as difficult to get speaking invitations from major groups as it is to get coverage in the media. A few
legislators who are good speakers, who have gained publicity in the
press, or who have cultivated good relationships with groups may get
most of the opportunities to speak to them while most legislators are
largely ignored.

The opportunities that legislators have to meet with and speak to
groups in their own districts depend on the type of area that the member represents; some parts of the metropolitan area are better organized than others. It also depends on the boundaries of the district; some
coincide with communities, while others cut across community lines
and organized groups. Another factor is the initiative and persistence
of the legislator in finding groups and establishing contacts.

The older parts of cities exhibit a higher level of organized activity
than the newer suburbs. Ethnic neighborhoods are often well organized. Black legislators emphasize the importance of churches for maintaining constituency contact. A black legislator from Louisville visits a
different church in his district every week. A San Antonio legislator,
representing a partially Mexican-American district that combines a
number of small communities with an urban area, says that there is an
endless string of activities in each community—barbeques, turkey

shoots, dances, parades, and homecomings. He attends these regularly
and mingles with his constituents. A legislator representing a district in
the center of Louisville regularly attends the neighborhood picnics,
church meetings, and goes with his grandmother to bingo parties to
stay in touch with constituents. Although many of these social occasions allow no opportunity for speech-making, the legislator gains visibility and finds out about problems in his community. Constituents
who would not write or call him may be willing to speak to him in person about either community or personal concerns.

In addition to social events, districts have a number of organizations with interests in legislative matters. The most important of these
are often neighborhood organizations. A Louisville legislator has several neighborhood groups in his district that meet monthly, and he tries
to attend many of these meetings. A legislator representing part of the
metropolitan area of northern Kentucky (adjoining Cincinnati) maintains contacts with seven neighborhood organizations through a citizens advisory council that represents them; he also meets regularly
with community service organizations in the area. Some legislators
make a point of attending local hearings of governmental groups such
as planning and zoning or school boards. This is a good way of staying
in touch with local problems as well as meeting those citizens who are
most likely to be concerned about them. Among the other groups that
are most likely to be organized at the local or district level and would
welcome legislators as speakers are parent-teacher organizations,
churches, and service clubs in local communities.

Where political parties are well organized, legislators stress the importance of staying in touch with local party organizations. In Denver,
Louisville, and several Ohio cities, I found legislators who were in close
touch with local party leaders. Such contact with the party is epit-
omized by the practice of one Louisville legislator I interviewed who
has monthly meetings with Democratic precinct captains and with
members of his own political organization to discuss local needs and
legislative issues.

Those who are most successful in using local meetings are the legislators who are most aggressive in seeking out invitations to attend. A
legislator from Houston runs a boxed notice in his newsletter to advertise his availability:

### Need a Speaker?

Rep. [      ] is available to speak to your civic club, school, church
group, service or professional organization anytime on a topic of
your choosing that involves state or local government. To make arrangements, call the district office at [      ] or write [      ].

Some legislators hold forums, town meetings, or similar meetings from time to time. A Denver legislator, for example, holds a monthly open meeting which all elected officials in the district attend. A Louisville Democrat every few months holds a series of open meetings in five different sections of his district. A Tennessee legislator organizes meetings in constituents' homes to meet regularly with small groups. Most of those who hold open forums recognize that attendance is usually low, but they seem to believe that those who are particularly interested in a topic will attend. They also think that holding such meetings makes a favorable impression on those constituents who hear about them but do not attend; it demonstrates their accessibility.

A minority of legislators say it is difficult to use group meetings to maintain constituent contact. They represent primarily suburban districts or districts that cut across the lines of existing communities and groups. One legislator remarked that he has parts of four neighborhood groups in his district, but in each case the major part of the group is located in another district. A Texas legislator represents a district including a small corner of a metropolitan county and an adjoining rural county. He finds that in the rural community there are good opportunities to speak to groups: "People still come out in the local towns to hear political speakers." But in the bedroom communities of the metropolitan county there are few organized groups and little interest in politics. A Tennessee legislator in a middle-class suburb finds that the only groups of any importance are churches and service clubs, and these groups do not want to listen to a legislator very often; apparently months go by without any invitations. An Ohio legislator pointed to the dilemma of legislators in a state where the session lasts for much of the year. There are few invitations to speak, and many of these come on days when she has to be in Columbus for the session. Several white legislators in districts with heavy black populations indicate that they have some difficulty in getting invitations to attend black churches and social organizations, which are so important to black legislators.

Many of the sprawling suburbs of metropolitan America have a low level of social organization. So fluid are these districts that they present enormous problems to their representatives. A high proportion of residents in many suburbs have moved in since the last election and may be gone before the next one. In many sections of suburbia the only place where people are likely to meet neighbors is at the shopping center. The legislator has great difficulty in gaining visibility and learning about his constituents and their problems. The difficulty is compounded if the boundaries of his district cut across communities, subdivisions, or neighborhoods. In a sense, of course, it is impossible to represent the interests of a constituency if the constituents share no common interests and there are no media or organizations to facilitate communication among them. The legislator is reduced to representing them as individuals and may have no choice but to walk the streets of his district ringing doorbells in an effort to establish some limited form of contact and communication.

In those states with countywide at-large elections, such as North Carolina, the metropolitan legislators face problems of communication that are similar in some respects and different in others. Because they are not elected by districts, they do not have to find local groups where they can speak. They can deal entirely with groups organized at the city and county level. Not every legislator gets the same access to these groups; those who are most skillful in making speeches and getting media publicity are likely to get the lion's share of invitations to speak. Those legislators who are neglected by the city and county groups have a more serious problem than single-member district legislators, however, because they need countywide visibility and in some cases the endorsement of countywide groups if they are to win reelection. North Carolina legislators in metropolitan counties too face problems in getting coverage in the newspaper, television, and radio. The problem is more serious for legislators in multimember districts because they must develop visibility throughout the county; they cannot make much use of local weeklies because they have no district constituency.

Interviews with North Carolina legislators provide examples of how they cope with these problems. In Greensboro the Guilford County delegation has worked out a rotation policy with a local radio station; each week a different member of the delegation discusses the activities of the delegation. In somewhat similar fashion, that delegation holds a monthly forum, attended by all members, in different parts of the district. Similarly the Wake County delegation (Raleigh) has a meeting at the Capitol twice a month during sessions for citizens to attend, and there is a substantial turnout. Despite these examples of collective activity, it is clear that the more aggressive and articulate legislators get ample opportunities to speak to groups, while some other members are frustrated by their lack of contacts.

Legislators from metropolitan counties in Indiana are elected in multimember districts of no more than three persons; in Marion County (Indianapolis) there are five three-member districts. Consequently they share the need to communicate through media and groups at the county and city level, while they must concentrate their efforts on district communication. Actually the three-member districts are large enough that there may be more organized groups and recognizable communities within the district than would be true in many single-member districts. The three Democrats from Marion County, for example, represent a predominantly black district and are able to get good coverage for their activities in the black media.

There is often evidence of cooperation among the three members representing the district. Members of the same party frequently campaign as a team and this cooperation carries over into the session. Republicans in one Marion County district, for example, jointly conduct a poll that they distribute to local newspapers and groups. In many metropolitan counties, notably Marion, legislators work closely with local party organizations, meeting with them regularly during the session, sending newsletters to their members, and maintaining informal personal contacts. Because there is an unusually high degree of straight-party voting by Indiana, it is less important for legislators to become highly visible to constituents as a whole and much more important to maintain the contacts with the party organization that will assure renomination and assure that the organization will work hard for the ticket in the November election.

The specific problems faced by legislators in metropolitan districts vary with the character of the metropolis and the vagaries of district boundaries, but the general problems are common to most. Legislators must compete with their colleagues for the limited attention of the media and the major interest groups. Except for those elected at large, legislators must gain visibility at the county level while they build a solid political base in the district, whether or not the district is a well-organized entity. Those representing single-member districts share the advantages of a compact and usually relatively homogeneous district, one where personal contact is relatively easy to achieve if a person is willing to devote a great deal of time to it. Metropolitan districts offer both distinct advantages and disadvantages for communicating with constituents, characteristics that are virtually the opposite of those found outside the metropolitan areas.

*Nonmetropolitan Districts.* The single-member district composed of one county is the perfect district for a legislator interested in good communications with constituents. In the days before the courts imposed standards of population equality for apportionment, there were many such districts, but today they are rare. There are several advantages to representing such a district. As the only representative in a county, it is relatively easy to get attention in the media. A metropolitan legislator told me of her amazement in discovering that a colleague who was the sole representative of a county could get front-page publicity just by speaking at a luncheon in the county. If you represent a single county, you can concentrate on building contacts and becoming well known in that county; moreover, you have the advantage of being a resident of that county and avoiding the resentment faced by the member who must represent counties in addition to his own. Finally, there are advantages of having district lines that coincide with county lines because the normal channels of communication—both media and groups—are organized along county lines.

A much more common experience for the nonmetropolitan legislator is to represent a district that includes all or parts of several counties. In any multicounty district, it is almost impossible for a legislator to represent constituents in other counties as well as he can represent those in his own. Before entering the legislature, most members have built up a network of friends and acquaintances through their business or profession and their civic and social activities—and these are usually concentrated in a single county. Once they are elected to office, those who are part-time legislators continue to maintain a business, law office, or other activity that brings them into frequent contact with persons in their home county. Legislators frequently mention how easy it is to stay in touch with what is going on at home because of these continuing, informal contacts. But staying in touch outside the home county requires effort. It is necessary to establish contacts, make trips, and persuade local organizations to issue invitations.

In some sparsely populated rural areas the problem is principally one of geography. A legislator may have to represent such a large area with widely scattered communities that it is difficult if not impossible to make frequent personal visits throughout the district. Related to this is the problem of trying to maintain contact in a number of different counties and communities. This means visiting a number of courthouses regularly, becoming acquainted with a number of local editors, and arranging schedules to speak to many small groups scattered across the district. Some nonmetropolitan legislators find it difficult to keep up with the requests for speaking engagements; others have difficulty getting such invitations because they lack visibility in a sprawling, multicounty district. Some legislators establish regular schedules for appearances in the district even without invitations. One member visits each of four county courthouses once a month; another schedules monthly visits to six small communities outside his own county. Most multicounty districts are not served by any single newspaper. A legislator may have to establish contacts with editors and send press releases to as many as five to ten local, weekly newspapers. New legislators often find it difficult to establish such contacts, but once this has been achieved communication through the media may be relatively easy. It is not much more difficult to send copies of a column or a news release to ten newspapers than to one or two.

Legislators with large multicounty districts (and some with smaller ones) often face another problem: their districts do not follow county lines. In addition to having one or more whole counties in the district, a legislator may have part of a county, perhaps a very small part. Alternatively a legislator may represent no entire county but just parts of two or three. One Tennessee legislator, in fact, represents parts of five different counties, but all the county seats are in other districts. It is difficult to maintain good communication in part of a county, particularly if the section is relatively small, or excludes the county seat, or does not contain any whole communities. Both the media and the organizations that are so important for communication are lacking, and constituents in the area may not even know who their legislator is. One Ohio legislator whose district includes all or parts of five counties finds that he can maintain contacts well in the four counties where the county seat is included in his district, but he has no contacts in the fragment of the fifth county attached to his district—"they don't even know that I exist."

The problems of representing a district that cuts across county lines can be illustrated by one Indiana district, which contains all of one county, all but one township in a second, and from one to three townships in three others. There are seven weekly newspapers and one daily covering parts of the district, plus three metropolitan newspapers published outside the district but read by some in it—and consequently the legislator has to try to maintain some contact with ten newspapers although he serves only a small fragment of the readers of some of the papers. This legislator finds some advantages in the situation, however. After years of experience he has learned how to get news releases printed by the newspapers and carried by local radio stations; he believes anyone running against him would have great difficulty in reaching the media. He finds that the individual townships do not have many institutions and organizations that can be used for communication, and consequently he works through county groups—even though he represents only part of the county. Despite his extensive experience and contacts, he finds that he hears more often from the counties where he represents all or most of the townships. One of the counties that is partly in his district has only 19,000 persons but shares two senators and three representatives. He suggests that, if all the legislators tried to represent the whole county, as he does, it would be overrepresented.

It is difficult to determine whether a county that is divided between districts is overrepresented or underrepresented in reality. If a small county is divided among several members, none of whom live there and all of whom principally represent other counties, the needs of that county could be ignored. It would also be possible for a county to suffer from disagreements among several legislators representing parts of it. A similar problem may arise if a very small county is attached to a larger one. Probably the most obvious case of distorted representation occurs when a small portion of a county, with a few hundred or a few thousand persons, is detached from the main part of the county and attached to another district. Unless the legislator makes heroic efforts to overcome the communication barrier, he is not likely to be known by the voters in this fragment. More often than not, they will contact the legislator who represents the rest of the county; he may handle their problems or forward them to the other member. Where legislative district lines have created such fragmentation, many constituents are represented de facto by legislators for whom they have no opportunity to vote.

The problems of fragmented counties and those of large multi-county districts are both consequences of judicial demands for standards of population equality in districting. In Massachusetts these new standards deprived the islands of Martha's Vineyard and Nantucket of their individual representatives and linked them in a district with a part of Cape Cod. The islanders protested, and their rallying cry of "secession" created publicity for their plight. While the legislature considered a constitutional amendment that might give special consideration to the islands, as a temporary expedient it authorized a legislative aide for each of the two islands. The Speaker appointed to these positions the former members of the House from Martha's Vineyard and Nantucket. Although this gave the representative closer liaison with the islands than he could otherwise receive, press reports indicated that many constituents were not happy dealing with a middle man, and that the legislator found some difficulties in working with liaison persons whom he had not hired.

## Institutional Norms and Resources

The problems of communication faced by legislators and the techniques that are feasible vary according to the type of district, but there are also systematic differences from state to state in the commonly used techniques of communication. A major reason for variations among the states is that legislatures develop different standards or norms of behavior for dealing with constituents, and some legislatures provide their members with much more adequate resources than others do for communicating with constituents. One way of measuring these variations is to find out how often legislators used newsletters and conducted opinion polls in their districts; both are techniques that require substantial resources to be used effectively. Our interviews provide a rough measure of these activities.

In North Carolina and Massachusetts, very few members of the legislature make much use of newsletters, and very few of them try to carry out polls of their constituents.

In Colorado and Indiana, approximately one-third of the legislators who were interviewed send out newsletters, but most of these are sent to a few hundred or perhaps a thousand persons—including such groups as political party workers or interest group leaders. Very few send newsletters to all constituents. Relatively few legislators send out questionnaires, and most of those who do, send them to the same limited group who get the newsletters.

In Kentucky and Ohio perhaps one-fourth of the members send out newsletters; most of these in Kentucky and a majority in Ohio who do send newsletters distribute them to all constituents—sometimes using volunteers to distribute them by hand. About one-third of the legislators in both states make some use of opinion polls, but often these are sent to fewer than all the constituents.

In Tennessee at least half of the legislators use newsletters, usually sent to all constituents, and as many as two-thirds of them make some use of polls, in most cases being sent to all constituents.

In Texas about two-thirds of the legislators who were interviewed send out newsletters, usually to all constituents, and approximately the same number sent out questionnaires. In other words, most of those who use newsletters include survey questions in some of the newsletters.

Finally, all California legislators who were interviewed send out newsletters to their constituents as a whole, and almost all of these include questionnaires from time to time in the newsletters.

While the proportions in each state are approximations, they make the point that newsletters and constituent polls are much more common in some legislatures than in others. These differences can be explained by both the norms of legislature and the resources that are available to members for financing newsletters and polls. The idea of using any communication technique—a newsletter, poll, newsletter columns, or radio tapes—originates with a few of the more enterprising members, perhaps those with close districts, larger ambitions, or greater communication skills. Other legislators learn about the technique and decide to use it in their districts. If some of these techniques become widely adopted over a period of years, the incoming legislator discovers that most legislators are sending out polls or newsletters and decides to follow the practice. In states like California and Texas, for example, newsletters are used not only by particularly skillful and ambitious legislators but by others who would appear to lack both the skills and the motivation to use sophisticated communications techniques.

It is also evident that the availability of resources affects the use of these techniques. It is time-consuming to prepare a newsletter or to write a weekly newspaper column. Developing a good questionnaire takes time, and tabulating the totals of questionnaires from constituents can be a very time-consuming enterprise. Many of the legislators who told me that they did not prepare newsletters or newspaper columns said that they would like to do this, or they intended to in the future, but they just could not find enough time. In states like California and Texas where newsletters are most commonly used, legislators have staff assistants to help prepare them. In states like Colorado, Indiana, Kentucky, and Ohio, the lack of individual staff does not preclude the use of newsletters and questionnaires; it means that these are produced only by those legislators with the motivation and skill to do the job themselves. In some states the party caucus staff provides information to include in the newsletters, but does not seem to offer technical assistance with producing newsletters or preparing questionnaires.

To send a newsletter and/or a questionnaire to all the households in a legislative district can be very expensive. In most of the states included in our study the funds available to individual members for printing and mailing are much less than would be necessary to send a mailing to all constituents once or twice a year. In some states there is a modest allocation for office expenses that would pay part of the cost of a general mailing. Some states provide very limited funds for postage, and some pay none at all. This largely explains why legislators in Indiana and Colorado, for example, send out newsletters only to a select list of a few hundred constituents. In states where funds do not support a general mailing, some legislators pay the costs themselves, while others recruit political workers to deliver the newsletter or questionnaires to every house in the precinct. They may also publish a questionnaire in a column or a paid advertisement in a newspaper.

In Texas and California, the two states where newsletters are most commonly used, there are specific allocations of funds for mailing them. In Texas members are permitted 50,000 individual mailings a year; this makes possible at least two mailings to every household. California legislators are permitted four free mailings during a two-year term; the number used to be five, but it was cut to four because of criticisms that the larger number benefited incumbents politically. In a further effort to limit the political use of newsletters, California legislators may not make free mailings in the last few months before the election.

In one sense, the most important variable affecting the use of newsletters and polls is the resources available for preparing, printing, and mailing them. But it is the legislators themselves who authorize funds for hiring individual staff and for printing and mailing newsletters. Resources are allocated for these functions in legislatures where the members believe that the functions are important enough to justify the expense. Newsletters are often criticized as a means of serving the political interests of incumbent legislators, and many legislators agree with that criticism. This is obviously one reason why most legislatures have not provided funds needed to pay the full costs of mailing one or more newsletters a year.

Generally, most legislatures have been very cautious about providing individual members with professional staff, secretaries, and office and mailing expenses. Some legislators are sensitive to criticism that legislative costs are too high and that funds allocated to individual members gives them an unfair advantage in elections. Many legislators strongly believe in the concept of the "amateur," part-time member, and they resist efforts to make the position more professional and institutionalized. In some legislatures the leadership prefers to centralize staffing, rather than allocating staff resources to individual members. Massachusetts and Ohio are examples of states where the allocations of resources to individual members have been surprisingly limited, given the length of the sessions and the nearly full-time commitment of many members to the job.

California has led the states in the provision of staff and other resources to the individual member. A constituent entering a California legislator's office might easily believe that he had wandered into a congressman's office by mistake because the offices are bustling with staff members. The California legislators also have fund allocations for district offices, where much of the constituency service work is done. Even though the Texas legislature has a regular session only every two years limited to less than five months, the expense allocation to the members permits them to hire staff on a year-round basis (at a lower level than during the session) and permits them to have district offices, a provision that many of them take advantage of. In both California and Texas the district office is an important factor in facilitating communication and also in providing constituency service. In other states only a few legislators have established district offices, either by paying for them personally or by borrowing space in a local city hall or courthouse.

## Techniques of Communication

The character of the district defines the problem of communication for the legislator. The legislative institution determines the resources available, and fellow legislators provide norms and examples. How well the legislator uses his resources to communicate with the district depends on the skills and imagination of the individual representative. Those who work hardest and use the most sophisticated techniques tend to be younger and often more ambitious; they are more often located in metropolitan areas. Some of the older and more experienced members, particularly in rural areas, do not believe that these techniques are necessary or desirable; they rely on more informal, personal contact.

*The Media.* In my analysis of district variations, I described differences in the accessibility of media coverage, particularly in newspapers. The larger the number of legislators in an area covered by a newspaper, the greater the difficulties faced by any single member in getting coverage of his activities. Some legislators get better coverage than others. Some legislators know how to prepare press releases and develop contacts with reporters. Some are articulate in radio and television interview programs. Legislators with professional experience in press, radio, television, or advertising generally have little difficulty in getting media coverage.

Other legislators get more than their share of publicity because they are "out front on issues." They consistently take positions on important and controversial issues. Some are genuinely issue-oriented, and some have strong liberal or conservative orientations. Others may speak out on controversial issues primarily to get media coverage. The legislator who pays particular attention to needs in his district—better roads, improved parks, better storm drainage—can often get attention for his efforts. A few legislators told me that they deliberately avoid media coverage, particularly on controversial issues, because they thought it would do more harm than good. One legislator with a strong issue-orientation, after having been defeated for reelection in 1976 and then elected in 1978, decided to reduce his political risks by taking a lower profile on issues, by supporting the legislative efforts of colleagues rather than introducing bills on controversial issues himself. In short, despite the varied constraints on access to media, legislators with skill and determination can use the media as a significant means of communication.

While some legislators try to keep a low profile, most legislators recognize the risks of media coverage. There is not only the risk that publicity about their stand on a controversial issue will alienate voters, there is also the risk that the stands they take and their legislative activities will be distorted or criticized by the media. The press, radio, and television are not ideal media for communicating with constituents because they are not under control of the legislators. For this reason some legislators write a regular column, at least during the session, for use in the newspapers, or tape a report for use on radio stations. It is almost impossible for legislators to get a regular column printed in a major metropolitan newspaper. The prospects are much better in rural papers and in some of the suburban weekly papers in metropolitan area. Legislators may use the column to summarize major legislative activities, such as hearings or important bills that have passed—in some states a central legislative agency or a party caucus prepares a summary that members can use for this purpose—to describe bills they have introduced or projects they are seeking for the district, or to explain their voting record. Legislators often provide information about how they can be contacted or when they will be visiting or speaking in various parts of the district.

*Newsletters.* The newsletter serves the same purpose as the newspaper column; it gives the legislator an opportunity to publicize his voting record, speeches, and activities; the legislator can explain what he is doing and define the image that he wants to create, without any reporter acting as an intermediary. The legislator can describe efforts being made to help the district and can also advertise his accessibility, listing phone numbers, office hours, and services that are available to constituents. The format of a newsletter gives greater flexibility than a newspaper column; it should get more attention from constituents because it arrives in the mail. A newsletter may enhance a legislator's visibility and contribute to his image as one who seeks to stay in touch with constituents. The newsletter also provides a good vehicle for polling constituents.

A sample of newsletters shows them, as a whole, to be of professional quality. They compare favorably to congressional newsletters in terms of printing, style, use of photographs, and in the skill with which information is presented and the image of the legislator is portrayed. Most newsletters include a picture of the representative, and some show him meeting with important officials or constituents or hard at work in the legislative chamber. The content of the newsletters can be divided into reports on legislative matters, issues affecting the district, offers of services, and information about how to contact the legislator.

It is rather common to include summaries of major legislation passed during the session. One legislator offers to provide information about any of the bills or copies of them. Another includes a list of bills most likely to affect residents of his district. Some members evaluate major bills passed during the session or make judgments about how well the legislature performed in general. Sometimes newsletters are issued at the start of the session, with space devoted to describing the major issues likely to arise or those issues most likely to affect the district. Some of these reports clearly serve an educational purpose, explaining complicated issues, describing the pressures to raise or cut taxes, or discussing the need for new legislation. Several legislators print pie-shaped diagrams explaining how state funds are raised or spent. Here the legislator is given a chance to describe his own views and make his own arguments on issues that are pending in the legislature. Several legislators use the newsletter to explain constitutional amendments or initiative or referenda proposals that will soon be on the ballot. He can present pro and con positions, and sometimes he endorses or opposes the proposal.

Most legislators give particular attention to bills that they have sponsored. At the start of the session these may be described in some detail. A Texas legislator devotes half a page to his "agenda for '79," ranging from tax relief to the reduction of bureaucratic paperwork and providing better mental health care facilities in his city. He devotes space to his proposal to end the local property tax by offering local governments the chance to adopt alternative sources of revenue, such as a sales tax. One newsletter consists in large part of a series of articles on bills introduced and passed by the legislator (I will call him Brown) under such headlines as "Brown Bill Providing Tax Incentive to Home Owner Becomes Law"; "Brown Wins Fight to Reduce State Meals Tax"; "Three Year Brown Effort: New State Antitrust Law"; "Brown Joins Move to Raise Drinking Age." Another legislator included a description of his successful legislation under the title: Rep. [    ]'s Bills Become Law." (There was no list of bills that did not become law.) Although less attention was given to voting records, some legislators did provide brief descriptions of their voting records on some major bills. One legislator pointed out that he had a record of voting on 99.2 percent of the roll calls in the session, the best record of any member from his large county.

A substantial part of a legislator's efforts involves legislation and projects specifically for the district and various kinds of assistance to groups and neighborhoods in the district. The newsletters report some of the local legislation and projects, but they say little about the more specialized services for groups and neighborhoods—presumably because the newsletter is usually sent throughout the district, and these services are of interest only to smaller groups. One legislator from Texas, however, has published a newsletter that provides detailed statistical information about state services for his district. Two versions of the newsletter are printed, one for each county in the district. Residents can learn from the newsletter, for example, how many extension agents and 4-H Clubs are in the county; how large the livestock and crop production of the county is; how many students attended schools, how much was spent for their textbooks, and how many students from the county are attending public colleges; how many miles of roads are in the county; how many hunting and fishing licenses were issued; and what successes the state Industrial Commission had in bringing new plants to the county.

Many legislators provide specific information about services available from the state or directly from the legislator. One newsletter contains a list of free publications available from state agencies. Another legislator provides a list of state publications available from his office; he cites the heavy requests for these publications as a sign that constituents are paying attention to the newsletter. Several legislators provide a list of telephone numbers that can be called in the capital, or in their city, for information on a variety of governmental matters or of state and local services. One California legislator who represents a Spanish-speaking district included in his newsletter a full page, printed in both English and Spanish, explaining in detail the steps a person should take in dealing with a contractor if he wished to build or remodel a house, including information about calling the state licensing board to check on the contractor's record. At the same time the legislator described his bill designed to provide more protection to consumers in dealing with contractors.

Many newsletters contain information about how to contact the legislator by phone or letter, along with strong requests that constituents get in contact if they have any problems or want to express their views on issues. One legislator lists an office number in the state capitol, a twenty-four hour answering service number, and the member's home phone number. Another newsletter describes the location of a district office, inviting constituents to call the number or to visit ("There's always a pot of coffee brewing, so stop by and say hello").

One California legislator not only provides information on the location of his district offices in two counties but also includes pictures and descriptions of the jobs done by each member of his district staff. Several of the legislators list their regular office hours for meeting constituents in various parts of the district or "town meetings" scheduled in the district.

One California legislator puts out a detailed annual report, which is distributed to about five thousand persons on his mailing list. It is an eighteen-page report, with detailed sections on community service (with forty-four specific activities), legislation sponsored in the last session (and information on its success or failure), legislation he will sponsor in the next session, his record on major and controversial bills, his ratings (all highly favorable) by five interest groups, and three pages of examples of his service to individual constituents. There is no way to tell how carefully this report is read by constituents, but those who do not read it cannot fail to be impressed with their representative's record of service and will learn in detail where he stands on the issues.

*Public Opinion Polls.* These polls are used by most legislators surveyed in California, about two-thirds in Texas and Tennessee, about a third in Kentucky and Ohio, and smaller numbers in the other states. Where funds permit newsletters to be sent out widely, questionnaires are usually included. Elsewhere, questionnaires may be printed in newspapers, mailed to a smaller list of contacts in the district, or even distributed by hand when the legislator is walking a precinct or working a shopping center. Those who do not use opinion polls often indicate that they wish they had the resources necessary for conducting them; some, however, assert that polls are inaccurate or are unnecessary for making judgments about constituent opinion. Some legislators have given up polls because the response rate has been poor. Some legislators are sharply opposed to polls, arguing that they are nothing more than public relations devices.

Most state legislators who use opinion polls are well aware that the polls can be useful public relations devices, but they also believe that polls can provide them with a useful measure of public opinion. For the most part the questionnaires I collected from legislators seem to be designed to find out what constituents are thinking rather than to provide evidence of public support for the legislator's position. Most of the questions do not appear biased and are well constructed. They deal with topics that are on the legislature's agenda and are important and often controversial. Some of the legislators try to provide some background for the questions. One legislator whose questionnaire included a number of items on taxation provided in the newsletter a page of information on sources of tax revenue, allocation of spending, and comparison of average tax expenditures in Texas with that of other states. Legislators often ask constituents what is the most important problem facing the legislature or the state. Although the questions generally appear carefully prepared, it is not clear whether most legislators are aware of the difficulty of writing questions. One legislator indicated that 60 percent of his respondents were opposed to pari-mutual betting but that the same percentage favored it when it was described as a new source of revenue.

Obviously legislators, like anyone who conducts polls on public issues, face the problem of how to simplify complex issues so that constituents will understand them and will give useful responses. A number of the questionnaires on taxes and spending realistically avoid simple yes-or-no questions about cutting taxes. For example, one asks if local property taxes should be cut even if state funds must be increased to make up the deficit. One asks respondents to choose which type of taxes should be raised if the legislature should decide that a tax increase was necessary; another asks which tax should be cut if tax cuts are possible. Several questionnaires cover proposed changes in political institutions, such as a presidential primary, voter registration by party, or single-member districts in local government.

One interesting questionnaire describes a series of hypothetical situations "which are the kind I face often as your Assemblyman." The legislator asked, "Imagine yourself in my place—what would you do in the following situations?" The cases posed a series of choices: voting one's conscience or for the wishes of most constituents; making an endorsement in a local nonpartisan race; making a trade to get a bill passed that you are sponsoring in return for supporting an unneeded project sponsored by another legislator. The survey also asked constituents about how he should use his time in various situations, involving time spent in the district, in legislative hearings, attending a local parade, or going to social events. (A report in the next newsletter showed that a majority of voters wanted the legislator to vote his conscience, avoid deals, make the endorsement, and give priority to legislative business over district visits and parades.) Whether such advice from constituents is really helpful to the legislator can be debated, but it may serve as an educational function for the constituents concerning the choices actually faced by legislators.

My interviews and the examples of questionnaires indicate that most legislators use questionnaires not only to score public relations points but also to learn more about opinion in the district. The question is whether they are successful. It is impossible to answer confidently without much more data, but most legislators believe that they learn something from the polls. Often the effect of the poll is to confirm the perception of district opinion that the legislator already has. One legislator who described his poll results in those terms added, "The poll gives me a little backbone." In a similar vein, one legislator explained that when interest groups made demands which she knew would be unpopular in the district, she would show them poll results confirming the district attitude. One legislator said that he often asked the same question over a period of years and was able to keep track of changes in the direction or intensity of district opinion.

Although legislators often mentioned that polls confirmed and reinforced their perceptions of constituent opinion, most indicated they were sometimes surprised by the results. Some said they were not surprised by the direction of the majority viewpoint but by the size of that majority. One Texas legislator who knew that his district favored the dealth penalty was startled to find that 97 percent of those responding to the poll favored it. The same legislator was surprised to find a majority (60 percent) of the same constituents favored the registration of hand guns. Several legislators reported that polls showed their districts were about evenly divided on the abortion issue, while the organized pressures on that issue had led them to believe that a solid majority were opposed. Polls may also demonstrate whether a legislator is successful in arguments that he is making to his constituents. One legislator was disappointed to find that his working-class constituents were opposed to passage of an income tax, as an alternative to part of the sales tax, despite his explanation of how the income tax would be less burdensome to them.

There is a huge variation in the proportion of persons who return the questionnaires (through newsletters or other means). Many legislators reported responses numbering only a few percentage points. Some legislators have given up using polls because of the low response rate. A fair number of members report responses in the 10 to 15 percent range, which would have to be considered an excellent rate for such surveys. A few legislators report responses from mailings of questionnaires to the general public to be as high as 30 to 50 percent—totals that are difficult to believe. It would be interesting to know what distinguishes the legislators (and the questionnaires) who get 10 percent or more from those who get very few responses. Legislators seemed to be more concerned about the low number of responses than about the risk that the responses might come from an unrepresentative sample. A few members, however, were alert to this problem. One checked the parts of the district the questionnaires came from. Another explained which groups or types of constituents normally were overrepresented and said that he took account of this distortion in interpreting the results. One legislator, acknowledging that those persons who felt strongly about the topics would be more likely to answer the questionnaire, pointed out that those persons were of particular interest to him because their intensity of feelings might lead them to remember his stand on the issue on election day. One legislator, a sociologist well aware of the unrepresentative sample, said that the poll was a good way to learn the views of the attentive public.

It would be a mistake to assume that legislators only count the number of pro and con responses to questions. A number of them noted that constituents often wrote in comments on the questionnaire, and that these comments were often the most useful parts of the responses. One legislator noted that constituents who would not take the time to write letters would write their viewpoints on a questionnaire. Another said that some constituents who would not take the trouble to fill out a questionnaire would be motivated by it to talk to him about issues on the poll when they had an occasion to see him.

Instead of sending out a questionnaire to all constituents, some legislators send one to a few hundred or a thousand persons—those on the mailing list, party workers, community and group leaders, etc. This may be done because it is cheaper than a general mailing, or the legislator may believe that this smaller group is better informed and more likely to respond, or that the opinions of this group are more important. Some legislators get a substantial response, as high as 50 percent, from such a select group. One Indiana legislator sends the questionnaire to active party workers in the district to keep in step with this group, on whom he depends for renomination and reelection.

One Texas legislator, in addition to sending out a poll in his newsletter at the start of the session, uses them on specific topics throughout the session. A university professor conducts these polls for him, using a stratified sample of 1,000 persons in the district. The legislator finds these polls to be more reliable and useful than the questionnaires sent out with the newsletter.

Most legislators who regularly use polls take them seriously as a source of information about opinion in the district, but this does not mean that they rely on polls as the only source. They often seem to regard polls as a useful supplement to other sources of information about opinion. Most of the contacts from constituents are organized, and legislators often wonder how accurately the vocal and organized minorities reflect the viewpoints of the whole district. Despite the limitations inherent in measuring opinion through questionnaires, with returns that may be small and unrepresentative, some legislators find that this provides a good balance to the organized opinion.

Of course there are other ways of tapping the viewpoints of groups and individuals and balancing the organized pressure. A legislator can initiate contacts with persons whose judgment and knowledge he trusts, who are community and group leaders. One legislator who described in some detail the variety of techniques that she used to solicit opinions on specific issues said that she also used questionnaires about once a term, not because they were better or were a substitute for these other activities, but that if she used all the sources available for measuring and evaluating opinion, she could get a good picture of what her constituents are thinking.

*Mail.* One of the most important ways of maintaining contact with constituents is through mail. Legislators may specifically encourage mail through their newsletters or when they are speaking to groups in the district. Anything that a legislator does to increase visibility, whether visiting the district or speaking out on controversial issues, is likely to lead to an increase in mail. Those legislators who have enough staff to answer their mail regularly and promptly are also likely to receive more mail.

Mail may be valuable to the legislator as a source of information about opinions on issues and as a means of alerting the member to problems in the district. Legislators recognize, however, that mail may not be representative of district opinion and that large amounts of mail on an issue are usually the result of an organized campaign. Although the legislator can encourage constituents to write, it is impossible to structure the flow of mail in order to make it representative. From the legislator's viewpoint, mail is a passive form of communication. The member who wants to get advice from his constituents, or from specific constituent groups, cannot simply wait patiently for the mail to come in. It is necessary to take the initiative, to seek out those whose views are important on the issue.

*Personal Contacts.* To a large extent legislators develop personal contacts with constituents through organized groups, a more efficient and practical method than trying to reach them one at a time. The availability of organized groups depends to a large extent on the social structure of the community or communities that lie within the district and the congruence between the boundaries of the district and the communities.

Most members take advantage of invitations to speak to organized groups, unless they have conflicting commitments. Legislators often find that these invitations come most frequently during the session when they have the least free time. Some members encourage such invitations; others get more requests than they can handle. A Massachusetts legislator who goes to many meetings says that he is trying to cut down on the number he attends because the district has been increased in size. A Texas legislator whose heterogeneous district spans three counties says that during a single year he gave 457 speeches and that the question-and-answer session following the speeches provided valuable feedback on public opinion in the district. A California legislator reports that he averages ten invitations a day to attend meetings and that half of these include invitations to speak. Not every representative is overloaded with speaking invitations.

The member can also organize forums or town meetings in various parts of the district, perhaps in conjunction with other public officials; or he can attend political party meetings, public hearings, or other gatherings where public business is being discussed and where he can make his views known and find out what constituents are thinking. A Cleveland representative organizes town hall meetings in his district on topics of interest to his constituents and brings in state officials to talk to them; 500 attended a meeting on utility rates. A Chicano legislator in Denver holds a monthly meeting with other public officials in the district and gets a good turnout of citizens. An Ohio legislator in a suburban district has held about forty meetings during a two-year term in the various townships of his district, but averages only about ten in the audience. A California member finds that attendance at such meetings is better if they are co-sponsored by some group, because its members as well as the general public will attend.

A number of members in states with well-organized political parties attend regular meetings of party workers, as often as once a month. A Cleveland legislator regularly attends the Democratic party ward clubs in his district and stays in touch with ward leaders. Some Ohio legislators meet regularly with local township officials or with mayors to stay informed about local problems. Some legislators attend local school board or city council meetings or planning and zoning meetings when controversial issues are being discussed to find out what constituents are thinking. This may increase the risk that they will become involved in strictly local issues—a risk that some legislators carefully avoid but others appear to welcome.

A California legislator regularly consults persons and group leaders who are expert on a topic or are most likely to be affected by a bill when she is considering introducing legislation or is trying to make up her mind about a bill. Some legislators send out copies of bills to groups in their district that would be affected by them to alert the groups and to get feedback from them. A few legislators have organized advisory groups representing a cross-section of the district and consult these groups with some regularity. An Indiana member, for example, has a "liaison board" of twelve persons who have contacts with major interests in the district. A legislator from a low-income district in Los Angeles has set up a group of advisory committees on a variety of topics and meets with each group every couple of months; some members of the group are volunteers recruited through her newsletter. Several legislators establish networks of elected officials and community and group leaders throughout the district who can provide quick feedback on issues that arise.

Many legislators devote a great deal of their time in the districts to attending social functions of all kinds. Occasionally they are invited to say a few words or are introduced to the group; more often they simply go there to make personal contacts. Legislators attend these functions for a number of reasons. It gives them visibility, which may be important in remote parts of a large district. They often find that constituents will talk to them about legislative issues, local needs, or personal problems at such gatherings, thus providing legislators with opportunities to learn something about unorganized opinion in the district as well as to provide services to persons who would not call them or come to a district office with their problems.

The types of social events mentioned by legislators are as varied as the characteristics of their districts. A number of legislators attend social functions, such as potluck suppers, at churches. Black legislators often find that churches are the center of the social and political life of their community. Legislators from all types of districts attend high school games. Rural legislators attend auctions, square dances, fish fries, or barbeques. Legislators from ethnic neighborhoods go to local festivals, fairs, and parades.

Legislators view these social functions with varying degrees of enthusiasm. Many politicians throughly enjoy social life and would rather spend their evenings attending social events than at home reading a book or studying legislation. Other legislators attend these functions simply because they think it is good politics. Another group of legislators avoid these events, unless they are invited to speak. One California legislator who believes it is important to attend these functions lists on his calendar as far in advance as possible the important social events scheduled by the groups and communities in his district so that he may attend as many as possible. Some legislators are quite imaginative in making their presence felt around the district. A veteran Ohio legislator, whose district extends into parts of three counties, presents a plaque to any couple that has been married over fifty years, and this provides an incentive to visit communities all over the district and to maintain contacts throughout the area.

One of the best ways of being accessible to constituents is to maintain a district office with a staff member and a telephone; if the member can be found at the office on a regular basis, the accessibility is even greater. Relatively few states provide money for district offices; in our group of nine states, all the California legislators had district offices, as did most Texas legislators (at least when the legislature was not in session). Some legislators in other states have found ways to maintain some form of district office or to maintain regular office hours in various locations throughout the district. A legislator in a blue-collar suburb of Cleveland has established an office in the city hall, using that switchboard to get phone calls. I visited another Ohio representative in his district office—a small room in an old house conveniently located in his lower-middle-class district, where he handles a heavy case load with the help of a secretary. Some legislators whose districts encompass a number of counties, cities, or towns hold regular office hours, every week or once or twice a month at each county courthouse or town hall. This is a common pattern in Massachusetts. One member from that state, for example, holds regular office hours once a month in each of the three towns in his district, at which he meets people with individual problems. A rotation policy such as that is, of course, less useful to constituents than the existence of an office that is accessible all the time.

The most ambitious and demanding efforts to maintain contact with constituents are made by those legislators who walk the precincts. Because it is such a slow, time-consuming way to maintain contacts, we may wonder why such legislators use it. One answer is that the technique proved effective for many legislators when they were first elected, and they believe it remains an effective technique. It makes a favorable impression on constituents, who expect candidates to ring their doorbell but not officeholders, particularly when there is no campaign in progress. Those legislators who use the door-to-door technique find it gives them a good picture of constituent attitudes, of what issues are of concern to the ordinary citizen.

Legislators generally do not try to cover the entire district with door-to-door visits during a term. They are most likely to visit a few blocks in a precinct once or twice a month, but those who follow this practice believe that from visits to a small sample of homes they can gain both public relations advantages and some useful feedback. It is interesting that several of the legislators who mentioned such precinct visits were California members, whose districts are much larger than the average in population. The most devoted disciple of precinct visits whom I interviewed is a representative in San Francisco, who walks a precinct every Friday when he returns to the district from Sacramento. At the same time every member of his staff is also expected to visit a precinct. In addition, he expects his staff members to visit organizations and groups throughout the district every week to establish contacts and make them aware of the services available through the legislator's office. One final example of personal contacts comes from a Cleveland representative who use a telephone instead of shoe leather. During a weekend afternoon he will make random phone calls to persons in his district, identify himself, and ask them about issues and problems that concern them. He estimates that he reaches at least a thousand persons a year and that he gets useful feedback about the issues of concern to his constituents, as well as about the limitations on their knowledge about public issues.

## The Goals of Communication

Probably the most important variable affecting a legislator's accessibility is his motivation. Some work much harder and use more ingenuity than others; the younger, more ambitious members tend to be more willing to devote the time and energy necessary for good communication. An examination of communication from the viewpoint of the legislator and not the constituent risks exaggerating the effectiveness of communication. The average unattentive citizens are not listening very hard to the messages coming from their state legislators, and relatively few constituents make any effort to contact their legislators. Some constituents cannot or at least do not make any clear distinction between their congressmen and their state legislators. Until we have data on constituent perceptions of the state legislators, our picture of communications at this level will remain incomplete.

Communication is a two-way process. Both aspects are important to the legislator, and the techniques employed by legislators often incorporate both. Legislators who send out newsletters ofter incorporate questionnaires that will provide feedback; when they give speeches, they normally leave time for questions and comments; and legislators prefer the kinds of personal contact that will facilitate exchanges of views and information with constituents. Some legislators use newsletters to explain public issues, some emphasize their legislative accomplishments, and some seek to encourage and facilitate constituent requests for service. The newsletters, and presumably columns in newspapers and public speeches, are used to serve the varied goals of the legislators. The legislator who conducts a poll, initiates contacts with group leaders and other local elites, or talks to many average citizens in touring the district is trying to become as familiar as possible with the views and concerns of his constituents, to avoid being dependent entirely on the organized presentation of views and demands from the district.

Just as we lack constituent perception data that would help us to evaluate how well legislators are communicating, we lack constituent opinion data that would enable us to judge how accurately legislators perceive opinion in their district, how good their polls and other sources are. Most legislators I talked to seem to be quite confident about their assessment of constituent opinion. They think they know what issues interest and concern constituents, and what the direction and intensity of opinion on these issues are. They recognize how few constituents are well informed, and how few issues stir up much interest. Some legislators rely rather heavily on their polls to reinforce other sources of information; others believe that such polls are either unnecessary or unreliable.

Effective communication is important as an end in itself and also as an essential ingredient in representation. Constituents expect their legislators to be accessible, to listen to them, and to explain what is going on in government. Effective representation requires that legislators become throughly familiar with the needs and interests of the district, a requirement that cannot be met by waiting passively for mail or telephone calls. It is equally important that the legislator explain his activities and the decisions of the legislature to constituents. While the communication techniques that are suitable and feasible vary with the character of the district and the resources of the legislature, the success of these techniques depends largely on the personal skills and initiatives of the member. The legislator who is not an effective communicator not only risks defeat at the polls; he may unknowingly misrepresent the district because he fails to understand its needs and evaluate the demands that reach him. Even those legislators who may be less effective as communicators usually are sensitive to and interested in constituent opinions.

# 4. Policy Responsiveness: The Ingredients

What is the relationship between the views of constituents on issues and the perceptions, attitudes, and behavior of the representative on these issues? How does the legislator make judgments about constituent opinion and policy matters that are salient to his district? The underlying premise of policy responsiveness, according to Eulau and Karps (1978, p. 63), "is the presence of a meaningful connection between constituent policy preferences or demands and the representative's official behavior."

I will begin by examining major categories of issues because the ingredients of policy responsiveness differ from one kind of policy to another. The next step is to determine how constituent demands are organized and perceived by legislators. I will then examine two aspects of representation that have attracted much attention in the literature—focus and style—and attempt to clarify these often misunderstood concepts. In Chapter Five I will examine the factors that affect how legislators make choices in responding to needs demands on policy issues. I will then look at the concept of legislator responsibility to the district, concluding with a brief effort to integrate this analysis of representation into a larger theory of legislative decision-making.

## Policy Issues

It is useless to generalize about demands or the focus and style of representation without distinguishing among various types of policy issues. It is pointless to talk to state legislators about how they represent their districts without specifying the policy areas we are talking about. Members recognize that some issues are more salient than others to constituents; some are salient to broad groups of constituents while others are salient only to much smaller groups, usually organized ones. Some issues arouse intense feelings among constituents; most do not.

A study titled *A Policy Approach to Political Representation* by Ingram, Laney, and McCain (1980) provides some useful insights on this topic. "The attitudes of voters on issues are fragmented and multidimensional, with clusterings of issues that voters see as related" (p. 11). "We expect to find that representatives' attentiveness to and agreement with constituent opinion varies with issue clusters" (p. 12). The legislator will pay more attention to constituency on an issue that he believes is more salient to constituents (or arouses strong feelings among constituents) or a significant proportion of them. Even when a particular issue is not highly salient, the legislator may recognize that it is related to a cluster of issues on which constituents have opinions. This leads Ingram and her associates to suggest that certain issue domains may "activate certain cues because of the basic interests and concerns of the persons and groups involved" (p. 13). Legislators may be accustomed to hearing from certain groups of constituents on certain types of issues, and they may assume that those issues will be salient. When those issues arise, they may look for cues from constituent groups or even alert those groups to the bills that have been introduced.

The importance of issue dimensions has been recognized by others who have studied representation and legislative decision-making. One of the major findings of the studies of Miller and Stokes (1963), based on the 1958 survey of legislators and constituents, was that the congruence between constituent attitudes and the congressman's vote is higher on issues with high salience and intensity of feelings, such as civil rights. On such issues the congressmen's perceptions of constituency attitudes were also more accurate than on issues like foreign policy. Clausen's (1973) studies of roll-call voting patterns in Congress have emphasized the differences among major issue dimensions although he has not directly explored the differential impact of constituency.

John Kingdon (1977, 1981) has offered a model of the legislative decision-making process in which legislators ask themselves a series of questions about issues that arise and seek voting cues on the basis of answering those questions. The first question is whether the issue is controversial. If it is, the congressman examines the positions of the various forces or actors in his political environment—one of which is his constituency—and if there is consensus among them, votes accordingly. If the congressman encounters disagreement among them, he makes a judgment according to his major goals: satisfying constituents, gaining influence in Washington, and achieving policy objectives. Kingdon hypothesizes that "the congressman considers the constituency interest first. He may not end up voting with the constituency, but he always considers it when it is above the minimum level of importance" (1977, p. 578). At an early stage the congressman determines whether an issue is salient to his constituency, or significant groups within it. Issues are pertinent to this model because on some issues the legislator might be expected to recognize that constituents (or other actors) would normally be concerned—the issue would be salient to them.

For the purposes of studying policy responsiveness, it is useful to divide the issues facing legislative bodies as follows: 1) major issues that affect important groups of citizens generally—a) traditional issues, frequently economic ones, on which major interests and groups have established positions; b) newer issues, generally social ones, which often arouse strong emotional feelings and often cut across existing political alignments; 2) narrow, parochial issues of concern to specialized groups but of little interest to the general public, including bills affecting local governments; and 3) issues, however broad or narrow in scope, that are not salient to organized or unorganized interests in the district.

As I interviewed legislators in nine states, I regularly asked them about the issues that aroused most interest and generated most response from their districts, those that would fit one of the two categories of major issues, defined in 1) above. Certain types of issues were mentioned frequently enough in one or usually several states to provide a brief agenda of the issues most pertinent today regarding policy responsiveness of state legislators. The most frequent issue among the traditional, economic ones was collective bargaining for public employees, or specifically for teachers. In some states the issue of public employee salaries was mentioned, particularly in the context of constitutional or legislative limits on taxes. A labor issue broader in scope than public employees was the effort to adopt or to repeal right-to-work laws; some legislators mentioned that much of the pressure on that issue was coming from organized groups outside the state. Other aspects of educational financing were mentioned often, particularly in Ohio and Colorado. In several states the issue of taxes and controversies over establishing and implementing "tax caps," or limits on the state taxing or spending levels, were questions that stirred up constituent interest, particularly from organized groups of public employees. An economic issue of major importance at the time I was in Texas was an effort to raise the level of interest rates that lending institutions could charge. Several legislators were wrestling with the bottle bill and were getting input from their districts concerning it.

There are a number of traditional economic issues that seldom produce much input from constituents. Broad questions of budgetary policy generate little response, although proposed cuts in specific areas will arouse complaints from citizens—particularly employee groups. Legislation affecting the regulation of business or labor is of direct concern to specific interest groups but seldom arouses large numbers of constituents. Even tax policy, which concerns all taxpayers, produces a relatively small volume of mail and phone calls. Constituents are more likely to grumble generally about high taxes than to express their views about specific proposals to change the tax laws.

Some of the social issues mentioned by legislators are traditional ones such as changes in the laws regulating liquor or some aspects of gambling. But most of the social issues that arouse the strongest emotional responses in the districts are relatively new. There was a high degree of consensus within the states and among most of the states on the importance of these issues; some were currently on the agenda, while others had been tackled within the last session or two or were anticipated in the near future. Two of these are familiar ones, often associated in the minds of legislators: the Equal Rights Amendment (ERA) and abortion. In several states, particularly southern and border ones, capital punishment was a major issue, while in others gun control was a current topic. Busing continued to be an important legislative issue in some states, although it has faded in importance. A relatively new issue is the efforts by members of church-supported private schools to reduce state regulation. Finally there are emotional issues that arise from time to time involving various aspects of animal abuse and that produce surprisingly heavy constituent response. In Ohio the issue involved the hunting of mourning doves; in Texas it was instances of abusing dogs and using live rabbits for training greyhounds. (A few years ago in Ohio the issue involved a "bucking strap" used in rodeos to insure that horses would be bucking broncos.)

The reasons for making these distinctions (rather than other types of classifications) among types of issues will become clear in the discussion of the demands that are made on legislators. The types of groups that make demands, and the intensity of constituent opinions, are perceived by legislators as being different from one category to the next. These distinctions are also pertinent to an understanding of how legislators respond to constituent pressures.

## Constituent Demands

To understand the nature of constituent demands made on legislators regarding policy issues, we need answers to several questions: How are these demands communicated to the legislator, and to what extent are they organized? How does the nature of the issue affect the way demands are communicated and organized? Do demands arise differently from different types of districts? How accurately are demands perceived by legislators? How do legislators determine whether the demands communicated to them (often by organized groups) reflect the views and needs of unorganized constituents?

*Organized and Unorganized Channels.* It is useful to begin by summarizing the ways in which demands are communicated to the legislator from his district. In so doing, we should distinguish between organized demands and unorganized demands, even though in practice the distinction between the two is not always clear-cut.

1) Organized demands are made by the leaders and members of interest groups, businessmen, and local government officials: a) The leaders and paid lobbyists of groups, businessmen, and local officials may visit the legislator in the district or the capital, call or write to him, or send him questionnaires about his views; b) Rank-and-file members of interest groups may be mobilized to visit the legislator in the district or the capital or to participate in letter-writing campaigns; c) The legislator may get feedback from leaders or members of groups when he speaks at their meetings or visits their headquarters; d) The legislator may take the initiative in soliciting the views of these local elites and leaders by sending them copies of bills, asking for their advice, establishing advisory committees, or using other techniques to tap organized and expert opinion in the district.

2) Unorganized demands are made by individuals who are not part of the local elite and are not mobilized by them: a) These individuals may initiate communication with the legislator through letters, phone calls, or personal visits in the district or the capital; b) Individuals may communicate in person with the representative when they attend meetings where he speaks, or meet him in the precinct, at shopping centers, or wherever he goes to establish contacts; c) Individuals may respond to questionnaires sent out by the legislator; d) Individuals may communicate their concerns indirectly by writing letters to the newspaper editor read by the legislator or by talking to local elites who in turn contact the legislator; e) Individuals may use any of these channels to communicate purely personal concerns and problems that alert the legislator to broader problems that may require a legislative solution or better oversight of administrative agencies.

Traditional economic issues are most likely to be raised by leaders of the established, organized groups. The legislator is likely to be familiar with the positions of groups on these issues; the groups are often trying to preserve vested interests or to win a modest advantage. Occasionally an issue may be sufficiently controversial or have enough popular appeal so that the group will be able to mobilize members to write or visit their legislators. On the newer, more emotional, social issues some of the established groups, such as churches, have well-established positions, but much of the pressure comes from relatively new organizations, often single-issue groups such as those aligned on both sides of the abortion issue. These are issues that are salient and emotional enough so that group leaders may be successful in mobilizing mass participation in the lobbying efforts. These are also issues more likely to be salient to the unorganized constituents. The issues described as narrow and parochial are likely to attract the interest of only the group leaders, public officials, and other local elites. Some of these may have intense interest in the issues, but they will not be able to enlist broad popular support in their campaigns.

*District Variations.* The nature of the district affects the quantity and types of demands that are made, in ways that are rather obvious. The larger the number of organized groups that have a constituent base in the district, the greater the number of organized demands that will be made on the legislator. Some rural legislators emphasize the advantages of not having many groups, at least conflicting ones, in their district, and particularly the advantages of having no labor unions based in the district. Suburban legislators may have districts that do not follow political boundaries and therefore may lack recognizable group interests, though they may be contacted by groups with a base in the metropolitan area. Legislators in multimember and particularly countywide districts, such as those in North Carolina, are subject to demands from the broad variety of groups based in their largest districts. Because of the greater diversity of countywide districts, legislators are more likely to be subjected to conflicting demands from organized groups. In countywide districts the volume of organized mail is likely to be heavier than in single-member districts, but there may be relatively little unorganized or spontaneous mail from individuals because constituents lack the firsthand contact with members that is more likely to be found in single-member districts.

Legislators often describe their districts as being either issue-oriented or not very interested in issues, measured in terms of the amount of mail and other forms of communiction they get on issues. The most obvious variables affecting this are the level of education and the socioeconomic status of the district. Constituents in high-status districts are much more likely to raise issues on their own initiative; they are also more likely to be recruited as correspondents by interest-group leaders. In districts with lower educational levels, legislators often report that they receive little or no mail or phone calls on issues. The constituents do not initiate such contacts, and group leaders find it difficult to mobilize them. Most representatives of such districts do not seem to be bothered by the lack of input from constituents; they claim to know what the needs of their constituents are either because these needs are clear (better housing, health care, day care centers) or because they maintain such close contact with the district that group leaders and rank-and-file constituents can talk about their problems.

*Perception of Demands.* Since Miller and Stokes (1963) included perceptual accuracy as an aspect of their study of representation, a few political scientists have explored various dimensions of the question: how accurately do legislators perceive the views of their constituents? The existing research on this question is often methodically flawed and leaves many loose ends (see the summary of research in Clausen, 1977), but some generalizations can be made about the accuracy of these perceptions. The most important of these generalizations is that legislators will tend to exaggerate the extent to which their views are shared by their constituents. The legislators most likely to have an accurate perception are those who are more senior (unless constituent attitudes are changing rapidly) and those who represent relatively homogeneous districts. In addition, legislators are likely to more accurately perceive opinions on those issues they recognize as being salient to constituents.

Although many factors can impinge on the ability of legislators to accurately perceive their constituents' opinions, probably the most important and pervasive is the legislator's tendency to perceive greater agreement between his own views and those of his constituents than, in fact, exists. One reason for this is that the legislator's channels of communication may produce more input from those individuals and groups who do agree with him. He may send out newsletters and questionnaires to his supporters and get feedback from constituents at meetings of organizations that are friendly to him. Moreover, constituents and groups that are sympathetic to him may initiate more contacts, while those that are completely hostile may have given up trying to influence him. Of course the legislator may deliberately maintain communications with those individual and groups that are sympathetic to him and may be expected to vote for him at the polls.

Misperception arises when the legislator believes that he has an accurate perception of the full range of viewpoints in the district but is actually basing his judgments on a small sample of constituents or is misinterpreting some of the inputs that he gets from the district. Dexter (1977) concludes from interviews with a number of congressmen: "Some men automatically interpret what they hear to support their viewpoint" (p. 11); "A congressman's conception of his district confirms itself, to a considerable extent, and may constitute a sort of self-fulfilling prophecy"(p. 8).

My interviews with legislators shed some light on their perceptions of district opinion and their own evaluation of how accurately they can judge constituent opinions. It is impossible from the interview data, however, to determine how accurate these perceptions are or whether the legislators exaggerate their ability to judge opinions in their districts.

There is a high degree of consensus among state legislators that a large proportion of the mail they receive is organized mail, or programmed mail as one legislator described it. Most legislators believe that they can easily recognize organized mail. The most obvious sign of organization is the volume of mail. One legislator said that when he gets a thousand letters from his district on an issue, as happens from time to time, he is certain that the mail is organized; independent letters on an issue rarely total more than twenty-five. Legislators pay attention to the source of their mail, and most mail that comes from outside the district (or perhaps outside the county for a metropolitan legislator) is organized. Other indications of organized mail are similar or identical wording of letters or postcards or the use of a postal meter in a large mailing.

Legislators recognize that it is easier to organize large volumes of mail on emotional issues on which the letter writers have strong opinions—issues such as ERA, abortion, gun control, and the death penalty. Although the traditional economic interest groups continue to make some use of mass mailing campaigns, the experience of legislators suggests that it is the new organizations devoted to social issues that are currently making the greatest use of this technique. Other, less weighty emotional issues sometimes provoke a flood of mail. A legislator from Dallas reported getting 1,900 letters protesting the abuse of dogs after the media had publicized an individual case of alleged dog abuse.

State legislators recognize that most mail they get is organized by interest groups, but that does not necessarily mean they discount its importance or ignore it. On the one hand, organized mail does not reflect a cross-section of district opinion; on the other hand, some legislators believe that groups capable of organizing a mass mailing are also capable of mobilizing people to vote as a bloc at the polls. There is no consensus among legislators about how organized mail should be evaluated. An experienced, sophisticated Ohio legislator believes that organized mail tells something about district opinions because constituents must have some interest in an issue to send a letter; the mail is organized and not manufactured; and it assumes more importance because other sources of constituent input are so limited. A Tennessee representative evaluates organized mail in a fashion typical of many others. He believes that organized mail is not as dependable as individual letters as an indication of the opinions of the people in his district; he prefers to rely even more heavily on personal contacts to stay in touch with thinking in the district. A California legislator who has developed a variety of communication channels has established the practice of calling up persons who write to her with criticisms of a bill to find out why they oppose it, whether they understand it, and whether they have written simply because someone asked them to do so.

The most experienced legislators tend to be dubious about the mail they get not only because it is organized but also because they perceive that most constituents—even those who are persuaded to write—have little interest in or understanding of most issues. A veteran Kentucky lawmaker argues, "Almost without exception issues are generated; they are not real." Except for a few emotional issues, or something as threatening as a tax increase, he believes that the public has scant interest in issues even if they belong to organized groups whose leaders take stands on the issues. The problem, then, of evaluating organized mail is not only to decide how representative it is of constituent opinion but to determine whether a significant public opinion actually exists.

Some legislators who complain about the unrepresentative quality of organized mail also are frustrated by the relatively small number of independent, spontaneous letters that they receive. A couple of legislators from Denver, for example, voiced this complaint. One said, "To be honest, I don't get as much feedback from constituents as I would like; I get a lot of mail, but most of it is junk mail from various organizations, and I get very little unorganized mail from my district." The other made the point that most of the mail he got was either organized or was sent by persons who were reacting to some issue that had received media publicity. What he failed to get was much mail on the ordinary day-to-day issues concerning people—mail alerting him to problems in the district.

Many of these legislators, however, believe they have reasonably accurate perceptions of opinion in the district. Often they claim to know the district well and to stay in touch with its people. Some legislators use questionnaires because they cannot rely on the mail as a measure of constituent opinion, though many legislators are suspicious of opinion surveys. A more general, widespread source of information is the informal, personal contact with rank-and-file constituents and with trusted community leaders and friends. One North Carolina legislator, who says that he receives "stacks and stacks" of organized mail, gives it relatively little attention and says, "I learn best about public opinion by going around talking to people, and I think I have a good feel for what people want."

Most legislators quickly learn how little most constituents know and care about the issues confronting the state legislature, and many are frustrated by this knowledge. The perceptual problems most often faced by state legislators do not result from their inability to recognize organized communications, or even from a shortage of other means for measuring opinion. Rather, the legislator's constituents tend to lack the awareness and information required to form an effective opinion, even on issues that stir up organized responses or significantly affect the district. Perception fails because there is little or nothing to be seen.

## Areal Focus of Representation

Political scientists have been interested in legislators' perceptions of the geographic area they represent since the publication of *The Legislative System* with its emphasis on the areal focus of representation (Wahlke, Eulau, Buchanan, Ferguson, 1962, ch. 13). That study clarified Burkean notions of representation by distinguishing between the geographic focus of representation and its style (trustee v. delegate). The authors found that some legislators were district-oriented and some state-oriented, while some combined the two. A typical district-oriented legislator said his job was "to represent his constituents in matters that vitally affect his district" (p. 289). It is important to note the subtle and complicated distinctions among types of district representation. It is generally recognized that not all issues, but only a subset of them, are salient to interests in the district. It has also become clear that the range of possible foci of representation is broader than district and state. A legislator may represent the district, or a smaller constituency within the district, or a broader constituency that has some ties or roots within the district. Each of these possibilities needs to be examined.

*The District.* We can assume that most legislators are familiar with and sensitive to the interests of the whole district, and that they respond to demands that arise from the district on those issues that are salient to groups within it. A district orientation means a sensitivity to broadly defined attitudes and interests in the district, and more specifically a sensitivity to particular groups. Eulau, Wahlke, Buchanan, and Ferguson (1978, p. 117) have pointed out that "if a district interest, so-called, can be specifically singled out, it is more likely to be the interest of a politically salient group in the district than of the district as an undifferentiated entity." When we say that a legislator is oriented to the district, we mean that he is prepared to represent any and all groups rather than giving priority to some groups or interests in the district.

A district orientation does not mean that a legislator always gives priority to district interests; many issues are not salient to the district or to particular groups in the district. It does mean that the legislator is sensitive to district issues and aware of those issues that are most salient to the district; when an issue assumes major importance to the district, the legislator gives priority to the district's demands and interests. The authors of *The Legislative System* distinguish between legislators who are oriented to the district and those who are oriented to the state. In my interviews with state legislators, I did not gather the data necessary to make that distinction—largely because of doubts about its importance. It is difficult to believe that there are many legislators who ignore the interests and demands of their district if these are deeply felt and effectively articulated. Legislators are seldom forced to choose between the interests of their district and those of the state. The choices more often come between interests that are strong in their district (among others) and those that are strong in other parts of the state; when this occurs, there is a strong incentive to give priority to the interests of one's own district. Some legislators are more parochial than others, and some are particularly sensitive to district interests, but a simply dichotomy between district and state interests is artificial.

When I talked to legislators about their focus of representation, I was trying to distinguish between those who perceived themselves as representing the whole district and those who gave priority to subgroups within the district. Most legislators asserted that they represented the district, rather than some subgroup within it. Some of them were explicit about their responsibility to represent the whole district. Many members from heterogeneous districts represented areas composed of blacks and whites, and these members considered it essential to represent both racial groups. A Chicano representative from Denver, with a district more than one-third Hispanic and black, said that it was important to represent all ethnic groups in the district, not merely because the district wanted that, but because her influence in the legislature would be reduced if she was stereotyped as being just a Chicano representative. Several white Tennessee legislators who represent districts that used to be primarily white and are becoming at least half-black are very sensitive to the problems of trying to represent both groups.

*Smaller Constituencies.* In his study of congressmen and their districts, Fenno (1978) noted that a congressman perceives his electoral support in his constituency as a nest of concentric circles. The geographical boundaries of the district include: 1) the reelection constituency—those perceived as voting for the member; 2) the primary constituency—the strongest supporters who could be relied on in a primary election; and 3) the personal constituency—the close political advisers and confidants. Although Fenno deals with a congressman's various subconstituencies as they affect his electoral success, such subconstituencies carry implications for the member's representation of the district as well. A legislator must frequently make choices among competing groups and interests within his district, and these choices are likely to be made with due regard to the potential electoral support a group or interest can provide. It should be kept in mind that Fenno's conclusions about representing subconstituencies are not based on an empirical study of how congressmen respond to these groups on specific issues; they are based on watching the "home style" of congressmen and particularly their efforts to maintain the electoral support of these groups.

Do state legislators have similar perceptions of specialized constituencies that are the basis of electoral support, and, if so, do they feel particularly accountable to these constituencies on policy matters? In my talks with state legislators, I found much less awareness of and responsibility to such constituencies than Fenno found at the congressional level. When asked about sources of electoral support, many legislators were able to define parts of the district that were the best sources of electoral support. But they often did so in rather general terms, with less precision than might have been expected. Often voting support was defined in terms of party registration in various parts of the district; sometimes they cited voting statistics in precincts; and sometimes emphasis was placed on areas where they had strong personal contacts. Relatively few defined a reelection constituency precisely, and very few talked about what Fenno would call the primary constituency.

Among those who did define a reelection constituency, only a few said that they felt any greater responsibility to such groups or types of voters. Generally, state legislators do not seem to be particularly responsive to those groups who provide their strongest electoral support. There are some exceptions: a few legislators, for example, indicated rather explicitly that they tried to represent the views of the partisan majority that elected them. A conservative Republican in Indiana said, "You may have to address yourself first to the concerns of the group that you feel represents a majority"; he defined that group as those who shared a conservative philosophy. Another Indiana Republican representative said that he felt an obligation to the people who elected him, and particularly to the active party workers; he kept in close touch with the views of this constituency and found a high consensus on most issues. Some legislators who belong to ethnic minorities articulate a particular concern for that segment of the district; others emphasize the importance of representing all groups within the district.

Why is there so little evidence of state legislators being responsive to supportive constituencies in the district? Part of the answer may be methodological. Legislators may believe it is more acceptable to assert that they are responsive to the entire district rather than to admit giving priority to particular constituencies. The best way to collect evidence on this question may not be to ask it directly. Moreover, legislators were not consistently asked about this; after many legislators had told me that they represented the whole district, I gave little priority to the question in later interviews.

Differences between state legislative and congressional districts help to explain a reduced sensitivity to supportive constituencies at the state level. Most House districts at the state level are much smaller and more homogeneous than congressional districts. One consequence is that a larger proportion of state legislators win general elections by lopsided margins and consequently have less reason than congressmen to pinpoint their sources of electoral support. A second consequence of greater homogeneity is that legislators have more difficulty identifying particular socioeconomic groups that vote Democratic or Republican. In some rural districts, for example, Democratic and Republican voters may be distinguished not by their socioeconomic status and interests but only by traditional voting loyalties. Some suburban districts embrace a large proportion of voters who vote independently despite their nominal party affiliations. Thus, state legislators may find it difficult to define a reelection or a primary constituency with distinct socioeconomic characteristics or interests. The reelection constituency in a homogeneous district may be made up of persons with traditional party ties, while the primary constituency includes a lot of friends and neighbors. Some state legislators, too, are relatively inexperienced politicians who may be less adept than congressmen in defining such constituencies, particularly if they are not obvious in the more homogeneous districts.

Several legislators suggested another reason why legislators may not be particularly responsive to supportive constituencies, even in those districts where they can be identified. They pointed out that the most volatile issues of recent years—abortion, ERA, gun control, cap-

ital punishment—cut across traditional party and interest group alignments. A Democratic legislator, for example, may try to be responsive
to the working-class Democratic voters who regularly support him but
may find that they are deeply divided on such issues.

Legislators who represent multicounty districts can find it difficult
to maintain contacts outside their home county. But these members,
with rare exceptions, try to represent the interests of the entire district.
In the rural multicounty districts, there is little variation in the interests of the counties. There are some examples of legislators from multicounty rural districts who have closer contacts in, and in a sense are
more responsive to, those counties generally supportive of the member's party. A couple of Kentucky legislators fit into that category.
They clearly recognize that their reelection constituency is concentrated in two of the three counties of the district and maintain contacts
more effectively in these areas. But, as one of them pointed out, Republicans and Democrats in the district do not differ on the issues, and
therefore he can be responsive to the entire district in taking positions
on issues.

Occasionally legislators are confronted with the problem of representing a multicounty district that includes fragments of counties; if
the composition of the counties varies, the member may have problems
representing the divergent needs of a large majority and a small minority. Even in such situations, few legislators admit that they are responsive only to the majority. One Kentucky legislator, whose district was
largely rural but included a fragment of a county with a college town
in it, admitted that he made little effort to represent or maintain contacts in that town; but his response was completely atypical.

When legislators are elected at-large in metropolitan counties, we
might expect some of them to be particularly responsive to smaller
groups, interests, or communities. The only legislators I interviewed
who were elected at-large were in North Carolina, and they consistently emphasized that they represented the whole county and did not give
priority to groups within it. In 1967, when I interviewed legislators in a
number of metropolitan counties, those in Indianapolis and Denver
were elected countywide. Most asserted they represented the whole
county, but a few indicated that they were particularly sensitive to the
needs and problems of persons and local governmental units in their
own communities. This sensitivity was related more to individual problems and local projects, however, than it was to legislative issues. Despite the claims of legislators to represent the whole county, there were
doubtless minority groups in these counties—ethnic, partisan, eco-

nomic, or geographic—who believed they were not adequately represented by legislators who were elected by majority coalitions in which they did not participate.

*Constituencies Outside the District.* Under certain conditions, legislators consciously respond to interests beyond the boundaries of the district. For the most part these interests are not in conflict with the district ones but represent a logical extension of district interests. The best examples of this occur in metropolitan counties where legislators have a sense of responsibility to interests outside their district. A legislator whose district includes part of the inner city may think of himself as representing interests throughout the city because there are no conflicts or differences between the constituents he represents and those throughout the city. A good example is an Indiana representative whose two-member district covers half of an industrial city; he says people throughout the city consider him to be their representative.

Many districts in metropolitan counties are small, divided by artificial boundaries. Leaders of organized groups in the metropolitan area contact all the legislators in the county or all who are expected to support their goals. A metropolitan legislator may attract attention beyond the district by being active on particular issues, getting media coverage, being black or a woman; and such legislators usually respond to these demands of groups and individuals that come from outside the district. A representative in a Kentucky metropolitan district noted that he had worked with the League of Women Voters in the county even though few members of that group lived in his middle-income district. When I interviewed metropolitan county legislators in 1969, I found that about one-third of those in single-member districts articulated a countywide areal focus; some of these originally had been elected in a countywide at-large election before recent shifts to single-member districting.

There is another sense in which many metropolitan legislators are responsive to countywide interests. When there are institutions in the county, projects proposed for it, or legislation designed to serve particular county needs, members of the county delegation generally feel a sense of responsibility to serve these needs even though there is no direct and immediate benefit to their district. A legislator from Knoxville, for example, tries to serve the needs of the University of Tennessee; the university is not in his district, but many of its students and employees are. The construction of a city park, the remodeling of a county courthouse, or the expansion of a hospital in the city serves the interests of the whole community and not just the persons in the district where the facility is located. Legislators in a metropolitan county meet regularly with city and county officials to find out what legislation and what new appropriations should have priority. The legislators often work closely to achieve these goals. Because most metropolitan legislators participate in such efforts to some extent, it is correct to say that they tend to be responsive to interests outside their district.

Some legislators may be particularly sensitive to countywide interests. An example is a Louisville legislator who was chairman of the Jefferson County delegation and therefore was more concerned than most with concerns of the entire city and county; at the same time he described a number of district problems he had worked on, such as getting traffic lights installed. Another example is a Republican legislator from Houston who argued strongly that the shift to single-member districting in Harris County had made the delegation much less effective—partly because members were too concerned with parochial interests of their district and no one gave enough attention to the broader needs of Houston, a topic that he had given priority to.

The fact that many metropolitan legislators are responsive to interests broader than their district does not mean that there are no conflicts of interest within metropolitan counties. In fact such conflicts do occur, and the establishment of single-member districts has led to a decline in cohesiveness among metropolitan delegations in some counties that in the past had at-large elections (Jewell, 1969; Hamm, Harmel, and Thompson, 1979). It is not surprising to find legislators from higher-income, suburban districts voting against those from the central city on a variety of legislative issues.

Members of a metropolitan county delegations are sometimes divided on proposals and projects for their counties, and these divisions have become more frequent in counties where single-member districting has occurred. Most legislators elected from single-member districts in a metropolitan county probably have a dual geographic focus: a primary loyalty to their district and a secondary loyalty to those other interests in the metropolitan area that do not clash with those of the district. While most have a sense of responsibility to the entire metropolitan area, they need not agree on what is needed for that area; they view needs from the perspective of the interests that dominate their own districts.

North Carolina legislators who are elected at-large in metropolitan counties generally argue that a countywide district is valuable, and perhaps even essential, for preserving unity within the delegation, particularly on legislation and projects for the county. They generally operate under a unit rule that provides for united support for the position a majority takes on local government questions. Legislators in metropolitan delegations in Texas and Tennessee (both of which were elected at-large at an earlier period) often disagree on matters affecting their counties. How often they disagree depends in part on the extent to which they represent diverse ethnic, partisan, and economic interests and in part on the success or failure of efforts by delegation leaders to achieve compromise. It also depends on the kinds of issues that divide the delegation. A particular divisive issue in some metropolitan counties is annexation. When legislation is proposed to change the ground rules concerning annexation, there is little agreement within a county delegation between those legislators representing districts already in the central city and those representing districts whose citizens are resisting annexation. It is noteworthy that legislators in Davidson County (Nashville) have fewer problems in agreeing on local issues in part because of the metro government established in that county. As one legislator sad, "We are all concerned with the same budget, the same issues, and the same local needs."

Another group of legislators who are responsive to groups and interests outside the district are the members of ethnic minorities. They frequently are contacted by individuals and groups belonging to that minority from other parts of the metropolitan area, nearby counties, or other parts of the state. They often feel a particular sense of responsibility to represent the interests of that minority throughout the state. They see no conflict between serving those interests and serving their districts, which usually include a substantial number of members of that minority. Several of the black and Chicano legislators I talked to are very active in statewide organizations of these minorities and clearly serve as spokesmen for these interests within the legislature and in the wider political arena. One black legislator in Indiana suggested that black representatives are still defining their roles and trying to decide how best to respond to the large demands made on them, in terms of both legislation and service requests. These demands are likely to remain heavy, and minority legislators are likely to continue to be perceived as representing a constituency that is broader than the district.

A few legislators articulate a statewide focus of representation. These are experienced legislators holding important committee responsibilities who are absorbed with issues that are statewide in scope, such as taxation or education. Some hold or have held leadership positions in the legislature, and some have ambitions for statewide office and tend to have a broader perspective. A statewide focus of responsibility may mean that they pay relatively little attention to parochial concerns of the district or that they are prepared to cast votes on legislation or appropriations that will hurt their district in the interest of statewide needs. A veteran legislator from Indianapolis, for example, indicated that he opposed a tax proposal that might help his constituents because he thought it would shift too heavy a tax burden on the farmers. A Denver legislator, who had previously served in a leadership role, described himself as trustee and noted that he had opposed a plan for school financing that would have helped Denver because he thought it was bad for the state as a whole. I found too few examples of legislators who articulated a statewide focus of representation in specific terms to draw any firm conclusions about the reasons for choosing the role, but most of those who did were persons who had held or were seeking committee or leadership positions in the legislature or elective positions outside it that required them to develop such a broad perspective.

The district is the principal focus of representation for state legislators in those cases where the district constitutes, or coincides with, a meaningful political entity or community. State representatives are less likely than congressmen to identify subconstituencies within the district as important because state legislative districts are smaller and more homogeneous, with fewer conflicting interests. Where districts are part of a larger political unit, such as a metropolitan county, it is almost inevitable that the focus of representation will be broader than the district because interests are organized along county or metropolitan lines and there are relatively few interests that are distinct or unique to the district. Where the district boundary lines are drawn arbitrarily with little regard to other political boundaries, there is even less reason for the legislator to concentrate on district interests. In fact it may be impossible to define such interests. While it is true that some legislators have more parochial interests than others do, nearly all legislators give careful attention to those interests that are local in nature, whether or not these are organized specifically along district lines.

## Representational Style

The authors of *The Legislative System* (Wahlke, Eulau, Buchanan, Ferguson, 1962) described a variety of legislative roles, but none has attracted more attention or inspired more replication than the representational role—the now familiar distinction between trustees and delegates. The *trustee* is one who follows his own judgment, based on his factual knowledge and understanding of the issues and/or on the principles in which he believes. It is a role based not only on a normative definition but also on the fact that constituents may be uninformed or uninterested in an issue or their views may be impossible to determine (pp. 272-76). The *delegate* is one who follows instructions because of a normative assessment of his role or because it appears necessary to get reelected. Although the term is usually applied to those who take instructions from constituents, it is defined by the authors broadly enough to apply to those following other clients—interest groups, party leaders, the chief executive, etc. (pp. 276-77, 467). The authors also defined a middle category, the *politico*, who may shift from one orientation to another, depending on circumstances or issues, or who may attempt to perform both roles simultaneously, creating role conflict (pp. 277-80).

Wahlke and his associates classified the legislators on the basis of answers to general questions about how they perceived their job. A number of other scholars have used these categories to classify legislators in various state, national, and local legislative bodies (sometimes omitting politicos). Some have used similar broad questions as the basis for classification, while others have devised more precise questions. Some have followed the trichotomy or dichotomy, while others have defined representational role as a continuum. But the main thrust of this research effort has been to classify legislators in terms of their representative style, based on interviews or written questionnaires, and then to search for variables that explain the classification of individual legislators and to test the ability of representational role to predict various types of behavior, particularly roll-call voting. (For a summary of previous research, see Jewell, 1970; for analysis of the impact of role on behavior, see Gross, 1978; Kuklinski and Elling, 1977; McCrone and Kuklinski, 1979; Friesema and Hedlund, 1974.)

These studies have provided some insights into the variety of ways legislators view their responsibilities as representatives, and they have demonstrated that there are some significant differences. Some legislators are confident of their own judgment, and others are more inclined to find out what constituents (or other significant groups) think and, if constituent opinion is strong and united, to vote accordingly. The major weakness of these studies is that representation is a much more complex subject than they suggest, and the role orientations of most legislators are much too complicated to permit stereotyping them as delegates or trustees on the basis of their answers to a few questions. Most legislators shift their representational role depending on the issue and are not exclusively either delegates or trustees. (In that sense, they may all be politicos, but that term is neither well chosen nor well defined by its authors.)

Eulau and Wahlke (1978, p. 14) have criticized the effort to use role orientations to predict legislative behavior. First, they argue that "we have never assumed that role definitions in response to interview questions would yield anything more than definitions; and definitions certainly do not predict behavior." Second, they assert that it is inappropriate "to impose on legislators' own definitions of a role or on their role orientations a predictive burden that the relevant role concepts cannot possibly carry and are not meant to carry." Whatever the potential for predicting behavior from role orientations, I would agree that developing simple stereotypes of roles from interviews or questionnaires does not provide a full enough understanding of the complex process of representation to make possible useful predictions about behavior.

This study of representation does not include an effort to classify legislators according to representational orientation or to use such a classification to predict behavior. The first concern is to define more carefully the ways in which legislators may represent constituents. The constituents whom the legislator is primarily representing may be either a narrower or a broader group than the population of the district.

Pitkin (1967) suggests that, in the debate about representational role, both the trustee and the delegate orientation fit the definition of representation if neither is carried to its logical extreme. There is room for varied approaches to representation, as long as the following ingredients are maintained: the representative must be able to act with independence; he must act in the interests of constituents and normally in accord with their wishes; if he acts contrary to their wishes, he must be prepared to explain why (pp. 164-66).

These aspects or styles of representation are neither mutually exclusive nor contradictory. A legislator might follow one style on one bill and another style on a later bill. It is also possible to practice several styles of representation simultaneously, consciously or unconsciously. I believe much of the confusion about representative style arises from the assumption that such styles are incompatible or contradictory. The three aspects of representation on policy questions are defined as follows: 1) the legislator's opinions and attitudes are typical of those of his constituency; 2) the legislator uses his own judgment to determine what position on an issue will best serve the needs of constituents, acting as a trustee; 3) the legislator responds to what he perceives to be the demands of his constituency, acting as a delegate.

*Legislator Who Typifies the District.* The concept that a legislator typifies the district is the lowest common denominator of representation. Most legislators are typical of their districts in the sense that they share the dominant views and attitudes of the district. Although better educated and from a narrower range of occupations than the constituents, most legislators have lived in the district or at least in that part of the state for most of their lives and are likely to reflect the dominant ethnic identity and religious affiliation. The more homogeneous the district, the easier it is for a legislator to be typical; but if the district is heterogeneous, the electoral process enhances the likelihood that the legislator will share the interests and views of the majority rather than the minority.

The idea of representing a district by sharing its dominant views and attitudes is not normally considered to be a style of representation. In fact it is often associated with the more familiar styles. A legislator described as a trustee may say that he knows the needs and understands the views of his constituents because he is typical of them. A legislator described as a delegate may assert that his perception and evaluation of constituency demands is accurate because he shares the underlying views of the district. Most legislators, in fact, are typical of their district and can represent it even on occasions when they are neither responding consciously to demands nor making conscious decisions about the welfare of the district. The fact that legislators are typical means they often can act and vote as their constituents would want them to and in a way compatible with their interests even in the absence of perceived demands or conscious judgments about the district. Moreover, if we recognize this as a style of representation, it is easier to understand how elections affect representation. Even when issues play little part in elections or affect very few of the votes that are cast, it is likely that voters will choose a candidate who shares many of the attributes and the underlying attitudes of the constituents. In fact, if one legislator is more typical than the others, he is likely to be elected, partly as a consequence of the fact that most districts are usually controlled by a single party.

The persistent theme in my discussion with legislators was their feeling that they are typical of their district and have internalized the beliefs and sentiments of the constituents. Many pointed to the fact that they had lived for years in the district. A particularly thoughtful representative from Ohio says, "In some ways I am fairly representative. If I react to a problem or a situation in a particular way, I am confident that many others will react that way." A Colorado legislator who asserts that he is a trustee (using exactly that term) also says, "I am very much a part of the district. I am very much in line with what they think—I reflect fairly well the composition of the district." A Kentucky legislator who has lived in his middle-class district for thirty-one of his thirty-six years says that he knows what people think because he is typical of them and because he has lots of contacts in the district; this enables him to judge whether the groups that make demands on him are really representative of views in the district.

A liberal white legislator from Memphis, representing a middle- to lower-income district with a slight black majority, agrees that he is not typical in a socioeconomic sense, or in terms of his life-style, but argues that he is generally in tune with the viewpoints of the district, that he shares their attitudes and understands their needs. A rural Tennessee legislator, who grew up in one of his two counties and lives in the other, says that he feels comfortable representing the district: "I understand my constituents, and I think they understand me." A Republican from a working-class district outside of Cleveland, a normally Democratic district, might not appear to be typical, but she asserts that she is: "I think I almost typify the district; by following my gut feeling I seem to succeed in representing it." She describes the district as very conservative, though Democratic: "they think like Republicans, but they don't know it."

Some legislators who claim their viewpoints are typical of the district may be misperceiving district attitudes, but those who make this assertion also claim to stay in close touch with the district, and not merely to have grown up in it. It is probable that some who claim to be typical really mean that their views are typical of those shared by a majority—perhaps their reelection constituency; where the district is heterogeneous and its viewpoints diversified, it is not possible to be typical of everyone. Although some members may exaggerate the typicality of their viewpoints, we should not underestimate the importance of this central fact: most legislators believe that they share the general attitudes and viewpoints of the majority of their constituents. This is one important reason why the conflict between the roles of trustee and delegate is more apparent than real. Representatives believe that their judgments on most issues are compatible with the views of their constituents. When demands are made on them to take contradictory positions on issues, most legislatores believe they can determine whether these demands are representative of the views held generally in the district.

*Legislator as Trustee.* The trustee has been defined as one who follows his own judgment, based on his own knowledge and principles. In what sense, or under what conditions is the legislator who follows his own judgment representing the constituents? Are there conditions under which the case can be made that a legislator who follows his own judgment is not representing constituents? Using Pitkin's definition of representation, we would have to say that a legislator who follows his own judgment is representing constituents if he acts in their interests and either follows their wishes or explains why he has not done so. This line of reasoning would suggest that the legislator who follows his own judgment without regard to, or obviously contrary to, the interests of his constituents cannot be regarded as effectively representing them. We should keep in mind our conclusions about the focus of representation: a legislator may define his constituency more narrowly or more broadly than the geographical district.

Within this framework, under what conditions does a trustee represent constituents? The most important condition must be that the legislator is familiar with and sensitive to the needs and interests of the district. This means that the legislator must know the district well, understand its problems, and keep in touch with what is happening. The role of the trustee does not suggest an ivory tower theoretician or a legislator who never visits the district. Understanding the district and its problems requires information, not merely intuition. When the legislator makes a legislative judgment that takes into account the needs and interests of the district, whether or not the judgment is correct, this decision fits the definition of representation. Many legislators who say that they rely on their own judgment emphasize that they make continuing efforts to stay in touch with the district; most legislators believe they understand the needs and problems of their districts and can judge the attitudes of constituents on basic issues. Many legislators, including trustees, believe their views are typical of those that dominate the constituency. In fact some of the legislators who are most vocal in asserting that they rely on their own judgment are equally insistent that a majority of constituents share their basic political values. The impression one gets from talking to those legislators who might be classified as trustees is that most of them meet these conditions of representation; they make judgments informed by a high level of familiarity with the district and its needs and with the interests and viewpoints of their constituents.

A second condition for trustee representation pertains to those issues that have no effect on the district at all. Many issues, some important and a great many parochial or trivial, have no effect on the district or its significant constituent groups. On these the legislator may follow his judgment or rely on the advice of lobbyists, executive agencies, or other legislators. His responsibility to the constituency is a simple one: to consider whether the issue might have some effect on the district—a task that is usually routine and automatic. In a sense the legislator is representing the district adequately as long as he takes into account that possibility; at least he is not failing his representative responsibilities when such issues arise.

Other factors mentioned by legislators who rely on their judgment support the assumption that they are representing constituent interests. Some legislators assert that their constituents trust them and expect them to follow their own judgment. The validity of this argument depends on the accuracy of their perceptions. Some legislators justify following their own judgment and convictions by saying that they made their views known to voters before the election and therefore have a mandate to vote in accordance with those convictions. Some legislators who say that they follow their own convictions emphasize that they must be able to explain their views and voting patterns to their constituents. These legislators are articulating their accountability to constituents, an important element in representation.

*Legislator as Delegate.* The final aspect of representation involves the legislator who responds to what he perceives to be the demands of a constituency. This delegate role appears on the surface to be a simple one, but it is complicated by two problems faced by any legislator acting as a delegate: determining the accuracy of one's perceptions and deciding to which constituency to be responsive. In a sense the job of a delegate is much more difficult than the job of a trustee. Accurate perception of demands requires the development of effective means of communication.

Demands may arise not from the district as a whole but from specific groups—often organized—within the district, and the legislator who acts as a delegate must choose to which of these groups to respond. Demands may come from such a broad range of groups and individuals in the district that the member may safely conclude there is a consensus within the district on an issue. Alternatively, demands may come from a broad range of the member's supportive constituency—those to whom he feels particularly responsive. In either case, the legislator as delegate has no serious difficulty in making a choice. More often demands arise from smaller groups within the district (or occasionally outside it). Then the legislator must determine whether there is conflict among these groups, and which if any of these are among the supportive groups to which he feels particularly responsive.

When demands are made on him, the legislator must evaluate the accuracy of his information about the opinions of groups. He must make judgments about the degree of consensus, strength of feelings, and level of information of groups making demands. Where conflicts occur among groups, he must take into account these characteristics of each group and consider whether each is part of his supportive constituency. If the issue is relatively broad in scope, the legislator must also consider whether the demands are compatible with what he understands to be the interests of the district (including those that have not been articulated).

*Conclusions about Representational Style.* When a legislator makes judgments about the interests of the district, a trustee must be well informed about the needs and attitudes of the district. The legislator cannot act effectively as a delegate without making judgments about the demands made on him and the nature of the groups making those demands. One of those judgments is whether articulated demands are compatible with what he understands to be district interests. In theory there is a clear distinction between making judgments and listening to demands, but in practice the representative style of an effective legislator must contain elements of both. It becomes clear not only that both the trustee and the delegate role are legitimate styles of representation but that a legislator may, and frequently does, follow both styles in making decisions about any important or complicated issue. The more sophisticated legislator dealing with a complex issue over a period of time is constantly weighing the demands that are made on him against what he knows and about the issue and what he judges to be its effects on the welfare of his district and particular constituencies within it.

# 5. Policy Responsiveness: How Choices Are Made

The process of representing constituents on policy matters requires legislators to make a number of choices. What factors affect those choices? To this question we now turn.

When legislators discuss the process by which they make decisions that are important to constituents, the discussion is not abstract; it is issue-specific. Just as the decision-making process differs by issues, it differs by individuals; no two legislators perceive the process exactly the same way. The terms trustee and delegate define broad approaches to decision-making. We are interested in the personal perspectives and the reasons given by legislators to explain their approaches. We are also interested in the effects that district and electoral characteristics have on their choices—as perceived and explained by the legislators.

## Factors Affecting Representational Choices

The legislator usually faces few decision-making problems on the traditional economic issues. Most districts are fairly homogeneous, the major interests are clearly recognized, there is a dominant point of view, and the legislator usually shares the viewpoint. If there are divisions of opinion, he is likely to recognize which one predominates among his supportive constituency. Sometimes the interests of the district are so obvious that there may be little if any organized pressure on the issue. Where such pressures exist, they are more likely to reinforce than to challenge the viewpoint of the representative.

It is the newer issues, often social in content, that arouse the strongest emotions and cause the most difficulty for legislators, issues such as ERA, abortion, capital punishment, busing, church schools, gun control, and more traditional social issues such as betting and liquor. These issues are likely to be particularly salient to the voter, leading not only to organized pressures but to independent contacts from constituents. Some of the organizations are the single-issue groups that threaten to defeat legislators who fail to support their position.

Some of these issues split the district down the middle and, because they cut across party lines, some split the reelection constituency. On issues like abortion or capital punishment the legislator may have strong convictions, which are not necessarily compatible with those of a majority in the district.

The legislator may believe that on some of these issues the strongest demands come from a group that does not represent majority opinion in the district; abortion is a good example. The legislator may believe that some of the groups are ill informed, on the consequences of capital punishment for example. This is the type of issue on which the legislator is most likely to have to make a choice between the demands that are best organized or loudest on the one hand, and his own conviction or judgment about the interests of the district on the other hand. In practice, legislators who have described such choices sometimes say that they have stuck to their convictions and sometimes say that they have abandoned conviction to go along with the majority demand.

There are also a great many issues that are narrow in scope and are of concern only to small groups. One example would be bills introduced at the request of local officials to deal with problems of local government. Legislators tend to be highly responsive to such demands, and only occasionally do they encounter opposition from other groups. When demands are made on narrow issues by small groups, and there is no opposition, legislators tend to be supportive, unless they perceive some damage to district interests or unless other political actors, such as state agencies, express strong opposition. Because these issues seldom relate to matters on which the legislator has convictions, he has few difficult choices to make. If a couple of groups are contesting an issue, such as doctors and optometrists, the legislator must exercise judgment, or must try to determine which group is more important from the legislator's point of view.

*Personal Factors.* If most legislators adapt their style of representation to particular issues, it is also true that some legislators rely more consistently on their own judgment and others are more sensitive to constituent demands. It is these differences that have led to stereotyping some members as trustees and others as delegates. We can reject simple stereotyping of legislators and still seek to understand the reasons why legislators differ in their outlook on representation and in the emphasis that they give to constituent demands.

Earlier research (Jewell, 1970, pp. 470-83) has suggested a number of personal variables that have some effect on the choice of representational role. Psychological factors appear to have some effect, giving some members more confidence in their own judgment. There is also some evidence that legislators with higher education and higher status occupations are more likely to be trustees. There is inconsistent evidence about the effect of ideology on representational role, though one might expect strong ideologues to be trustees. There is some evidence that political experience outside the legislature and seniority in it are likely to encourage a trustee orientation, presumably because the member learns that the public is often uninformed and apathetic about issues. Most of these relationships examined in earlier studies are statistically weak, even though some of them appear to be very logical. Part of the reason for such weak associations is the difficulty of defining and measuring such categories as delegate and trustee with any precision.

This study is not designed to classify state legislators by representational role or to discover variables that correlate with such roles. Instead, the goal is to understand better how members make representational choices by examining the reasons that they provide for these choices. Legislators represent districts in three ways: by typifying the views of constituents, by making judgments about the interests and needs of the district, and by responding to perceived demands from their constituents. Most legislators believe that they are typical of the mainstream of attitudes in the district, and most of them are probably correct. This feeling is so pervasive and the reasons for it are so obvious that there is no need to explain it further.

The reasons that legislators give for a trustee orientation are varied, but they fall into certain identifiable patterns, within two broad categories: a distrust of constituent demands, and a confidence in one's own judgment.

Legislators generally report that most of their mail is organized, and many of them regard organized mail with caution if not suspicion because it does not necessarily reflect broader viewpoints in the district. They often express the wish that a larger proportion of mail were unorganized. Legislators who share this perception of organized mail differ on how much weight should be attached to it. Those who value it more highly believe that the groups that are capable of organizing mail campaigns and making other types of organized demands are the most important political groups in the district and must be listened to.

But one of the major arguments advanced by legislators who say that they generally follow their own judgment is that the mail and the other organized demands are unrepresentative of broader opinion in the district, and these demands are often in conflict with what the legislators perceive to be the best interests of the district. A veteran Kentucky legislator representing rural counties says: "I think I know the district well enough to judge what it wants and what its best interests are. I don't ignore the mail, but I have to be concerned with what is right for the district, not just for a few people or groups." A similar point is made by a representative from Ohio who believes that the leaders of groups in her district are out of step with the majority of people in the district, who share her conservative views. A couple of Ohio legislators make the point that many of the controversies of greatest concern to interest groups are of no interest to the large majority of constituents; both used the example of conflicts between medical doctors and optometrists over putting medication in patients' eyes. The general suspicion of mail as a measure of district opinion was summarized by one experienced legislator in these words: "You can never truly know what the will of the people in the district is, certainly not by counting the mail you get. It is never a large enough sample."

One of the most important discoveries that most legislators make after some experience in office is that most constituents are poorly informed about legislative matters. Even those individuals and groups who are attentive and interested enough to make demands on their legislators often do not understand the complexities of issues and frequently are misinformed about specific provisions of legislation. An Ohio legislator believes that "the issues are too complex these days, and people don't really understand them (and are embarrassed by their ignorance); moreover, there are so many issues, the people can't keep up with them." Legislators who make an effort to determine public attitudes are often most realistic about the low level of public understanding. One such legislator believes that polls are a useful guide to the mood of the public, but they cannot be followed blindly because "often the voters don't have the whole story, or they don't have the accurate facts of a situation."

A Kentucky legislator who believes she is in close touch with public attitudes in the district concedes that voters sometimes provide information on a topic that leads her to find out more about it. But "when I feel that the voters who contact me are not well informed on an issue, I vote as I wish. People often misunderstand what a bill actually does." Another Kentucky legislator provides an example of voter misinformation, involving the formula for distributing education funds to local school districts under the minimum foundation program. Constituents who have contacted him see this as a plan that would make it easier for local school boards to raise taxes. He believes that he has a better understanding of the plan, and that it will serve the interests of the district. Another Kentucky legislator says: "I have a philosophy about this: I have access to certain information that is not generally available to the constituency, and I make a decision on the basis of that information. It may not be to their immediate liking, but I feel that I am voting in their long-run best interests." Similarly, a Massachusetts legislator asserts that he is typical of the district, that conflicts rarely arise between his views and those of the district and occur only when constituents are poorly informed, usually on complicated or esoteric topics.

Those legislators who decide to reject the demands they get from constituents are often closely in touch with the district and responsive to it and share the underlying attitudes in the district. Most demands that are made on them from the district, even from the leadership of organized groups, reflect a simplistic approach to an issue that the legislators know to be complicated. When the demands pertain to a specific bill, they often come from persons who misunderstand the bill, or have not read it, or do not know that it has already been amended to solve the problems that concern them. The demands are seldom pertinent to the important choices that the legislator must make. Constituents may demand that a bill be defeated, when the crucial issue is how to amend it. They may ask for unrealistic levels of funding for a program. Their advice may be of no help to the legislator who has to decide how much of a compromise to make or what priorities to assign to programs that are competing for limited funds. The legislator more often turns for advice to a lobbyist in the capital instead of to group leadership in the district, because only the lobbyist has advice and information that are timely and pertinent.

It is obvious to most legislators that relatively few issues are salient to constituents; what disturbs many of them is that most appear to care so little about issues that should interest them and that will have some effect on them. Legislators often rely on their own judgment out of necessity because their constituents, or at least the unorganized ones, do not express their views. Some legislators believe that they have a good sense of what constituents want even though they do not hear from them; others are clearly frustrated by the lack of information. According to an Ohio representative: "There is no way that you can get enough contacts so that you can say that you know how everyone out there feels; you go into a lot of votes with no idea what people want, because on most of the votes down here the public doesn't really care about them until after the fact." Another legislator concludes, "I am never faced with deciding whether to vote for what my district wants or my preferences because I don't know how my people feel—except in the most general terms."

There is a second broad reason why legislators rely heavily on their own judgment; not only are constituent demands unreliable, but they have confidence in their own judgment and often believe that constituents share that confidence. One of the most common assertions of legislators who might be classified as trustees is that voters expect them to use their own judgment on most issues. It is easy to make such an assertion of course, and we might wonder how valid it is. But legislators who make such assertions are often ones who are in close touch with their district and seem to be familiar with its viewpoints. Some report that they are seldom pressured by organized groups, while others argue that such groups are unrepresentative of more than minority viewpoints. They make a convincing case that most constituents trust them to use their own judgment on most issues:

People seem to be saying—we elected you; we have confidence in you and expect you to use your own judgment.

The district trusts me to follow my own judgment. They elected me, not to read the results of questionnaires but to exercise judgment on issues.

I don't feel obligated in all circumstances to vote the majority view in the district. I think the people elected me to look at things myself and they trust me to make a decision. They want me to make objective decisions on issues.

In a somewhat similar vein, legislators assert that constituents respect their independence and their willingness to take a stand on issues:

I am sure voters prefer to have you take a stand on things; they tell you that they would rather know how you stand even if they disagree. And I have a reputation of having taken stands on controversial issues.

I take a stand on issues openly. A majority of people have agreed with me. They know my stand and respect it. They may not agree with me but they respect my willingness to make my position clear.

A Kentucky legislator who is particularly able and well informed said that groups in his district often contact him at the request of state organizations with which they are affiliated, but they are often apologetic about these requests. The local groups tell him: "You know more about this issue than we do." Constituents not only trust the judgment of their legislator but recognize that he is better informed on the issues.

Some legislators justify their policy of relying on their own judgment by saying that they promised to follow this policy when they ran for office. They argue that they have a mandate to be trustees:

My philosophy has always been that I try to listen to all sides, and I study the issue, but the bottom line is that I follow my conscience—and I tell them when

I campaign that I will do this. As a general rule the public accepts this approach, though some groups will try to cut your throat on an issue.

When I campaigned, I said that if the voters wanted someone just to conduct polls and vote according to public opinion, they should vote for someone else. And, if you trust the mail and other contacts, I have voted against the majority position on a few emotional issues.

Other legislators say that they have sometimes voted according to their own convictions, and against an apparent majority in the district, on issues, but that these were issues on which they had made their position clear during the campaign. They are not really arguing that they have a mandate to vote in that way, but that the voters knew what to expect when they made their choice. A good example is the Massachusetts legislator who voted against capital punishment even though he believes the district favors it by a two-to-one majority. He says, "I campaigned on that issue—I am being up front about it."

Another variation of a mandate theory comes from a conservative Republican legislator from Ohio, strongly issue-oriented, who perceived his district to be generally conservative on issues. He says that the constituents recognize his conservative views and approve of them. They leave him free to follow his own judgment as long as he remains consistent. "If I changed my views on something like state financing of education, the district would not tolerate it."

Some legislators explain their choice of a trustee role largely in terms of the need for leadership:

I try to analyze bills in terms of whether they are needed, are good for most of the people, and are fiscally responsible. If you only analyze bills in terms of whether they will cost you votes, the tough decisions will never be made. That is one of the reasons why we are lagging in education in Ohio—because no one is willing to make these tough decisions.

Any legislator who simply counts the mail is not a thinking legislator and is not doing the job. You can just let the district drag you along. If my opinion is different from that of the district, because of my background on the issues, it is my duty to vote according to my opinion, and explain it to the district.

I think our job is to do more than simply respond, and more than simply to follow our conscience. Our job is to lead, to explain to people the issues, the pros and cons, and the reasons why we vote as we do. You can't represent everyone in the district anyway. You have to strike a balance and the way I strike it is to try to be aware of the way the major groups in the district feel. Go in with your eyes open, knowing how people will react. And recognize that most people don't make a judgment on just one issue.

As this last comment in particular indicates, those who emphasize the importance of legislative leadership do not necessarily ignore the views of organized groups in the district, but try to keep them in perspective. Likewise, they do not overlook the political risks that may be involved in a trustee's role. But some believe there are also risks in trying to satisfy all the constituents. "You sometimes run into issues on which district opinion is divided. The district is so diverse that whatever you do will make someone unhappy. I tend to do what I think is best—I vote my conscience on those issues. If you try to straddle the fence and try to please everyone, you will end up satisfying no one. You save yourself a lot of grief by doing what you want to do—it is politically smarter."

A somewhat similar view is expressed by a legislator who has opposed the views of a majority in his district on some emotional issues, like the death penalty and abortion. "I tell my constituents that I am opposed to such bills, I cannot vote for them; if you want them passed, vote for someone else. If you still want me, you know that I will take these stands. I am a political scientist and have read Edmund Burke. I would not advise my colleagues to do this, but it works for me. You will lose some votes, but for every one you lose you gain four or five from people who say, 'I disagree with him but I respect his integrity.' "

Some legislators who follow their own judgment at the risk of alienating organized groups in the district are realistic in assessing the risks of such action. A Kentucky legislator says that there are a few issues on which he differs with significant groups in the district and on which he decides to vote against them. "I may have to take the heat for a while. You worry about possible opposition even if you haven't had any. If they thought they could beat you, some groups would run someone against you. You don't want to hand an opponent an issue he can beat you with. But it is harder to justify a vote that you don't believe in than one that you do." A California legislator who has been "out in front" on a number of controversial issues believes that he gains some name recognition from such stands, and "I hope to get support from people who recognize that I am forthright and that I have reasons for my position, even when they disagree with me." He believes he will also win support as a Democrat from the partisan majority in the district, but he realizes that there are political risks with being controversial and being out of step with a majority on at least some of these issues.

My experience has been that some of the legislators who are most outspoken about the importance of relying on their own judgment represent districts in which the dominant political attitudes are very

close to their own. This does not mean that there is no risk in the legislator's following his own convictions; some groups may be opposed to
his stand on some issues. But it does mean that the legislator can count
on a strong base of political support for his decisions. Some legislators
who articulate a strong trustee orientation also devote considerable effort to staying in touch with constituents. One of the most forthright
statements of a trustee position comes from a conservative Indianapolis
Republican: "My feeling is this—if I can't be my own man, if I can't
represent what I feel is right and good in government, then I am going
to quit the legislature. When the day comes when I vote out of fear of
some pressure group, that is the day I leave office." That legislator,
however, is one who feels a strong sense of obligation to the political
party organization that helped to elect him and stays in close touch
with the organization on policy as well as political matters.

Many of those who articulate a trustee role are issue-oriented in the
sense that they have strong convictions but also in the sense that they
devote much of their time as legislators to initiating and trying to pass
(or defeat) bills. Obviously the more prominently they are involved in
controversial legislation, the greater the risk of alienating constituents,
and some legislators admit that the choice of issues to support requires
some care and restraint. A Tennessee legislator, who estimates that he
is somewhat more liberal than his district and who says that he votes
his convictions on the major controversial issues, says that he picks with
care the issues that he is willing to be identified with, and he approaches some issues rather obliquely.

A liberal Democrat representing a rural district in Indiana that is
normally Republican says that he works consciously to develop issues
that are of importance to his district, such as opposition to the inherit-
ance tax, opposition to higher property taxes for schools, and an effort
to cut utility rates. He does not automatically accept all the proposals
of the state Democratic party, but concentrates on those that are compatible with the district's interest. He is something of a maverick on
such issues as energy and the environment, but he takes care to show
his constituents how his positions on them serve the district. A Colorado legislator provides a good example of exercising caution on issues.
He is very interested in legislative questions, and is one of the most active and well informed members in debates on the floor. But, after being defeated in one reelection bid, he has decided to develop a lower
public profile on legislation, to introduce fewer bills and to concentrate
more of his attention on amending and supporting bills introduced by
others.

The number of legislators who clearly articulate a delegate role of representation is smaller than the number who clearly define themselves as trustees, but it is not difficult to find examples of the delegate orientation:

I have a very naive and narrow-minded attitude toward the representative form of government. I believe that I should vote my constituents' wishes when they are known to me—and I have told the constituents that. Unlike some of my colleagues, I am not so sure that I am better informed than the constituents or that there is a good excuse for voting against their wishes.

I can't think of a time when I have voted contrary to the district, because I vote the way they want me to vote. I am a representative; I am typical of my district, and if conflicts arise I go along with their views.

Broad statements of a delegate orientation, such as these, do not shed much light on how the legislator actually "votes the constituents' wishes" or votes "the way they want me to vote." Some of those who articulate such views say that conflicts between their views and those of the district rarely occur. A more important factor is that these delegates generally admit that constituent opinion often cannot be followed because it is poorly informed, not clearly articulated, or sharply divided. A North Carolina legislator says, "I try and represent the people in terms of my own philosophy—I believe that is what they sent me to do." But he admits that, in a district with divided attitudes, he tends to represent better the county whose residents share his generally conservative philosophy. Similarly a Colorado legislator says, "I try to subordinate my personal views to the interest of the district. I think that is what representative government is about—to know what the people in your district want and what their interests are." But he then explains that his constituents are divided on the issue of annexation, and he must support one point of view and explain it to those who disagree with him.

General statements of a delegate orientation can tell us little about the conditions that compel delegates to respond to the demands of constituents, but a clearer picture emerges from other interviews. Many of these are members who usually rely on their own judgment or who generally agree with the viewpoints that dominate their district, but who believe on occasion they must subordinate their judgment or convictions and vote according to the wishes of the district. Legislators are most likely to follow that course when they are convinced that a large majority of their constituents, and not just the most vocal ones or the best organized, are in support of a position on an issue and feel strongly about it. A Tennessee legislator, who generally feels in tune with his district, describes his relationship with his constituents as follows: "I am a representative, and when they clearly speak, I am going to represent them. When they do not clearly speak, that is when leadership comes in." He encountered two such issues: capital punishment and professional negotiations for teachers. He supported capital punishment, despite his convictions, and opposed professional negotiations despite the fact that he was a teacher and had close ties to teachers' organizations.

Other legislators echo the view that when a clear and substantial majority takes a stand on a salient issue they find it necessary to vote that way:

When public opinion is overwhelming and the opinion is strong, you have to give weight to it. My district is overwhelmingly for the death penalty and I voted for it, although I had great doubts about it.

I personally am opposed to capital punishment, but the feeling in the district was overwhelming, and I voted for what I thought was the feelings of the constituents; I had heard from lots of people throughout the district.

The one rule that I laid down when I took office was that my own ideas were secondary and the district's view would come first. I favored a bill for liquor by the drink because the district was three-to-one for it.

The examples that legislators give of the issues generating such strong sentiment are few in number and are mostly emotional issues. Capital punishment was mentioned most frequently, and inevitably where there was a conflict the legislator opposed it or had doubts and the district favored it. Another issue was the question of ERA. A third was the issue of abortion, although legislators were not likely to find lopsided margins in their districts on this issue. A few legislators mentioned liquor questions. The example concerning the professional negotiations bill for teachers was the only one involving economic issues. This does not mean that economic issues such as this are never salient to voters, but they are less likely to be salient to large majorities in the district. Moreover, there is less likely to be a conflict between the legislator and a district majority on economic issues. If there is a serious split in the district on such issues, the legislator is likely to find that his views are compatible with the majority that normally supports him.

There is another category of issues on which some legislators subordinate their views to those of constituent groups: issues of relatively trivial importance that are of concern to relatively narrow groups in the district. A Tennessee legislator says that he votes his convictions on the "big, tough issue like capital punishment." He feels the most pressure on issues that are marginal, that he does not really care about, and he may go along with whichever group is stronger or more vocal. A Texas legislator claims that he can vote his convictions on most of the issues that are really important, but "the flack I receive is on real trivia; the trivial issues can give you trouble—though they are really meaningless." Given the fact, he sometimes acts like a delegate on trivial issues.

When I interviewed legislators about their use of questionnaires to measure district opinion, I did not find any "poll-watchers" who slavishly followed the majority opinions revealed in the questionnaires. But a few of those legislators with relatively strong delegate orientations do rely heavily on their questionnaires to determine when there is a strong majority on a salient issue and when that majority is strong enough that they should follow it. A Massachusetts legislator who makes consistent use of polls and gets a good response says that when there is a lopsided majority in the poll on an issue, "I would obviously follow that majority." A Texas legislator who regularly conducts polls, and gets a good response, says, "I've always felt that on crucial issues I need to follow the guidelines of the people who elected me; using a poll on the major issues makes that possible." Another Texas legislator, who sends out several questionnaires a year and claims to get a 30 percent response, relies on the poll with some limitations:

We try to follow the poll as closely as we can, recognizing the limitations of yes and no answers. Most of us have a few issues on which we feel so strongly that we would not change regardless of the poll results. (For example, I totally oppose a state income tax.) But on many other issues I follow what the constituency wants, unless I believe that it would really hurt them. For example, I supported a proposal for a public utilities commission, which I believed would do more harm than good, because 78 percent of the people favored it in the poll. I struggled with the issue, but I finally voted for it.

The more carefully we examine what legislators say about representation, the easier it is to understand the difficulties of predicting legislative behavior from stereotypes of trustees and delegates. In a sense, most legislators share a dual role orientation: they are both trustees and delegates. They may differ in emphasis: the extent to which they trust their own judgment and their sensitivity to constituent demands. Some differences of emphasis may be caused by variations in districts. Most legislators who say that they rely heavily on their own judgment try to stay in contact with their constituents and express confidence in their perception of public attitudes. Whatever their professed role orientation, most legislators share a suspicion of organized mail and a desire to use other channels to evaluate constituent opinion. Those legislators

who appear to be most willing to base their decisions on the clearly expressed demands of constituents recognize that there are few issues on
which opinions are so strongly expressed and lopsided, and even fewer
on which such constituent opinion clashes with that of the legislator.
Most legislators are comfortable with the general policy viewpoints
that they perceive are dominant in their districts; they believe that
their own views are typical of those in the district. Consequently their
role orientation does not lead trustees and delegates to vote differently
on legislation that is pertinent to those viewpoints. When more specialized groups make demands on issues that are salient to the majority
of constituents, all legislators face similar problems in determining
whether such demands serve the broader interests of the constituency.

*Influence of District.* One variable affecting how legislators make
choices is the character of the district: its homogeneity, socioeconomic
level, and electoral structure. In a district that is basically homogeneous in socioeconomic character—all rural or all urban working
class, for example—the task of representation is relatively easy. There
is likely to be a high degree of consensus on major issues, although social issues sometime divide a constituency that is united on other matters. In such homogeneous districts, it is easier for legislators to determine public attitudes and to make judgments about whether they are
compatible with organized group demands. The greater the homogeneity, the greater the likelihood that group demands will be compatible with broader district opinion and that there will be few sharp conflicts between groups.

Most of the black legislators I interviewed represent central city
districts that are heavily black and lower or middle income. These
members agreed that their districts were easy to represent because conflicts among interests were few and they had no difficulty in determining the needs and wishes of the district. Similar comments came from
many of the legislators representing districts that were overwhelmingly
rural. Some of them mentioned specifically that such districts had few
organized groups and that conflicts between district groups were rare.
They described their districts as being easier to represent than metropolitan ones. Many of these rural districts are sparsely populated and
therefore sprawling geographically, but the problems of transportation
and maintaining contacts are alleviated by the homogeneity of interests.

There are differing points of view among the legislators who represent heterogeneous districts. Some may find such representation easy
because they deliberately choose to represent a majority interest—but I

have found few examples of such choices. More commonly, legislators see an advantage in representing a heterogeneous district because no single group can dictate to the member, or he can ignore conflicting points of view that will cancel each other out. Such legislators argue that they have more freedom to choose if they are subjected to conflicting pressures. While one might suspect that such legislators are trying to make the best of a bad situation, they sound sincere and even convincing in their explanations.

Some legislators believe that the diversity of interests give them an opportunity to be less parochial. A Colorado member says that she is able to cast a "statewide vote" instead of just representing the interests of a bedroom community. A Tennessee legislator remarks that his district is a "microcosm of the city of Memphis," and therefore he can represent broader interests. A California member says that having a diverse district "probably causes me to give more thought to issues, because I am not free to do just what I want; it is probably an advantage in making me consider the range of interests in the district."

A more common statement about the advantages of a heterogeneous district is that it provides members with more freedom and flexibility. An Ohio legislator, who describes his district (with its industrial-rural mix) as a microcosm of the state, says that when there is so much diversity "no single interest can kill you," and you have a great deal of freedom to make choices among the conflicting claims of groups. Similarly a California legislator who says his district is probably the most heterogeneous in the state (in ethnic as well as economic terms) says that he can be "more aggressive and take greater risks on issues" because "it is hard for any single group to challenge you."

Those legislators who describe the advantages of heterogeneity note particularly the absence of certain types of pressures or the balance among them. A Colorado member says, for example, that no single minority ethnic group dominates his district. Others note that no single labor union is too powerful. A Kentucky legislator from a district that is primarily rural describes not only the absence of dominant groups but their overlapping interests: "I am fortunate that the district is varied and that no single group—unions, coal interests, or particular business—can dictate to me. The farmers are a major group in the district, but farmers often have other business interests, and so they are not tied to a single viewpoint."

By contrast, some legislators emphasize the problems in dealing with a diverse district. There is no obvious reason why legislators react differently to similar circumstances, although those who are most conscious of the difficulties of representing diverse interests may be more sensitive to constituent demands. The problems of representing a heterogeneous district are well outlined by a California legislator whose large district encompasses almost every socioeconomic group: "Undoubtedly it is more difficult to represent a district so heterogeneous. In a more homogeneous district you would have fewer conflicts; you could be right more of the time to more of the people. Part of what you are supposed to be doing is representing, and you simply cannot "represent" the views of such diverse groups when there are sharp conflicts, on an issue such as growth in the community."

Some of the legislators with racially diverse districts find problems in representing them. A Chicano representative from a district that is about two-thirds Hispanic (with that percentage increasing) is criticized by those in the district who think he represents only Hispanic interests and finds the situation difficult. Religious diversity may cause problems. A Dallas legislator who represents an inner city that is also diverse in ethnic and economic terms finds that in most respects he has no difficulty representing district viewpoints, but there is a Baptist group (both black and white) with strong views on blue laws and gambling, for example, that are out of step with the majority in the district.

Conflicts may follow class lines. An Ohio legislator from a heterogeneous urban district says that he gets support from low-income groups on welfare bills that he has introduced but gets criticized by those in the lower middle class who have steady employment. His consumer legislation is appreciated by most constituents but not by a number of small businessmen. A conservative California Democrat from a district that spans a wide socioeconomic range runs into criticism from liberal members of a university community and also from labor unions who disagree with him on a farm labor bill. Several legislators whose districts may be relatively homogeneous in other respects have difficulty in representing constituents some of whom live inside and some outside some major cities; the conflicts arise over questions of annexation and related tax matters.

Many of those who describe the problems of representing diverse districts have clearly decided what policy to follow—which group to support and which to oppose. But they seldom describe this choice in terms of the groups that do or do not provide electoral support to them. Some legislators have difficulties because they want to win the support of diverse groups whose interests often conflict. One of the problems they face is that this diversity sometimes makes it difficult to determine which groups are stronger or which viewpoints are more broadly representative. A Colorado legislator on the edge of Denver, whose district runs from suburbia up into the mountain area, finds that the residents of these two principal areas are quite different in their interests and priorities. She describes the difficulty of representing such a district: "I hear more from those groups that are minorities than from the people who make up the bulk of the district. This makes it hard to judge what the district opinion is. On capital punishment, those who attended hearings and came from the district were all against it—but a majority in the district probably favors it."

The socioeconomic level, as well as the heterogeneity, of a district may have some effect on representation. Generally legislators who represent central city districts that are below average in income, education, and occupational levels report that their constituents make relatively few demands on policy issues. The level of group organization and membership is less, and constituents seldom initiate legislative requests (in contrast with requests for services). Legislators from such districts (including many black and Chicano members) emphasize that they know what their constituents need and that the district trusts them to vote in its interest. Some seem surprised by questions about how much mail or other contact they get on issues; they are not surprised by the absence of such mail. Generally districts with higher income, education, and occupational levels are more issue-oriented, as described by the legislators. There are more organized demands and more individual ones. While the constituents may be willing to let the representative use his judgment, they want to be kept informed about what the legislator is doing and are more likely to expect an explanation of legislative votes.

Is the role of a representative significantly different in single-member and in multimember districts? Single-member districts, being smaller, are likely to be more homogeneous; multimember districts are increasingly likely to be heterogeneous as the number of members elected increases. Multimember districts are almost by definition heterogeneous if they include an entire metropolitan county, like many of those in North Carolina. Most of the metropolitan legislators in that state do not believe it is difficult to represent such districts, and they echo the arguments we have heard elsewhere about no single group being able to dominate. One North Carolina legislator, for example, thinks that the Christian schools could exert considerable pressures on legislators in some rural counties, but they represent too small a segment of a metropolitan county to cause problems. The troublesome issue most often mentioned by metropolitan legislators in that state is that of annexation. Because they represent all constituents in the county, they are cross pressured on legislation that would change procedures for cities to annex territory.

Some of the multimember districts in North Carolina include clusters of rural counties. One legislator in a three-member, five-county district, which sprawls along the western part of the state, must represent rural, suburban, and industrial areas. He finds that there is no single interest group to dominate the district but also that there are fewer organized interests of any kind that make demands. Moreover, because no single newspaper or television station dominates the district, there is little coordinated media focus on issues. The only real problems arise from purely local issues, such as conflicts between school districts over funds.

The difference between single-member and large multimember districts involves not only levels of heterogeneity but also relative visibility of the legislators. The legislator representing a single district is more visible to constituents and at least theoretically is more vulnerable to pressure from groups that are concentrated in the district. In districts represented by a number of legislators, no single legislator is as visible or as likely to be subjected to direct pressures. Whether this theory accords with reality may depend on the way in which interests are organized and where their political strength is located. The legislator in a single district may be less vulnerable if he shares the views of the dominant interest in that district—as often occurs—or if there are no dominant interests identifiable there.

Is it possible to determine whether legislators in multimember districts are more likely to be trustees, and those in single-member districts delegates? Is the form of the district important enough to overshadow personal reasons for choosing role orientations? In the late 1960s, when I studied the changes in districting methods used in metropolitan areas of seven states, I classified state legislators according to their representational roles (1969, p. 30). I found that legislators were more likely to be trustees in states using multimember districts, somewhat more likely to be trustees where a recent shift had been made from multimember to single-member districts, and slightly more likely to be delegates where single-member districts had long been used. Moreover, in some of the states where the shift to single-member districts was being or had recently been made, some legislators argued that legislators would be forced to play a delegate role to win reelection in a single-member district.

Since that time I have become convinced that classification of legislators as delegates or trustees is both theoretically dubious and methodologically hazardous. Consequently, I have not classified the legislators in this study and cannot replicate the previous analysis; moreover, the number of legislators from multimember districts is not large enough in this study to make valid comparisons. If forced to quantify the results of interviews, I would have to say that the trustee orientation is a stronger and more pervasive one among legislators, whatever the structure of the districts. It appears to me that there is a particularly strong trusteeship orientation among the North Carolina members representing countywide multimember districts. In Indiana, where almost half of those interviewed came from single-member districts, there was no obvious difference in the balance of representational orientations between members representing the two types of districts. It would be interesting in multimember districts to compare the orientations of members representing the same constituency, but there were not enough examples of this in these two states to draw any conclusions.

Single-member districting makes the legislator more directly responsible to constituents. This fact may make some legislators more sensitive to demands from the district—more likely to be delegates. The form of districting clearly affects the focus of representation; this may be more important than the effects of districting on the style of representation.

*Effects of Electoral Variables.* There are several ways in which the political environment and the circumstances of a political campaign might affect a legislator's responsiveness to his constituency on policy matters. Most of these are easier to describe in theory than to document in practice, and we have little evidence regarding most of them. A fundamental way in which elections affect policy responsiveness is that voters choose legislators who are identified with a particular political party, organized group, or interest; as a consequence of that identification they represent one point of view rather than another. When legislators say that they are "typical" or "think like their constituents," they may be referring to those groups or interests that are in the majority and that contributed to their election. Thus there may be important policy consequences in elections even when policy issues play little or no role in the campaign.

Legislators may, however, take stands on some issues during the campaign. When this occurs, the number of voters who become aware of these issues and who base their voting decision on these issues is probably very small. (There is no data to substantiate that assumption, but it is true in most congressional elections and is probably true in legislative races as well.) Whether or not large numbers of voters are influenced by policy issues, some legislators may perceive their election as a mandate or endorsement to vote in accordance with their announced positions. Interviews with legislators produce numerous examples of members who say that they have emphasized issues in their campaigns. For the most part, however, the members are not arguing that they feel bound to vote certain ways because of the stands they took on issues in the campaign. Instead, they feel free to vote in accordance with their views on particular issues (even when these may conflict with apparent majority opinions in the district) because they were open about these positions during the campaign. No legislators say that they were compelled to take positions during the campaign to win needed group support and are stuck with these positions during the legislative session. My interviews probably underestimate the influence of election campaigns on members because this was not a major aspect of the study, but it is still noteworthy that campaign promises are cited almost entirely as a reason for justifying the position that legislators want to take.

When reasons were given for following a trustee orientation, some members said that they had taken such positions during the campaign; some said they promised during the campaign to follow their own judgment. A North Carolina legislator says that he generally takes a stand on issues during a campaign, "and I stick to that stand when the issue comes up to a vote; I suppose I have lost some votes on such issues—but not many." A Tennessee member says that on most issues he follows his own judgment. "I run on my own position on issues; and so I assume that people who have elected me, knowing my stand, have endorsed my position on the issues." A North Carolina legislator says that she has run on her record, has led the ticket in the primary and the general election, and thus concludes that her record satisfied the voters. Finally, a Kentucky legislator described his stand on issues in terms of his electoral majority: "I told the voters in advance how I stood on the issues. I believe in majority rule—the majority puts me in—and I have to follow the majority whose positions I have committed myself to. I'm not a statesman."

A number of those who have sought to explain the effects of district variables on roll-call voting behavior of state legislators have speculated that legislators who have been elected by narrow margins would be particularly sensitive to constituent demands, but the results of empirical studies in the states have been contradictory (Robeck, 1972; Dye, 1961; Sorauf, 1963; Pesonen, 1963; Patterson, 1961; Flinn, 1964; Grumm, 1965; LeBlanc, 1969). Fiorina (1974, pp. 90-108) has demonstrated the weaknesses of most of the theorizing about the effect of marginality on voting, a factor that often coincides with, but is theoretically less useful than, the factor of homogeneity. This study is not designed to test the effects of marginality on voting behavior or on representational style of legislators. In most states, of course, a large proportion of seats are safe rather than marginal. Nothing that emerged from the interviews about representational style and district characteristics would support the assumption that legislators from the relatively few marginal districts consistently view the job of representation differently or are more responsive to policy demands than are other legislators.

## Accountability to Constituents

Pitkin (1967, pp. 55-59) has criticized the idea that the essence of representation is accountability, but she incorporates the concept in the institutional context of free elections for a representative assembly (p. 235). In the last analysis, legislators are accountable because they must win the votes of their constituents to remain in office. But we may use the term accountability, or responsibility, in a somewhat broader sense. A basic definition includes, among others, these requirements (Pitkin, pp. 209-10): "The representative must act in such a way that there is no conflict [between the representative and the represented], or if it occurs an explanation is called for. He must not be found persistently at odds with the wishes of the represented without good reason in terms of their interest, without a good explanation of why their views are not in accord with their interest." It is this necessity to explain to constituents what the representative has done, and face the consequences of his explanation not being accepted, that I am defining here as accountability.

Fenno (1978, p. 240) argues that the process of representation is inextricably bound up with the political process by which a legislator builds support within his district: "Nearly everything he does to win and hold support—allocating, reaching, presenting, responding, communicating, explaining, assuring—involves representation. It is a view of representation as a process. It is a view of representation as politics, with all of the uncertainties of politics. It is a view, however, that has the net effect of making representation less policy-centered than it usually is." Accountability, defined in these terms, means more than explaining votes on policy matters. It encompasses all the dimensions of representation.

The process of communication is an instrument of accountability.

By reporting his activities and votes in newsletters, press releases, and speeches throughout the district, the legislator is not only gaining publicity and building support but is also explaining what he has done and why. By making himself accessible to requests and questions from constituents, the legislator is practicing accountability. Communication is not only the instrument of accountability, but it is one of the responsibilities of the legislator. Constituents expect the legislator to be accessible, as well as to vote in their interest. Other dimensions of representation include securing resources for the district and providing services to constituents. It is worth noting that legislators often believe their constituents are more interested in services than in most policies, that many of them devote extensive communication efforts to advertising their accessibility and explaining what they have done for the district and its constituents. Moreover, some legislators believe that an active, effective program of services gives them somewhat more flexibility in pursuing policy matters.

In this section we are primarily concerned with accountability in policy matters, and specifically with the ways in which legislators explain their stands on policy issues to their constituents. Fenno (1978, ch. 5) devotes a chapter to the question of how congressmen explain their Washington activity to their constituents—primarily explanations of their policy positions and activities. He defines explaining as "description, interpretation, and justification of behavior" (p. 136). Kingdon (1981, pp. 47-54), in his study of congressmen's voting decisions, also devotes considerable attention to how congressmen explain their votes and emphasizes that the process may have "a subtle, but important effect" on how they vote (p. 47). In my interviews with legislators, I found that they were as cognizant as congressmen of the importance of explaining their votes on policy matters, and I found a widespread belief that most voters will accept such explanations.

Some legislators explain their trustee orientation by saying that the voters trust them to follow their own judgment. If that trust were deep enough, there might be no need for legislators to explain their votes. Many of those who emphasize that they follow their own judgment, however, also stress that it is necessary to explain—or be prepared to explain—how they have voted. They believe that voters have confidence in their judgments and are ready to accept their explanations but want to hear those explanations. Many legislators are confident that in most cases they can either convince voters that their vote was correct or at least persuade them that it was a reasonable and informed action. A good summary of this position comes from a Texas legislator: "The key is to make sure that, if I make a decision on an issue where I have received a lot of input, I communicate my rationale for making that decision, and then even those who disagree with me will accept it." In a similar vein, a Colorado legislator says: "You can explain your vote to people who may disagree with you on some issues—that is the only way a politician can succeed. Most people will accept your decision if you give them a rational explanation."

Legislators often find that explaining their vote is an opportunity to educate their constituents. Those who complain about the member's vote usually do not actually understand the bill and its implications. A number of legislators are frustrated by the lack of time and opportunities to educate voters, particularly their critics, about the details of legislation.

Some legislators have discovered that there are limits to their powers of explanation:

I think, given a chance to explain my vote, constituents will buy my explanation and respect me, even if they don't completely agree. But there are some you can't reach.

People often don't understand an issue, but when I explain it to them they generally appreciate my vote. Sensible people will listen when you explain your vote. But a few fanatics won't listen at all.

You have to try to explain your viewpoint and vote, and the ability to persuade is one thing I think I have; and I can accomplish that. But some of the single-issue groups can't be persuaded.

As this last comment suggests, the groups that often cannot be reached by explanation are those that are strongly committed to a single issue, particularly an emotional one. But not all legislators believe that explanations directed towards such groups are a lost cause. Some of them have found that they can turn the issue around in explaining their votes: "Even on moral issues, members of single-issue groups can be persuaded that I have made up my mind and have a reason for it. They respect my belief on an issue like capital punishment. When people disagree with me, I try to give them a rational reason, but some of the issues are so emotional, you can't use a rational reason—and so I take a moral stand. And people respect my moral position."

Legislators recognize that it is organized groups, more than individual citizens, who want explanations for specific stands and votes. A Republican representative from Ohio, who described himself as a moderate, said that he had to pay particular attention to right-wing Republican activists in the district, who did not always agree with him but respected him for explaining his votes. Similarly union rank-and-file members respected him for going to factories and debating with union leaders over the issue of public employees having the right to strike, which he opposed. He concluded from his experiences: "If you explain your votes to people, and sound knowledgeable, and report back often, they will forgive a few votes that they may not agree with." In a similar fashion a Massachusetts Democrat describes how he dealt with groups that disagreed with his positions on gun control and on abortion: "I voted against the views of a lot of these people, and I told them my stand. I will lose some votes from these groups, but not all of them. People will generally trust you if you are straight with them and don't try to waffle on the issue." A liberal Democrat from Texas concludes that explanations directed at groups that disagree with you may serve an important purpose in neutralizing if not persuading the opposition: "When I go into conservative areas where my support is not too strong, I tell people how I am going to vote and what my stand is on issues. If I give them a logical reason for my vote, they may disagree with me, but they won't fight me. They may not vote for me, but they won't work actively against me, as long as they think I'm honest."

John Kingdon (1981, pp. 47-48), in his study of the voting decisions of congressmen, suggests that the prospect of having to defend and explain an unpopular position to constituents may cause some representatives to change their mind about how they will vote: "But there is more to the phenomenon of explaining than simply devising a justification for a vote. Congressmen sometimes find themselves in the position of being unable to devise an acceptable explanation. In such a situation, especially if they do not feel intensely about the matter, they often vote so as to avoid the predicament. In such an instance, it can be said that the necessity to explain one's vote has had an impact on the congressman's behavior." My interview with legislators did not provide explicit examples of this phenomenon. On the other hand, a concern with explaining one's vote may have been implicit in the statements by those legislators who said that, particularly on emotional issues where a strong district preference was clear, they voted against their own convictions and in support of the position favored by the district.

The legislators who talked to me about explanation, however, saw it as not only a duty but an opportunity to follow the course that they believed was best. For the most part they had confidence in their ability to explain complex issues to voters and win their respect even when they did not win their agreement. This view of the significance of vote explanation parallels the conclusions that Fenno (1978, p. 151) draws: "There are at most only a very few policy issues on which representatives are constrained in their voting by the views of their reelection constituencies. . . . On the vast majority of votes, however, representatives can do as they wish—provided only that they can, when they need to, explain their votes to the satisfaction of interested constituents. The ability to get explanations accepted at home is, then, the essential underpinning of a member's voting leeway in Washington."

In the last analysis, accountability means not merely explaining your record to voters but submitting it to their judgment at the polls. Some legislators claim a mandate from voters because of the stand they have taken on issues during campaigns, but they do not seem to feel constrained by campaign promises. There is little evidence from this study to suggest that legislators who have been elected by narrow margins are particularly responsive to constituent demands. It is also worth repeating that voting studies (at the congressional level) do not support the assumption that many voters make decisions in legislative races primarily on the basis of issues.

The question to be asked at this point, in the context of examining what accountability means to legislators, is whether they believe that their stands on issues and their ability to explain their record satisfactorily to organized groups have a major impact on their reelection prospects. How likely is it that legislators will be defeated because their positions on issues are unpopular? How carefully do they assess the electoral consequences of their actions?

There is evidence on both sides of these questions. The fact that many legislators devote so much attention to developing communication patterns and that many of them emphasize the importance of explaining their record suggests a sensitivity to the possibility of being defeated by issues. More specifically, they know that particular groups who feel strongly about issues and disagree with the legislator may seek to defeat them. State legislators are aware of the growing importance of single-issue groups and often criticize them for judging—and threatening to defeat—legislators on a single issue. Some legislators who seem to be quite secure electorally complain about opposition from groups that often would appear to be relatively weak and hardly threatening.

Legislators usually discuss their electoral situation in terms of groups and try to assess their potential impact. A North Carolina legislator, for example, notes that fundamentalist groups (seeking to abolish state control over Christian schools) have been vocal but their members have not been very active in politics. On the other hand, a group that has organized to oppose tax increases has made endorsements and handed out slates at the polls. A California legislator who has been criticized by labor unions is acutely aware of a threat by a union leader to run a candidate against him in the next election. A Kentucky legislator believes that he has had close competition in the primaries because his opponent has exploited the legislator's pro-abortion stand. He notes that extremist groups usually do not work actively in political campaigns. He also notes that he had to work hard to win the support of city firefighters, who opposed him in past elections and finally endorsed him in the most recent one. He is not arguing that issues alone determine election outcomes, but he is conscious of the support given by organized groups to him or to his opponents, and obviously these endorsements are affected by stands on issues. Other legislators make it clear that they do not expect to get support from certain groups (often labor unions in the case of Republican legislators) because of their position on issues. Many legislators thus perceive issues as having electoral consequences to the extent that they result in the mobilization of organized groups in political campaigns.

Policy issues rarely have much impact on electoral outcomes. Although organized groups may make endorsements on the basis of issues, this may have limited impact on voters. Moreover, there are relatively few issues that are particularly salient to constituents and on which legislators believe they must take a stand that is contrary to the views of many or most constituents. Many legislators recognize the validity of these points and echo them in their comments. A Republican legislator from Ohio who is experienced and thoughtful asserts, "There are few issues so important that you have to take a stand contrary to that of the district and risk getting beaten." But he has followed politics closely enough and knows his district well enough to conclude that constituents do not watch the votes of legislators carefully enough so that the risk on any particular issue is very great. An Indiana Republican legislator, from a two-member district, notes that the other member from that district is a Democrat who votes differently from him on most issues. Both of them win reelection, which leads him to the logical conclusion that, in his district at least, one's position on the issues is not crucial to the election outcome, which is more likely to be determined by name recognition and contact with the voters.

Some legislators believe that electoral risks occur not because of the obvious, major issues, on which the risks can be calculated, but on unexpected issues. A particularly thoughtful and articulate Texas representative says: "I can't take too seriously the claims of groups that make extreme demands, because I do not think that many people have strong feelings on issues and will vote you out of office because of them. What may defeat you is not some major and obviously controversial issue, but something that is unexpected." An experienced Ohio legislator agrees that, beyond a few clearly controversial issues, it is hard to predict the issues an opponent may try to exploit. He cites an example of a rather technical issue involving formulas for distributing educational assistance that affected the various parts of his district differently.

During the course of a session a legislator must cast hundreds of votes, most of which appear to be noncontroversial and not at all salient to voters. These make the legislator vulnerable because it is generally difficult to tell what issues a prospective opponent may try to exploit. Clausen (1973, p. 133) describes the problem faced by congressmen in these terms: "My image of the constituency is that of a somnolent giant usually oblivious to the representative's existence. However, this giant has certain tender spots that must be protected from the prodding opponent who would like to arouse the giant and turn its wrath on the negligent representative. To guard against this eventuality, the representative must constantly reexamine the otherwise placid constituency to locate the tender spots and provide the needed protection against the pesky opponent." The state legislator's problem is similar, but is perhaps less severe. One reason is the state legislative district is smaller and usually less complex; consequently it may be easier to locate and protect its "tender spots." Moreover, it may be more difficult for an electoral challenger to attract much voter attention to issues because state legislative campaigns usually have so little visibility. The state legislator, like his congressional counterpart, can also benefit from those activities and accomplishments, such as constituency service, that are likely to be more salient to constituents.

Perhaps the most realistic description of the electoral consequences of voting is the "string of votes" thesis, advanced by Kingdon (1981, pp. 41-42): "Even if it is granted that one vote out of the ordinary will not create lasting political damage, that fact alone is not all that congressmen may consider. It is possible to cast what one congressman called "a string of votes" against various elements of the constituency, the cumulative effect of which could be very serious. Even if each of them singly would create no great electoral problem, the string of them taken together would." No state legislator articulated this point of view, but it is probably pertinent to some of them. If the risk of damage from a "string of votes" is somewhat less at the state legislative level, it may be because legislators cast fewer votes in a session on issues that are salient, and few of them come from districts that contain a large number of well-organized and contending groups.

The final thing that needs to be said about the accountability of state legislators is that the data are still lacking to provide empirical evidence about the impact of issues in state legislative campaigns. To measure this properly would require not only analysis of the issues raised by candidates in a number of campaigns but also survey data from voters in a number of districts. Until then, we remain dependent on the legislators' perceptions of the consequences of issues for reelection prospects.

## Constituency in Decision-Making

This study is not primarily concerned with the decision-making process in state legislatures, but the study of representation would be incomplete without an effort to integrate our conclusions about policy responsiveness to the district with a larger theory of decision-making. American legislative scholars have developed a number of models of the decision-making process, which variously emphasize cue-taking, policy dimensions, predisposition-communication, consensus, previous behavior, and goals. Kingdon (1977), who has summarized these approaches, argues that they are not contradictory but are complementary, and he has developed a model that effectively integrates them. Here I seek to show how responsiveness to the constituency fits into Kingdon's model.

The model has several important assumptions (pp. 569-76): 1) The legislator establishes a repetitive pattern of decision-making that can be followed in vote after vote and that minimizes the cost of getting information and simplifies choices (p. 560). 2) The legislator has certain primary goals, including satisfying constituents, satisfying various actors in the capital in order to build influence there, and achieving public policy objectives (pp. 569-70). 3) In reaching a decision, the legislator searches for consensus among the set of actors who have possible influence over him, and, when that is lacking, establishes certain goals or priorities for making choices among them (p. 571). 4) When issues arise, the legislator sorts them into certain policy dimensions that are familiar, and on some of which his position is well established (p. 573).

These principles lead to a model, diagramed like a stimulation (p. 575). The legislator asks a series of questions: Is the issue noncontroversial? Is there conflict among the actors pertinent to the legislator? If there is controversy and conflict, is the issue pertinent and important to any of the legislator's goals? If so, is there conflict among these goals? If there is such a conflict and the legislator must choose among goals, the first priority is to determine whether the issue is highly important or salient to the constituency. If so, the legislator votes in accord with constituency interests or demands. If not, the legislator turns to consideration of other goals and actors.

John Kingdon, and the others whose theoretical approaches

he seeks to integrate, have focused their attention on decision-making in Congress, rather than state legislators. Is his model applicable to state legislators? I see no reason to doubt that it is. The assumptions underlying the model are equally plausible for state legislators. It may be even more important for state legislators to minimize the cost of getting information and simplifying choices, because they have less time and staff and deal with a large number of issues of relatively little importance on which they have little information or background.

Some models of decision-making (such as that by Matthews and Stimson, 1970) give little or no attention or priority to the constituency. In contrast, Kingdon (1977) assigns a high priority to the constituency. Whenever there is any conflict among the legislator's goals, Kingdon hypothesizes that "the congressman considers the constituency interest first. He may not end up voting with the constituency, but he always considers it first when it is above the minimum level of importance"(p. 578). The priority that Kingdon assigns to the constituency does not mean that most issues, or even many issues, are salient enough to the district so that constituency interests must be considered. Rather Kingdon is arguing that, when conflict arises, the legislator begins by asking whether the issue is salient to the district, and if it is the interests and demands of the district must be taken into account (if not always followed) as a decision is made. Although the legislator makes many decisions without any regard to the constituency, taking cues from other sources, he does this after he has considered and rejected the possibility that the issue is salient to the district.

The role that Kingdon describes for the constituency in his model of legislative decision-making is fully compatible with the description of representation that has been outlined in this study on the basis of interviews with state legislators. What needs to be done here is not to change that model but to amplify the constituency part of the model— to describe in more detail how the legislator determines whether an issue is salient to the district, how he determines district interests and assesses district demands, and how he weighs the interests and demands of the district against other goals and the demands of other actors outside the constituency. This description is based on the experience of state legislators, but it may fit national or local legislators as well.

How does the legislator determine whether an issue is salient to the district and how salient it is? Representation can only be understood in the context of issues. When an issue comes to the legislator's attention or when a bill appears on the day's calendar for floor action, the legislator places it in a policy dimension or category. Based on past experience with other issues in that dimension, the legislator can make a quick and accurate judgment about whether the issue or bill is salient to the district. Some bills, probably the vast majority, may have no effect at all on the district, such as local bills affecting other cities and counties. They may be relatively minor, noncontroversial matters that may be either broad or narrow in scope but that do not have any particular effect on his constituents. A bill making it easier for persons to renew drivers' licenses or permitting right-hand turns on a red light will help his constituents but is not particularly pertinent to the district.

Another category of issues and bills includes ones that the legislator knows are salient to the district. He may recognize immediately that the interests of the district or of significant groups in the district are affected. An example would be a bill to require higher property assessments, or a change in the procedures on annexation, or a bill changing the distribution formula for aid to education. Another category of salient issues (which may overlap the first) is one which he knows from past experience will provoke demands from groups in his district. Examples are bills pertaining to abortion, liquor regulation, or the right of public employees to strike.

There is a third category of bills and issues: ones that the legislator recognizes may be salient to important groups in the district. The legislator may contact group leaders in the district to warn them about the bill and to find out whether it affects their interests. The legislator may postpone judgment until he can find out whether the issue is salient. There may be a fourth category of bills: ones that the legislator dismisses as not being salient to constituents but on which pressures from the district subsequently develop. These are occasions on which the legislator may have to reevaluate the salience of a bill or an issue. Presumably this does not happen often to the experienced legislator.

These comments suggest that a model of constituency influence on decision-making must take into account variations in the time dimension. Some bills do not come to the legislator's attention until they appear on the calendar for decision. The member's busy schedule does not give him time to gather much information about most bills that are coming up for a vote. He must decide quickly whether the bill affects the district's interest, and if it does must use his own judgment about whether a positive or negative vote will best serve that interest. On some other bills that require a quick decision, the legislator may get information from some district group, or a lobbyist, or perhaps another legislator—information suggesting that the issue is salient to constituent groups or the broader constituency. The legislator must make a quick appraisal of that information (and its source), weighing it against what he knows about the district and constituent groups.

Other issues come to the legislator's attention long before they come to a vote. Some may have arisen in the previous session; some may have come up in the campaign; some may be major programs of the governor or important interest groups. In most cases it should be obvious to the legislator whether such issues are salient to the constituency as a whole or to smaller but significant groups within it. The greater the lead time on such an issue, the more opportunity the legislator has to determine how broadly salient the issue is and what are the intensity and direction of opinion among concerned constituent groups. On such issues the legislator should be able to make his decision with a full understanding of constituent demand and with his own evaluation of how the issue affects what he perceives to be the interests of the district.

This model of decision-making does not indicate that the legislator will always vote to support district interests and viewpoints in preference to all others. It does indicate that the legislator will take district interests and demands into account whenever the issue is salient to the district. The ultimate decision will involve a number of factors pertaining to the district as well as other factors, such as the strength of pressure from the governor or party leaders.

Perhaps the best way to describe how constituency factors influence decision-making is to outline a series of questions that the legislator will ask once he has determined that an issue is salient to the district. Some of the questions may be implicit or unconscious because the answers are so clear-cut, and when an issue arises on short notice the legislator may lack the time and information necessary to answer some of them. But on these issues salient to the constituency, when the timetable for decision-making permits it, I suggest that legislators follow this model and ask these questions in evaluating constituency interests and demands.

1) Does the issue have a clear and significant effect on the broad interests of the district, in the legislator's judgment? If it does, the legislator will normally vote to support those interests unless there are unusually strong pressures to do otherwise. Generally the state legislator will see no conflict between what he perceives as the district's clear interest and his own convictions. Where the perceived interests of the district as a whole are so clear, the legislator does not have to depend on organized or unorganized demands from the district though he will be

responsive to them as long as they are compatible with his perception of district interests. Where the issue does not affect district interests so clearly, the legislator must ask further questions.

2) Does the issue affect particular groups, organized or unorganized, within the district? If the answer appears to be positive, the legislator must make judgments first about the reliability of his communications from them.

3) Do the legislator's communication channels (letters, personal contacts, etc.) provide a clear picture of these viewpoints of constituent groups: how many are concerned, and the direction and intensity of views? If they do not, then the legislator may decide to seek a fuller picture by contacting group leaders, conducting opinion polls, or by other methods. The legislator then uses the information to evaluate group viewpoints.

4) Is there consensus on the issue among the groups that have communicated to him? If so, how numerous are these groups, and how strong are their feelings? If there is consensus, is this dominant viewpoint compatible:

—with what the legislator believes are the interests of the district?

—with his own judgment and the views of other political actors whose judgment he respects? If there are conflicts between the consensus of district groups and these other viewpoints, the legislator must make choices that may be difficult, weighing the strength of these groups, the intensity of their feelings, and perhaps taking into account whether these groups are politically active and whether they are part of his supportive constituency.

5) If there is disagreement within the groups in the constituency, the legislator, in deciding which group deserves support, must ask:

—Which group is more united in its beliefs and feels more intensely about the issue?

—Is one group numerically stronger, or does one group, more than the other, coincide with the legislator's supportive constituency? Despite our failure to find explicit recognition by legislators that they take this into account, it seems reasonable to believe that on some issues there will be such a difference and it will be a pertinent factor in the decision.

—Does the viewpoint of one group more nearly reflect, or coincide with, what he believes to be the interests of the district? State legislators often find themselves trying to balance the organized, articulated interests against what they believe are the interests of the silent majority.

—Which viewpoint is more compatible with the legislator's own judgment or with the views of other political actors whose judgment he respects?

At the risk of appearing redundant, it might be wise to add a caveat about how this model pertains to the state legislator. The decisions the legislator makes on issues salient to the district are usually less complex and less conflictual than those made by congressmen. When an issue affects the interests of the district as a whole or of major groups within it, there is usually little conflict or uncertainty about what the legislator should do. Many of the issues that cause conflict among groups are salient only to very narrow groups within the district. Although most mail comes from organized groups that may be unrepresentative, the skillful and enterprising legislator can tap the opinions of broader groups. The number of issues that are salient to large enough groups and that cause deep enough splits within the district to be really troublesome are very few. Consequently the job of representing the constituency in the legislative decision-making arena is a manageable one for most legislators.

# 6. Allocation and Service Responsiveness

Allocation responsiveness concerns the legislator's efforts to gain governmental goods and services for the district. They are general rather than individual benefits, but they frequently benefit one part of the district or one group more than others; this would be the case of a request for a stop light, a neighborhood park, or better police protection for a neighborhood. Service responsiveness pertains to the needs of individuals or groups who want help in dealing with government agencies. In some cases these may be national or local agencies, and not just state ones; occasionally legislators are asked by constituents for help in dealing with nongovernmental entities, like businesses.

In theory the distinction between these two areas is clear; it is between resources for the whole district or for public groups or sections of the district, and assistance to private individuals, businesses, and groups in dealing with government. In practice these areas may occasionally overlap; assistance to a businessman might help many employees and thus the whole community, or resources might be allocated to a group that is so narrow as to be essentially private. There are some other distinctions that need to be made. The requests for resources often come from local government officials and might include such matters as a new formula for allocating school funds or specific projects in the district. Local officials also seek legislators for help in getting legislation passed authorizing local governments to take certain actions. Such requests would fall under the category of policy responsiveness unless the legislative request was primarily for state funds. Legislators are sometimes asked by groups or individuals to intervene with local governments to get resources allocated for projects, and this falls under the resource allocation category. They are sometimes asked to assist individuals who are having problems dealing with local agencies—a form of constituent service. They may also be asked to intervene in local policy disputes, such as zoning conflicts or school board controversies. These cases, which legislators often try to avoid, fall into a no-man's land in our classifications system but will be discussed briefly in the context of constituent services.

These two broad areas of representation have several characteristics in common. They relate to demands from groups and individuals that are particularistic rather than general. They require the representative to work effectively within the district and with administrative agencies, and not primarily in the legislature itself. For the most part, the legislator can perform these services without arousing opposition in the district (although there may be intradistrict disagreements on some projects). If the legislator is particularly successful in getting benefits for the district and groups and individuals within it, no one in the district loses. The opportunity to provide these services has the potential for major political benefits for the legislator. Perhaps the major differences between these two areas, in terms of the roles and behavior patterns of legislators, is that most are actively involved in allocation responsiveness, but they differ greatly in the efforts that they put into service responsiveness and in their belief about whether the latter is a legitimate and important role. There is no need to explain why legislators participate in the allocation of resources, but we will try to understand why they differ in their attitudes toward service responsiveness.

### Allocation Responsiveness

The initiative for resource requests for the district comes largely from local officials. In metropolitan counties it is common for city, county, and school officials to meet with the legislative delegation as a group to explain local needs and discuss strategies for meeting those needs. In rural districts including several counties, the legislator has the responsibility of meeting officials from each of the counties and other local units of government. Some needs are purely legislative, and others involve resource allocation of various kinds. Some of these resources can be gained by special legislation or by amendments to the budget, and legislators can work directly to achieve these goals. More often, the resources must be gained from state administrators, who have the authority (under the existing budget) to repair a park facility, install a traffic light (or conduct a feasibility study for a new highway bypass around the city). In those cases where the funds must come from state agencies, local officials may use legislators as intermediaries to set up meetings with state officials or use their political skills to maintain pressure on the officials.

Legislators generally welcome the opportunity to play this role. A California legislator says: "We often provide assistance for local officials in dealing with Sacramento. It is part of the job, and it helps them to get the access they need. It builds good rapport with local officials, and if things work out it gives us good publicity." A Massachusetts legislator who represents seven towns says that he is able to play this liaison role better because he had eight years of experience as a town selectman.

Some legislators wish that local officials would make greater use of their services. An Ohio representative who reports that he works closely with the officials of forty-nine townships expresses the wish that they would use him more often to set up meetings with state officials. "I think they believe that they should not bother me, and I am trying to change that attitude." A Texas legislator representing five counties finds that there are considerable differences from county to county in how much help the local officials request. A Kentucky legislator serving his first term is still trying to develop his role as intermediary. When he took office, he found that his predecessor had not assumed that role, and local officials were accustomed to making their own contacts in Frankfort. He is trying, cautiously and tactfully, to change that pattern. In some large cities, and even in some rural counties, there are elected officials who have more political influence in the state capital than do most of the state legislators. In those situations, the legislator's role may be minimized.

Some legislators also work with the administration of universities and colleges in their districts to get more resources for them. A legislator from Austin says that the delegation from that county meets regularly with officials of the University of Texas to discuss both legislative and budgetary matters. They had recently worked on the problem of funding for bus transportation on the campus. A California legislator whose district includes the University of California at Berkeley finds himself swamped with university business. Some of it involves resources for new facilities, better salaries, and special projects; some involves constituency service on behalf of students or faculty members. Presumably the legislator's ability to serve constituent needs in dealing with the university administration is enhanced by his willingness to argue the university's case for more resources in Sacramento. Similar situations would presumably be found in most other districts that include colleges or universities.

The range of needs that legislators are asked to deal with is as broad as the range of needs at the local level. In Kentucky, nearly all the legislators mentioned specific projects that they had worked to get for their district. Perhaps because of political norms in Kentucky, legislators appeared to be more heavily involved in getting resources for the district than those in some other states. Legislators from metropolitan counties in Kentucky spoke about highway problems that ranged from extending and widening a major highway around Louisville to gaining grade crossings and a pedestrian overpass for schoolchildren. Perhaps the most commonly mentioned road project was the effort to get traffic lights installed at busy intersections. Success in gaining a traffic light can immeasurably enhance a legislator's reputation in a neighborhood. Another common concern is related to flood control, drainage ditches, and sewers. Legislators in lower-income districts spoke of getting health centers, youth centers, and improved housing. One legislator reported that he drove through his district on a regular basis looking for potholes that needed filling or housing in disrepair that should be inspected—problems that he reported to the local government.

In rural Kentucky, most legislators find that the greatest demand is for roads. Local governments and citizens want poor roads upgraded, worn-out roads repaved, and gravel roads blacktopped. One rural legislator estimates that 70 percent of the requests he gets from individuals are requests for roads. There are never enough funds to pave and to repair all the roads, and the problem is more acute in coal-mining counties where heavy coal trucks have been breaking up the roads. Although some state funds are allocated among counties according to a fixed formula, there appears to be enough flexibility in allocations so that legislators are under pressure to get a larger share for their counties as well as to support specific projects. (One legislator said, however, that a constituent had asked him to prevent a gravel road from being blacktopped, because he was afraid it would then be used by coal trucks.) Some of the larger road projects require a number of years to complete, of course, and require sustained efforts on the part of legislators.

There are a variety of other needs in rural Kentucky that call for allocation of state resources. Several legislators emphasize their efforts to get state parks in the district developed and improved. There are county fairgrounds that need repair, hospitals that need a surgical unit or expensive equipment, a county courthouse that needs to be rebuilt. For some projects federal funds are available, and the legislator may work to get the state funds that are necessary on a matching basis so that the county will qualify for federal funds.

Although it is possible that some of these proposed projects might arouse opposition from some groups in a district, the legislators who emphasize their role in securing projects rarely mention such conflicts. It is evident that the multitude of demands for repairing and paving roads in rural Kentucky sometimes confronts legislators with difficult choices in their recommendations, but such choices can be made with political skill. Although the efforts to obtain projects for the district can be time-consuming, I did not find legislators who complained about this chore or had any doubts that it was an important part of their job (unlike some of the comments on constituency service). A number of legislators describe with pride their successes in getting roads and other projects, and some are explicit in recognizing the political gains. Other legislators express frustration that they have been relatively unsuccessful in getting projects needed by the district.

This contrast in levels of satisfaction leads us to ask what factors determine how successful a legislator will be in getting projects. In Kentucky, where the governor is strong and plays an important role in the distribution of resources, legislators are more likely to emphasize the advantages of having close political ties to the governor. A veteran representative from rural Kentucky (who had emphasized the importance of roads) said: "I served with Julian [Governor Carroll] when he was a freshman in the legislature, and I know the other cabinet people. I know exactly where to go to get the job done. I can get my calls through quickly. An experienced legislator has a real advantage in getting answers from state officials." Another Kentucky legislator holding a leadership position agrees that such a position makes it easier to get a share of road funds. A freshman legislator says that it helps to be aligned with the governor and to know the key people in Frankfort: "If you are persistent enough you can get results." Another veteran legislator suggests that being known as friendly to the governor and his administration "is not an absolute must, but you can get more for the district if you are a supporter of the governor." One leader of the opposition party does not think it is a handicap to be a Republican, suggesting that he has been in Frankfort long enough to know how to get things done. But another Republican from a rural district expresses bitterness about his ineffectiveness in getting projects: "They don't give me the time of day in Frankfort." He is also frustrated by the fact that when decisions are made to build or repair roads in the district, he is not consulted or even informed of the decisions.

The position of legislators in metropolitan delegations, in Kentucky and in other states, is somewhat different from that of legislators who represent multicounty districts. In the metropolitan area, collective bargaining goes on, rather than individual bargaining, much of the time. One legislator from a metropolitan county in Ohio suggests that this reduces the pressure on individual legislators to make trades of votes in return for projects. It is also possible that other political considerations (such as the political power of the county or city administration or the governor's need to enhance his political standing in the county) may be more important in determining what projects are allocated to a metropolitan county.

Members of metropolitan county delegations do not always agree on priorities for allocating resources within the county or on specific projects. In several states that have shifted from at-large to district representation in metropolitan counties, there has been a resulting decline in the cohesion of the county delegation on matters pertaining to the county. Those representing the suburbs and those from the central cities do not always agree on what needs in the county are most urgent. Obviously the greater the disagreement, the weaker the ability of the county delegation to get administrative support for projects or legislative support for budgetary items and local legislation.

It is difficult and risky to generalize from a few examples about the factors that make legislators more or less effective in getting state resources for their districts. The individual political influence of a legislator may be more important in states like Kentucky and Tennessee, which have a long political tradition of projects being allocated by governors to counties whose leadership is supportive. Generally we would expect to find that in any state legislators belonging to the governor's party would be more effective in getting resources. In Ohio, however, which has divided government, some legislators believe that Democrats, who hold a majority in the House, are more successful than Republicans, who control the administration. There is another factor to be considered in determining the influence of political factors on resource allocation. Increasingly decisions on allocating resources must be based on more objective criteria—needs and priorities are determined by experts manipulating statistics—and are influenced by the demands of the federal government, which so often shares in the costs. The job of the legislator who is seeking funds for his district is not merely to develop political influence and learn how state agencies (and sometimes the federal government) operate, but it also requires him to provide evidence of the needs of the district. Legislators must play a broker role among local officials and among citizen groups in determining priorities in the district, as well as helping to keep them informed about the opportunities for both state and federal assistance.

## Service Responsiveness

Interviews with legislators about serving constituent needs provide contrasting impressions: for many legislators, constituency service is a major part of their job, absorbing their time and energy and a large proportion of their staff resources; other legislators perceive this to be a minor part of their job and actually devote very little time and few resources to it. A few figures will illustrate the contrasts. Some legislators say that they spend as much as half of their own time (plus most of the time of staff members) dealing with casework, while others rarely work on cases personally. At one extreme, there are some legislators who say that their office handles fifty to seventy-five (or more) calls and letters a week requesting service for constituents. One Massachusetts representative gets forty to fifty calls a day, most of which are requests for service.) There are many legislators, on the other hand, who rarely get more than four or five letters or calls a week requesting individual help, and some of these perceive that to be a relatively heavy load. A Colorado legislator said that she had received only ten requests for service after four months of the session; a freshman Kentucky legislator said that he had received one such request in the six-month period since the session ended.

Why is there such a wide range of legislative service responsibilities and activities? Why are some legislators much more oriented to, and much more involved in, constituency service than others? Can the differences be explained by variations in the demand for services, or by variations in the willingness or ability of legislators to provide those services?[1]

*Variations among the States.* Some of the differences that occur from state to state may be explained by the political culture of the state or by resources available in each legislative body. Although no precise quantitative data are available, it is possible to make some rough comparisons among the states in the attention devoted to constituency service. Among the nine states where I interviewed representatives, service responsiveness appears to have high priority in California, Massachusetts, Texas, and Ohio; medium priority in Indiana, Kentucky, and Tennessee; and low priority in North Carolina and Colorado.[2]

The first explanation for these differences is the political culture of the state, which affects the attitude and expectation of constituents. Political scientists have long recognized that there are cultural differences in various parts of the county, and some have argued that it is possible to distinguish the dominant political culture in individual states (Elezar, 1972; Patterson, 1968; Jewell and Olson, 1978, pp. 6-13). The history and tradition of the state, along with its social, economic, religious, ethnic, and geographic characteristics, lead to the development of certain attitudes and patterns of behavior that distinguish one state from another. Massachusetts has a long history of patronage, of political leaders providing various kinds of favors for voters. The citizens of that state are accustomed to bringing their problems to politicians, whether they need a job, better housing, or a welfare check. In a sense the state legislator is playing a role that a few years ago was played by the party ward leader. A similar political culture in Ohio and Indiana may help to explain the emphasis on constituency service that exists in those states.

Kentucky and Tennessee are examples of states where the traditional party organizations, with their reliance on patronage, are less common, although at one time they were very strong in both Louisville and Memphis. But in both states it seems to have been common for constituents to turn to political leaders for help in getting jobs, or getting a gravel road blacktopped, or for the satisfaction of other needs. Elling (1979, pp. 357-58) found that legislators in Kentucky stress casework more than Minnesota legislators do. He classifies Kentucky as having "job-oriented politics" and describes the "friends and neighbors' quality of Kentucky politics and the perceived importance of producing tangible, noncollective benefits for constituents in such a political milieu." He notes that Fenton (1957, 1966) has classified Kentucky as having job-oriented politics and Minnesota as being issue oriented. Fenton (1966) also places Ohio and Indiana in the job-oriented category.

If political culture helps to explain the emphasis on constituency service in Massachusetts, Ohio, Indiana, Kentucky, and Tennessee, it probably does not account for the high service priority in California, a state with a strong progressive, antipartisan tradition and no tradition of political machines or job politics. The low priority for constituency service in Colorado is compatible with one's impression of that state as being more issue than job oriented and lacking the machine politics that characterize some eastern and midwestern states.

No data exist on constituent expectations in the various states, but only the evidence reported by legislators. That evidence suggests variations by district in constituent attitudes. But Massachusetts, at least, stands out as a state in which legislators from most of the districts emphasize that their constituents expect them to provide service. On the other hand, Colorado is one state in which many of the legislators mention the low expectations of constituents.

The norms of the state legislature are probably also important in determining the emphasis on constituency service, although this is difficult to prove. The member who is newly elected to the legislature soon learns how much attention other members attach to constituency service and is likely to follow the pattern of activity that has become established. The attitudes of members toward constituency service also make them more or less willing to vote for the staff resources needed to facilitate constituency service.

There can be no doubt that resources for staff and for district offices contribute to constituency service in several ways. If a legislator has adequate staff, and especially if some staff members are located in the district, his office is accessible to constituents. The greater the accessibility, the more constituents will take advantage of the service. If the legislator had adequate staff help, he is more likely to be successful in answering the constituents' needs promptly and effectively, and word of that success will spread to other constituents, further increasing the demand. Moreover, where the legislator has staff assistance, he is more likely to give priority to constituency service, because this can be done without a great drain on his time. The legislator who has no help is more likely to become frustrated and impatient with the time-consuming efforts necessary to follow up on constituent complaints.

California is the best example of a state where the large individual staffs and the availability of district offices have made possible heavy emphasis on constituency service. With a heavy caseload, a wide range of services, and a large and well-trained staff, the legislative offices in California resemble congressional offices more than they do the offices found in most other state legislatures. The substantial staff support and money provided by the Texas legislature contribute to the high level of constituency service found in that state.

Some of the legislators whom I interviewed in both Colorado and North Carolina mentioned the lack of individual staff assistance as one explanation for the low priority they gave to constituency service and the low level of demand for such service. On the other hand, in both Massachusetts and Ohio constituency service ranks high on the list of priorities for most legislators despite a very modest level of individual staff assistance. Members of the Massachusetts House did not get an individual staff assistant until 1979; many of them indicated that they now use that assistant primarily to handle constituency service, a job they had done themselves for many years. In Ohio, there are very limited staff resources, particularly for members of the minority party, and yet many members devote a lot of time to constituency service. Several Ohio legislators, for example, have set up district offices, either by paying for them personally or by borrowing space from local governments. Finally, we should note that legislators in Kentucky, Tennessee, and Indiana all devote moderate amounts of attention to constituency service with little or no individual staff assistance; given the service-oriented political culture of those states, more adequate staffing might lead to a high level of constituency service.

It can be argued that in states like California, Massachusetts, and Ohio, where the legislature is in session for a large proportion of the year, members have greater visibility and are more likely to be contacted by constituents. On the other hand, some legislators in Kentucky and Tennessee believe they have more constituency contact because they are at home most of the time. The size of legislative districts may have some influence on constituency service, but there is no consensus on what that effect is. Members of the California Assembly believe that the size of their districts requires them to have the staff and local offices that facilitate service. Massachusetts recently cut the number of House districts from 240 to 160, with a resulting 50 percent increase in the size of each district. This increase was used to justify the addition of the staff assistant. Many legislators, however, have argued that the increase in size has made it more difficult for constituents to maintain close contact with their representatives, a change that could reduce the demand for services.

The states in which constituency service appears to have higher priority are generally ones that have the lowest turnover and that had the fewest freshmen in the session being studied. This suggests that the more experienced legislators and those with greater career ambitions are more likely to emphasize constituency service.

The nine states covered in this study vary also in a number of characteristics that may explain service activity: political culture, legislative norms, resources for staff and office expenses, length of sessions, and membership turnover. In such a small sample, it is impossible to determine with any precision the relative importance of each of these factors. We can only suggest that variations in constituency service by state have multiple causes and that a number of trends in state legislatures, such as greater resources and reduced turnover, are likely to increase the priority given to constituency services.

*Character of the District.* Despite some obvious interstate differences in services, there are also significant differences within the states, from district to district. Some of these differences in the demand for services are attributable to the nature of the district; others are attributable to variations in the responsiveness of individual legislators. It may be an exaggeration to describe districts or counties as having a political culture (comparable to that at the state level), but it is possible for traditional patterns of behavior and expectations to develop at the district level. Several Massachusetts legislators explain the heavy demand for services by saying that their constituents have developed high expectations as a result of the example set by previous legislators. One legislator said that his father had been a representative for ten years and "he took care of everyone." Several of the Boston legislators emphasize that there is a strong tradition in that city of representatives handling casework that involves local as well as state problems. This results in part from the use of at-large elections to the city council, but, whatever the cause, the tradition is a powerful one. A legislator in southeast Massachusetts, noting that many of his constituents were from Boston, believes that is why they expect so many services from their representative.

Generally it is accurate to say that the demand for constituent services is greater in districts that are below average in socioeconomic terms. A large proportion of those who come to their legislators for help need some kind of benefits from government: welfare, workmen's compensation, help in getting a state job. Obviously such requests are concentrated in lower-income districts. In districts with lower educational levels, constituents are likely to need more help in dealing with the bureaucracy or solving some of the other problems of living in a modern society. Although there are no consistent differences between urban and rural districts, the lower-income districts generating more requests for assistance are likely to be located in metropolitan areas. One of the most frequent comments by legislators is that constituents do not understand the complexities of government and do not know where they can go (what agency and what level of government) for answers to their problems; this is a particularly common observation by legislators representing districts that are below average in educational levels.

A good example of the service role of a legislator can be found in a working-class district in a medium-sized city in Ohio; it is 40 percent black and has a variety of ethnic groups. The legislator gets twenty five to fifty requests a week from constituents. He maintains an office in the district and devotes nearly full time to the job. He describes the range of services that are requested: help in getting food stamps, becoming eligible for welfare, getting workmen's compensation, getting relatives paroled from prison. There are constant requests for jobs, and the legislator tries to find jobs for constituents not only in local government but in private business. He regularly collects information on public and private jobs that are available and distributes the information through the churches.

Legislators who are black or Hispanic often represent districts that are below average in socioeconomic levels, and most of them devote considerable time to constituent services. These legislators often find that members of their minority group living in other parts of the city (who may have a white legislator) bring their requests to the minority legislators. An example is a Hispanic legislator from Houston, who gets forty to seventy-five cases a week, some of which come from Hispanic citizens in other districts; he is the only Hispanic legislator in that part of the city. A black legislator in the inner city in Indianapolis believes that "the novelty of having a black represent them leads blacks and others in the inner city to expect a lot from their representatives."

Legislators from higher-income, suburban districts tend to get fewer requests for constituency service, and some of them attribute the lighter load specifically to the fact that their constituents have fewer needs for certain kinds of services, such as welfare and workmen's compensations, or that the constituents need less help in dealing with government agencies. A legislator whose district includes the wealthiest parts of Houston believes that this fact helps to explain why he only averages one call a week for assistance. An Ohio legislator says that "most requests come from people who don't know how to find out where to go and how to get information; most of my constituents are better educated and don't need that kind of help." A few legislators from higher-income districts say that they have few requests for assistance because their constituents do not believe in asking the government for help; it would probably be more accurate to say that they do not need the help.

It would be a mistake, however, to describe constituency service only in terms of assistance to low-income groups. Legislators often mention the state agencies or institutions in their district in explaining the causes of casework. Those located in the state capital devote much of their time to handling complaints and requests from state employees; those in districts containing universities or colleges often get service requests from faculty and students. In states where staff resources are available and a pattern of extensive constituency service has developed, constituents from middle- and upper-income districts provide many requests, though they differ in character from those arising in lower-income district. Constituents want help in getting sons and daughters into college or professional school; businessmen have trouble dealing with state agencies; homeowners want local improvements or intervention in planning or zoning disputes. In short, both the extent and the nature of service demands vary with the character of the district.

The demand for constituency service also varies with the pattern of districting; it is substantially greater in single-member districts than in multimember districts, particularly the countywide at-large districts used in North Carolina. Most of the North Carolina legislators representing metropolitan counties who were interviewed said that they received few requests for constituency service; those who thought that they were handling more than usual generally had a smaller caseload than is common in most other states. The reason for this is the lower level of direct contact between constituents and legislators. Constituents are much less likely to be familiar with legislators, and they do not recognize a particular one as being their legislator. Likewise legislators do not advertise their availability, do not make it convenient for constituents to come to them. There does not seem to be any strong or consistent pattern of certain members of a county delegation specializing in constituency service, although a woman member of one metropolitan delegation says that she gets more contacts and requests from women throughout the county. North Carolina legislators appear to be satisfied with this situation and some explicitly recognize the advantages of not having to spend time on this function. Although some of the legislators recognize that single-member districts would have some advantages over the current system, the possibility of an increased service load is not one they mention.

In Indiana the use of two- and three-member districts may slightly reduce the demand for services, but these districts are probably small enough that this is not an important factor. Actually a number of the Indiana legislators from multimember districts, particularly those below average in socioeconomic level, emphasize the importance of constituency service. A veteran Republican representing a three-member district in Indianapolis finds that the constituency service demand is greater than it was when he was a representative from the whole county. I interviewed one legislator from Cincinnati who had been an at-large representative in the county during the early 1960s. He reported an increase in the constituency service load over that period of time and attributed it to both the establishment of districts and the fact that he was better known to constituents than in his early years.

One of the by-products of the drastic change in legislative apportionment during the 1960s was the decline of large, countywide, multimember districts and the establishment of single-member districts in a number of states: Ohio, Tennessee, and Colorado are good examples; the shift occurred in Texas in the 1970s. The result was to make legislators better known and more accessible to their constituents and to familiarize them with local needs. Because these changes occurred many years ago, I interviewed very few persons who had had experience with both types of districts; those few in Texas with long experience were divided in their judgment of the results. But the shift to single-member districts appears to be one of the reasons why in most of the states in this study, constituency demand for services is substantial. Districting also has increased the proportion of legislators who represent minority groups and of those who live in districts with lower socioeconomic levels. Such legislators are more likely to be recognized by, and to be responsive to, those constituents who have the greatest need for services.

One of the unexpected findings of this study is that the relative accessibility of state legislators is affected not only by the districting system used at the state level but also by that used at the local level. When state legislators representing a single-member district come from a city and/or a county where officials are elected at-large, the state representative may be the only elected official who is well known to the citizens and is familiar with neighborhood problems. Despite common theories about local government, the state legislator in these circumstances may be elected representative who is closest to the people.

One of the best examples of that situation is in Boston, where the city council consists of nine members who are elected at-large and who traditionally have not performed service functions for constituents. State legislators whose districts include Boston agree that they are expected to intervene in local problems and help constituents deal with city agencies. One such legislator says that 90 percent of his service calls involve city problems; he estimates he gets forty to fifty calls a day, mostly for service. He also expresses the view that the city council should be handling these problems because of the difficulty that a state representative sometimes faces in dealing with city agencies. Several years ago there was a proposal to elect the Boston city council by districts. It was not adopted at that time, but it had the support of some state representatives from Boston. It would have been interesting to see how long it would have taken for constituents, long accustomed to bringing their local problems to the state representatives, to use their city council members.

Several of the major cities in Texas, including Houston and Dallas, also elect city council members at-large; in Houston five of eight live in districts, which of course are too large (one-fifth of the city) for easy accessibility to constituents. This is one reason why Texas legislators from districts in large metropolitan counties receive many requests for local services. A legislator whose district is on the east side of Dallas and who maintains a store-front office in a shopping center says that he is the only highly visible elected official in that part of the city, and as a result he gets requests for help on a wide range of problems, including local ones. A San Francisco legislator who is highly active in constituency service, including a great many requests that are local in nature, says that one reason for this is that until very recently the city council there was elected at-large. He anticipates that the shift to city districts will have some effect on the demands directed to him, but believes that because he has a better staff "and because I am a better politician," he will continue to receive many local service requests. Finally, it might be noted that both Indianapolis and Denver have single-member districts for city government, which may help to explain why legislators from those counties do not receive as many local service requests as some of those in other states.

There is one other situation that explains demands from constituents for help in dealing with local prolems. Some legislators represent districts in areas where there is no incorporated local government. This is the case of one legislator from Harris County outside the city of Houston and a California legislator near Los Angeles. They get requests for help with local problems because there are no city officials and the county officials are too distant.

These examples from a number of states and a variety of districting systems suggest that the character of districting at both the state and local level can have a significant effect on accessibility of public officials, which in turn helps to determine how citizens get assistance in dealing with their problems. A more comprehensive study of constituency service ought to take districting into account as a major factor in understanding it.

*Legislator's Priorities.* The amount of time and effort a legislator devotes to constituency service depends on the norms and resources of the legislature and on the extent of demands made on him, but it also depends on the legislator's own sense of what is important and, consequently, the effort he makes to become accessible to constituents with individual needs. Legislators have considerable freedom to choose their roles. Some become totally absorbed in the lawmaking process; some devote much of their time to their constituents; and some make a conscious effort to do both jobs well. The more actively they become involved in constituency service, the more constituents become familiar with what the member can accomplish, and the more requests he receives for help with constituent problems.

Legislators may give priority to constituency service because it gives them a sense of satisfaction greater than they can get from passing legislation. One Texas legislator described his motivation in these terms: "One thing I like about politics is the feeling of being useful. I'm fairly religious, and I look upon politics as being a kind of ministry. I am not considered a heavyweight on legislation, but I put a lot of emphasis on service. I have always tried to emphasize constituency casework. One of the things I campaign on is personalized service—what you can do for the people back home." In a similar vein, an Indiana legislator says: "Serving constituent needs is one of the big satisfactions of being a legislator. The requests may seem trivial, but they are very important to these people, and I like being in a position to help people. I get more satisfaction out of this than anything else."

A California legislator who devotes a great deal of his attention and that of his staff to local problems and constituency service says that his highest priority is "being the ombudsman to society." His own background is in social work, and he has hired five social workers on his staff. He says that many legislators concentrate on lawmaking because their background is in law and they feel more comfortable with that role, but because of his background, "I feel more comfortable in the streets—and so I don't avoid that role." His sense of priorities is based not only on his background but on his perception of the process of representation: constituency service is the most important part of that process: "the legislative process could disappear and the service function would still be important."

This perception of the process of representation is shared by a number of other members who give priority to service activities. A Texas legislator finds that constituents are usually frustrated and angry, "at the end of their rope," by the time they reach his office; "if we don't get involved in these problems, we are going to lose representative government." One of the very few Republican members in Colorado who attaches importance to constituency service says that local needs and individual problems concern constituents more than policy issues. "Being responsive to these needs is what counts most because it helps to maintain the credibility of the process." Similarly, a Louisville legislator who devotes much of his time to local and constituency problems says, "Just cutting through the bureaucratic red tape for your people—if you do that you are doing 99 percent of what you were elected to do."

The attitude of legislators toward constituency service, and their activities that result from this attitude, have a direct impact on the number of requests that they get. When a legislator and his staff are working actively and effectively to handle constituent requests, word gets around the district and the number of requests increases. A Massachusetts legislator illustrates this point: "If I get a job for someone, sooner or later (and usually sooner) someone else in the family will call

about a job. The word gets around. If you do constituency work effectively, you create more work for yourself." One of the few Colorado
legislators who gives much priority to casework reports, "I get more requests because I have developed a reputation for being willing to
handle such things. I really feel it is a major responsibility."

Many of the legislators who attach priority to constituency service
do not merely wait for requests to come in; they actively seek casework,
and they make sure that constituents know what they can do. Some legislators are frank to admit that they solicit requests from constituents.
A Massachusetts legislator says: "If I didn't want much casework, I
would not try to attract it and would probably not get it. I do this for
two reasons: it is an important part of my job, and it is a politically
valuable thing to do." A legislator from California, where most members have heavy caseloads, says, "We do as much casework as we possibly can. This district would have a lot of casework even if I didn't solicit it, but I do."

The Ohio legislator from a working-class district, whose wide
range of service activities was described earlier, is a good example of a
legislator who clearly makes himself available and solicits work. When
he speaks to groups, he asks them to call him if they have any problems.
He hands out cards with his local and Columbus phone numbers on
them, along with a variety of toll-free "hot line" numbers in the state
capital. He maintains a local office where he is accessible.

Another Ohio representative devoted most of his interview to describing how actively he works on constituency problems. He has a
large staff of student volunteers from a university to work on constituency problems and this staff works on local and federal as well as state
problems. He notes that he has won a public service award for his work
on behalf of the local community. He hands out a brochure that emphasizes his interest in constituency problems:

Mike [      ] is in office to work for you. Mike's successful legislative record is
well known. But [      ] also devotes much of his time to solving everyday concerns for people who need help.
 During the last six years Mike [      ] has helped thousands of people with
questions or complaints about local, state, and federal government. He has
worked to solve problems involving utilities, housing, legal service, health,
education, welfare, employment, and social security.

The brochure lists his phone number and urges constituents to call if
they have "a question, a complaint or a problem with government,"
and it gives a number of examples of the kinds of problems that he is
prepared to deal with, such as the following:

Is there money to help senior citizens winterize their homes?
Is my grandfather eligible for workers compensation?
How can I get a dead tree removed from the alley?
When should I report child abuse?
Dogs are running loose in my neighborhood.
How can I locate my ex-husband for child support?
I've been overcharged by an auto mechanic.
How can I get a copy of the tenant-landlord law?

This sample from a list of twenty-five problems is noteworthy because it shows that this legislator is inviting constituents not only to bring him problems related to local, state, and national agencies but to request help in dealing with private businesses (auto mechanics) and in coping with personal matters (locating an ex-husband). That kind of advertising will produce constituent demands that are both large in number and broad in scope.

Although a majority of legislators express a positive attitude toward constituency service, there are some legislators who explicitly assert that constituency service is not a major part, or perhaps even a legitimate part, of their job. A Republican legislator from Colorado replied to my question about a constituency service: "If government is working properly, this is not a proper function for a representative. I think highly of my constituents, and they do not expect me to do that." A Tennessee legislator who is strongly oriented toward legislative activities responded in similar fashion: "I don't think that is what representing the people of my county is all about. My constituents send me up here for more than that. I don't see that as my function. My function is part of the policy-making process of state government."

Some legislators approach the question of their service role as a matter of time pressures and conclude it is not possible to do everything that is expected of them. An Ohio legislator says that every legislator faces incompatible demands on his time and must choose whether to be primarily an ombudsman or a lawmaker. He has chosen the lawmaker role; he finds constituency service to be very time-consuming. A North Carolina representative expresses a similar point of view: "I have been blessed by having only a small number of service requests. If I had a lot of such requests, it would drive me up the wall—I couldn't spare the time."

Just as some legislators attract more requests from constituents because their positive attitude and effective performance become known in the district, others succeed in discouraging such requests because of their negative attitude. A Texas legislator, with a reputation for devoting a great deal of time to legislative business, told me that he did not get many service requests from constituents because they knew that he would not do much for them. "I don't do it; I will not ask for favors or apply political pressure to help constituents. People know my attitudes and so they do not request it." An Indiana Republican explained that he did not get many requests for services because, unlike some colleagues, he did not encourage it when he made speeches in his district. The Tennessee legislator quoted above as believing that constituency service is not his function says that he does not get many requests, probably because "I haven't encouraged people to believe that I can get them jobs or help them with their problems."

*Substance of Constituency Service.* To get some perspective on the function of constituency service, we need to look at specific examples of what legislators are asked to do for their constituents. State government provides a great many services for individuals, and many problems arise when constituents have trouble getting the benefits that they think they are entitled to. An Ohio legislator points out that there are discretionary programs and that many of the complaints come from constituents who "fall into the cracks of eligibility." They have been rejected by the agency administering the benefits, or have been unable to get an answer, or have been referred from one agency to another. Some of these complaints come from persons who are clearly not eligible for the benefits that they seek, while others have a legitimate reason to seek an exemption or special consideration, or at least a speedier answer to their request. Examples are persons who are trying to establish eligibility for workmen's compensation, or for food stamps or other welfare programs, or those who are trying to get a relative admitted to a hospital or other health care program, or get them transferred to a facility that is better or more conveniently located. In cases such as this, the legislator may be able to get action expedited, or a case reviewed, but they are unlikely to succeed in forcing reversal of decisions already made.

Another category of cases includes the requests for jobs in state agencies. Some legislators in Massachusetts estimate that the majority of their requests come from constituents seeking jobs. Obviously there are not enough jobs to go around, and many require qualifications that particular constituents are lacking. Sometimes members can expedite the employment process or get waivers of civil service rules that seem unreasonable. A Kentucky legislator estimates that during a two-year term he might have been able to get a dozen jobs for his constituents, and there were about twenty applicants for each job. Although the proportion of successful job applicants was small, he wrote letters of recommendation for the others and helped them get application forms, so that the constituents had the impression that their legislator had done what he could. Legislators are also often asked to write letters for students applying to colleges, universities, and professional schools. Most legislators admit that they cannot get unqualified students admitted (and many would not want to); but constituents are often satisfied if their legislator will write a letter of recommendation.

Legislators who live in the state capital or who represent any district containing large state institutions of any kind find that state employees are among their most important clients. One legislator who is the only representative for the capital city estimates that he spend fifteen hours a week dealing with the problems of state employees. This includes questions of promotion, discipline, complaints of unfair treatment or discrimination, requests for help in getting transferred, and so forth. Although state employees may dominate the casework in the state capital, they constitute an important part of the load in any district where there are significant numbers of them, in state hospitals, prisons, or major regional offices or state agencies.

Those legislators whose district includes a state university have a wide variety of problems brought to them by faculty, staff, and students. A California legislator listed a variety of university matters he was asked to deal with (in addition to administration requests for help in getting resources or legislation): negotiations between employees and the university, recommendations for persons seeking faculty or staff appointments or promotions, and disputes over tenure. Legislators emphasize that they cannot get a tenure decision reversed or a constituent appointed to a faculty position; the most they can achieve is to get the university administration to consider a problem, review a decision, or give consideration to a person whom they recommend. But in a district that includes a major university campus, a large proportion of the constituents may have some connection with the university, and consequently a high proportion of service requests have something to do with the university.

Some of the problems legislators encounter concern the regulatory functions of state government, and often the request is that they persuade a state agency to make exceptions to its rules or ease its requirements. A Kentucky legislator who is on the health and welfare committee told me that, partly for that reason, he often got requests to help nursing homes that were under pressure from the state government to improve their facilities or close down. He felt that the regulations were often unreasonable for small nursing homes. A few months after that interview, investigative reporting by a Louisville newspaper about inadequate nursing home care had forced his committee to study nursing home conditions and had intensified the pressure for stricter standards. On an entirely different regulatory front, an Ohio legislator reported that he spends part of his time helping organizations to secure bingo licenses. Another Ohio representative was trying to help local television service repair companies that were having trouble complying with an attorney general's rule concerning how they make estimates.

Whatever the exact substantive focus of the request, legislators spend much of their time helping constituents cope with the bureaucracy. Many persons find the bureaucratic structure confusing and individual bureaucrats too often rude and unresponsive; it is also evident that many legislators share the frustrations of their constituents. One veteran legislator from Cleveland expressed his frustration in trying to get answers from state agencies: "They will give you the runaround, go to lunch, change their names—anything to avoid answering you." A Louisville legislator has had a somewhat different experience but is equally frustrated. When he calls a government agency and identifies himself as a representative he gets much better response than when he simply gives his name. He believes that bureaucrats should respond as promptly to citizen requests as to those from legislators, but experience shows that they do not, and that is why constituents have to turn to legislators for help. Legislators tend to use similar expressions in describing the problems that citizens have in dealing with state or local agencies:

When people come to our office it is almost the last resort. They have been kicked around. You can't solve all their problems, but you can bring the matter to a conclusion—either solving it or telling them it cannot be done.

The people who come to us don't know what agency or level of government to go to. Or they have been kicked around from one level of government to another. If we have to direct them to another office, we check to see if the problem gets handled.

Some legislators believe that certain types of problems recur—workmen's compensation in Ohio, for example—because the agency handling them is inefficient and unresponsive. Often the constituents do not understand what their rights are under a program, or what procedure they are supposed to follow. Lacking an adequate answer from state government, they turn to the legislator. One legislator described to me in detail the efforts he had devoted to a constituent who had been injured on the job, and who did not know what his rights were and could not understand what procedures he had to follow to substantiate his claim. The legislator had to track down the doctors who had handled the case and make repeated calls to the agencies that were supposed to be handling the case.

In many situations like this, legislators (particularly those who are lawyers) find that they are expected to provide free legal advice to constituents. They do not actually handle cases for them in court, but they provide free advice about their rights and about the course that they should follow in dealing with state agencies. An example is the Ohio legislator who was consulted by constituents about the problems they faced in a trailer park and who found it necessary to explain to them in detail what their rights were under the landlord-tenant act. A Kentucky legislator who is not a lawyer explained to a constituent what her rights were under a bill to compensate victims of crime and kept track of the case for an entire year. Some legislators, particularly those representing low-income districts, are asked to help in getting persons paroled from jail. One Texas legislator says that he gets a lot of those requests because he has been outspoken on behalf of prison reform. There is little that legislators can do about such requests, except perhaps to expedite answers to the relatives of prisoners.

Legislators may be asked to intervene in conflicts between individuals and private businesses, and the legislator may be able to do so effectively because of his influence or his negotiating skill. Such cases can have broader, and even public, implications. A California legislator told me how he intervened successfully to stop a plan to tear down a building in his urban district that had 275 housing units for the elderly, in order to put up a garage. As he described what happened, he singlehandedly stopped destruction of the building, even though only private property was involved.

There seems to be no limit to the range of problems that constituents bring to their legislators. One member said: "People really don't call you until they have a problem, and then it might be anything from a speeding ticket to a divorce case. It is hard to make some people realize that you can't solve all of these problems, but I do take the time to listen and where necessary to refer them to someone else." One of the most unusual examples mentioned by a legislator was the constituent who called because he found that there was salt water in his automobile gas tank, resulting from a leak in the underground tank at the gasoline station, and wanted help from the legislator in getting compensated. Finally there is the woman legislator from Kentucky who told me that a woman constituent, who had recently split with her husband, asked the representative to be on the lookout for a possible husband!

A constant theme in the comments of legislators about service requests is that constituents do not distinguish among national, state, and local problems or agencies. Whatever their problem, if it concerns government, they bring it to the state legislator. This is a familiar complaint among public officials, but because they are in the middle of the federal system, state legislators are more often asked to deal with problems involving both of the other levels of government, although their total load of casework is less than that carried by congressmen.

Many of the problems that are federal in nature involve the social security system, the veterans administration, or some other program of federal benefits. Since many programs of benefits involve federal money but are administered by state agencies, it is not surprising that constituents will turn to state legislators for help with any program—even ones completely administered by federal agencies. Another example of a federal program is one providing for loans to small businesses. Most state legislators develop over a period of time a working relationship with the congressman's office so that requests can easily be referred to the congressman's office in Washington or in the congressional district. Staff members in the legislative and congressional offices may work closely together on problems. Legislators who have the greatest interest in constituency service may request copies of all correspondence with the constituent in order to make sure that the problem is being handled promptly.

A Texas representative has a district that incorporates parts of three congressional districts within its one and a half counties. Two districts are large ones with distant congressmen (one including thirty-two and a half counties). Consequently the legislator directs all federal problems to the third congressman whose district is much more compact even though that individual serves as House majority leader in Washington and might be expected to be preoccupied with national issues. It ought to be pointed out that the relationship between state legislators and congressmen is reciprocal. Congressmen frequently get requests for help on matters involving state problems, which they can refer to the legislator. It is even possible for congressmen to get requests that are local in character. A city councilman in Kentucky once got a letter that had been addressed to the congressman and referred back to him; the constituent complained that dogs were running loose in his neighborhood.

For the most part, constituent requests for assistance from federal agencies can be easily dealt with by referring them to congressional offices, but requests involving local agencies or problems may make greater demands on the legislator's time. Some legislators refer such problems to locally elected officials—city councilmen or county commissioners. But sometimes the local officials are elected at-large and are not familiar with local problems or interested in handling constituent complaints. Often local elected officials have less staff assistance than state legislators for dealing with such matters. State legislators may believe that they can do a better job of handling such problems and/or prefer to take the political credit for handling them instead of sharing this with local officials.

We have noted that the existence of at-large local elections and district elections for the state legislature leads to an increased number of requests to state legislators that involve purey local matters. Legislators offer a number of other reasons why constituents bring local problems to them. One of the reasons is that some state legislators have previously served as local councilmen or commissioners; voters recall this previous connection, are accustomed to dealing with them on local matters, and think that they have experience and knowledge in local matters. A Louisville representative who had served as an alderman says that local business persons often call her: "Perhaps they can't get in touch with the new alderman, or they feel more comfortable with me." Some legislators believe that they are perceived as being more effective. "They think I can do a better job" is a frequent comment. Some legislators point out that they are better known than local officials. A Hispanic legislator from California believes that constituents come to him rather than the council member because of the ethnic factor "and because they think I will take a greater interest in their problems."

Some legislators try to avoid handling local matters, while others clearly encourage constituents to forward such requests to them. A Tennessee legislator who represents three counties tries to stay out of local matters that arise in two of the counties but deliberately intervenes in those affecting his home county. "I'm a citizen of that county, and I would get involved even if I were not in the legislature." An Ohio legislator says that local office holders sometimes get angry when he intervenes in matters that are strictly local, but he tells them it is part of his job to become involved whenever a constituent requests it.

Those legislators who encourage constituents to refer local problems to them normally do not simply refer these to local elected officials but deal directly with the local agencies involved, or perhaps with the mayor. A Louisville legislator says, "I have my own contacts in local government and work directly with them; I often have better contacts than the aldermen do." A Massachusetts legislator is very frank in describing why he does not refer local problems to local office holders: "Many of the requests I receive should go to local officials, but when we get requests we handle them ourselves. We are in a sense in competition with local office holders, and so we prefer to handle them ourselves. I develop my own contacts in local as well as state agencies."

Some legislators are asked not merely to help constituents in dealing with local agencies but also to intervene in local political disputes of various kinds. Some members who are perfectly willing to handle routine local casework try to avoid such intervention, while others seem eager to become involved. While the range of political conflicts is broad, several substantive problems are most frequently mentioned by legislators. One is disputes over planning and zoning and other aspects of land use. Major zoning conflicts (such as shopping centers) often involve state and even federal matters, such as environmental questions or highways, and thus there is a logical role for the legislator to play. One legislator described in some detail how he got a law passed to permit a local referendum on a countywide planning board; after it was passed and local officials failed to implement it, he got another law passed to name the members of the board.

Another type of local issue in which state legislators are often involved is the public school. At stake may be a proposal to consolidate schools, thereby closing some local ones; or to fire a school superintendent; or to change arrangements for busing. School controversies often develop over annexation questions, and sometimes the legislator must become involved because the state legislature has the authority to change the legal requirements for annexing territory. One legislator explains his motivation for becoming involved in local controversies in terms of the integrity of his district: "I represent an integrated area, and I have to work on local issues to preserve the character of the district. I also have to help protect the neighborhoods in the district." Perhaps the best example of a local activist is a California legislator who takes sides in local elections and local propositions that are on the ballot. Asked to explain why, he simply says: "I know it is risky to do this, but I am willing to take these risks because my personality and my views on issues lead me to become involved."

## Consequences of the Roles

Most legislators are involved in trying to increase the allocation of resources for their districts. A growing number believe that serving constituency needs is a legitimate and important part of their job, and they are devoting more of their time and their staff resources (where available) to this endeavor. What difference does it make? More specifically, what are the consequences for the legislature and representation if these roles assume increasing importance?

One possibility might be that as more attention is devoted to these roles, particularly constituency service, legislators will gain the experience and the incentive to carry out more effective oversight of state agencies. I made no systematic effort to find out whether such a linkage exists, but it was mentioned by a few representatives. A few others suggested that most casework was so narrow in scope and so routine that it had no effect on oversight. The most thorough examination of this question has been carried out by Elling (1979), who asked legislators in Kentucky and Minnesota about the effectiveness of casework for oversight. He concluded that there were some positive benefits, but also some serious obstacles, including the inadequacies of staff in some states, the limited number of cases handled by some members, and the fact that the bulk of these cases were limited to a few problem areas and agencies. He also doubted that many legislators saw any political advantage in pursuing the issues beyond the solution of individual cases.

Some legislators emphasized the importance of casework not so much for oversight as for inspiring legislation. One said that he had introduced a bill related to asbestos problems that grew out of the personal health problems of an individual constituent. Another legislator said that she is trying to pass legislation to deal with a problem frequently brought to her attention by individual constituents: the case of home repair companies that fail to do their work properly or in accordance with their promises and then place a lien on the house if the home owner withholds payment. Similarly she is working on legislation to deal with the problem of redlining neighborhoods for insurance and credit purposes, a problem that is frequently brought to her attention by constituents.

One possible implication of the constituency service role might be that by extending special favors, exemptions from rules, and patronage to constituents, legislators would be undermining the equitable treatment of citizens by administrative agencies. It is obvious that legislators do not perceive this to be the situation. Most legislators believe that a large proportion of the requests they receive from constituents are legitimate. A number emphasized that by the time individuals came to their office they were "at the end of their rope," discouraged because they had been shunted from one office to another and had been unable to get answers to their questions. The legislators do not believe that they are getting special favors for the undeserving; rather they are making the bureaucracy more responsive and helping constituents to find out more promptly what their rights are and whether they are entitled to benefits, exemptions from regulations, or other advantages.

One of the most obvious implications of the increasing allocation and service role for legislators is that attention to these roles provides political advantages to the legislator. They are able to claim credit for benefits gained by the district; individual constituents remember assistance provided by legislators; and these activities rarely inspire any opposition—in contrast to some legislative activities. Most legislators seem well aware of the political advantages of these roles, and some are quite frank in articulating them. As one Massachusetts legislator points out, the legislator can benefit even if he is not successful in gaining what the constituent wants: "As long as you return the call or the letter, and try to do something, people will appreciate it, and it will help you politically. you are not hurt if you fail to get jobs for constituents. People are not stupid; they know when you are making an effort. If you succeed, they will never forget you; if you fail, they will not blame it on you." I cited earlier the Massachusetts legislator who admitted that he was competing with local office holders to handle local problems because there were political benefits involved. Some legislators keep a file on all the persons they have helped and use this file at campaign time to recruit workers, funds, and votes.

Effective constituency service can have another important political advantage for the legislator: it enables him to take greater risks on issues, becoming involved in controversial questions and taking stands that may alienate some of his constituents. Legislators believe that voters who appreciate their concern with personal problems will forgive some stands on policy. In particular this view was expressed by several of the more liberal California representatives. A similar view was expressed by a Massachusetts Democratic legislator, who is well known for his liberal viewpoint and his involvement in controversial issues. He represents an issue-oriented district in Boston, with many well-educated constituents. But he wins reelection and is able to maintain his freedom on issues in large part because he takes care of constituency requests and local matters. These are the things his constituents talk to him about. He mentioned a Republican constituent who was active in the Reagan movement and disagreed with him totally on issues but who voted for him because the legislator could be counted on to handle local and individual matters.

A major theme of scholarly writing on congressional elections in recent years has been the large margins of victory enjoyed by House incumbents, which most writers explain in part by the increasing opportunities of congressmen to provide services for constituents and to publicize these services (Cover and Mayhew, 1977; Cover, 1977; Macartney, 1975; Fiorina, 1977a, 1977b). This present study shows that state legislators are similarly in a good position to gain politically from constituency service—particularly in those states where the staff resources are great enough to provide extensive service and where budgets will permit extensive efforts, such as newsletters, to publicize what the legislator is doing.

Can we demonstrate what are the specific political advantages for legislators of effective constituency service? There is evidence that legislators in some states are gaining electoral security and becoming less dependent on coattails and political trends. One of the explanations for that gain is presumably the opportunities for well-publicized constituency service, although the shortage of research on voting trends for state legislators makes it impossible to support this assumption with more evidence.

Do legislators recognize the political advantages inherent in performing constituency service and gaining benefits for the district? Many of them do, but some legislators do not regard service activities as a legitimate part of their job and others give it low priority. The political advantages of these activities are less universally recognized by state legislators than they are by congressmen. Legislators being interviewed often described their attention to constituency service in some detail without mentioning its political implications. One reason for this may be that the development of constituency service on a large scale is relatively recent in some legislatures. Moreover, those legislators who are less experienced and professional, and those elected from safe seats, appear to be less conscious than other legislators of the political consequences of their activities. It is even possible that some legislators do not believe that constituency service ought to have political consequences. One legislator I talked to had read Fiorina's work about the political advantages of congressional casework and recognized that it applied to him as well, but had doubts about whether legislators ought to be profiting politically from casework.

Some legislators who give relatively low priority to constituency service are concerned about the demands it makes on their time. They believe that their major responsibility is a legislative one, and that they should not be distracted from this. Some of the more senior legislators with heavy legislative responsibilities, such as committee chairmen, say that they find it difficult to spare enough time to provide constituency service and maintain contacts in their districts. In states with limited staff facilities, these time pressures are more acute, and it is possible that the growing emphasis on constituency service could weaken the legislative process. The conflict is less acute where more staff are available; in such states legislators usually find it possible to delegate most of the time-consuming details of servicing constituency demands to staff members. But a decision to use resources to provide individual members with staff assistance may mean that fewer resources are available for research on policy issues or oversight.

We may ask whether a legislative norm and a district tradition that combine to mandate a strong service role for legislators may affect the kind of persons who seek legislative seats. Do the high expectations for constituency service in a state like Massachusetts encourage candidates to run who enjoy such activities while discouraging those who are primarily interested in policy questions? Several legislators who were interviewed in that state expressed concern over the relatively small number of their colleagues who had a strong policy orientation; and some of those I interviewed appeared to be much more interested in the process of serving the district than in the process of lawmaking. Some retiring congressmen have voiced their frustration with the heavy demands of the allocative and service roles, among other things. It would be possible for a similar trend to occur in the states, although in most legislatures any such concerns are premature.[3]

One consequence of the legislators' emphasis on their constituency service role could be an enhanced public confidence in government. At a time when opinion surveys indicate that many citizens are alienated from government, a strong case can be made for any effort to make government more responsive to public needs. If citizens discover that legislators are effective in making the bureaucracy more responsive, they will not only use the services of legislators more but may be expected to become more supportive of state government. As government grows more complex and citizens come into more frequent contact with government agencies, the intermediary or ombudsman role of the legislator assumes greater importance. It is one thing to assert that these relationships exist; it is much more difficult to prove that effective constituent service on the part of legislators contributes to greater public confidence in government. That assumption remains untested in the research on state government.

I have defined the legislator's roles in allocating resources for the district and providing constituency service as two of the components of representation. I agree with Eulau and Karps (1978) and Fenno (1978) that representation must be defined broadly enough to include more than policy responsiveness. Consequently there is no need to ask whether these roles fulfill the legislator's responsibility as a representative; by definition they do.

These roles, and particularly the constituency service role, are not universally undertaken by legislators. Where they are not, it is because of the lack of resources for staff assistance, the lack of demand from the district, or the legislator's own doubts about the importance of the roles. Increasingly, legislators have come to believe that constituency service is important, both because it meets public needs and because it brings political benefits to the legislator. Those legislators who are more professional, or more skillful as politicians, take the initiative in seeking constituents with problems and in providing their services to local officials.

A major reason why some legislators are paying more attention to the service role is that they believe this is what constituents want. Many legislators who give relatively low priority to service have made this choice because they believe that it is compatible with the wishes of constituents. Most legislators believe that they are being responsive to whatever level of demand for services exists in their district; at the same time many of them have learned how to stimulate or to subordinate that demand through their action or inaction. We can describe legislators' perceptions of their districts, but we have no data on what constituents actually expect from their legislators. To answer that question, we must rely more on speculation than on evidence, but it is an interesting question that needs to be addressed to complete this assessment of representation in state legislature.

# 7. Representation: Public Perspectives and Conclusions

This study has analyzed state legislative representation from the viewpoint of the representatives rather than the represented. This strategy is dictated by the fact that the study relies heavily on interviews with legislators; resources were not available to survey constituents in the districts of the 220 legislators. A comprehensive study of representation requires some understanding of constituent perspectives: the public awareness, expectations, and perceptions about state legislators. I will seek here a more modest goal: to discuss the potential effects of public perspectives on representation and to describe some of the scattered data that are available concerning the ways constituents view their legislators. Because the data pertinent to state legislators are so limited, I will make occasional use of data relating to congressmen. I will seek also to summarize my most important findings about state legislators and representation and relate them to some of the more significant trends that are occurring in state legislatures—how these findings may affect, and are affected by, the changes that are occurring in the state legislatures.

Three aspects of public perspectives of legislators are awareness, expectations, and perceptions. Unless constituents have some awareness of their legislators, it is pointless to speculate about how they perceive or evaluate them. How successful are legislators in gaining visibility and in communicating with constituents? What expectations, if any, do constituents have about their legislators? How are they evaluated by constituents?

The questions raised in this chapter are broader in scope and more ambitious than the available answers. The fragmentary evidence we have should be treated cautiously; otherwise it will crumble into dust. It is important to ask the questions and to give some thought as to how they might be answered, as well as to think about how a variety of answers pertain to the important questions of representation.

The major reason for the shortage of data on public perspectives concerning state legislators is that very few academic surveys of opinion have been conducted at the state level. The highly useful national election surveys conducted by the University of Michigan have focused on presidential and congressional incumbents and candidates. The development of academic survey units conducting statewide polls is, with a few exceptions, a very recent development, one that makes it particularly useful for us to devote some attention to the questions that need to be asked and answered about public perspectives.

The 1978 National Election Survey provided much more useful information than past surveys had done about public perspectives on congressmen and congressional candidates. (It was the first such survey to use the congressional district as the primary sampling unit.) Future surveys, particularly in nonpresidential years, will provide increasing information about congressional elections and public awareness and perceptions of congressmen. These studies are valuable to those who study state legislators, and public perspectives on them, for two reasons. In the absence of comparable data at the state level, it is reasonable to speculate that some of the perspectives found at the congressional level also exist at the state level. (For example, state legislators are probably not better known than congressmen.) More important, in the long run, is that state surveys of opinion can replicate questions used at the congressional level, not only because these questions have proved to be methodologically adequate but also because such replication permits comparisons of public perspectives at the national and state levels.

## Public Awareness of Legislators

What do constituents know about their state legislators? Do they know who they are and what they do? Have they met their legislators or had other contact with them? Are the increasing efforts by legislators to develop visibility achieving that purpose? There is actually very little evidence available to answer these questions, and some of it is difficult to interpret.

A few surveys of public opinion have asked constituents if they could name their state representative and senator. In 1967 a Gallup poll showed that 24 percent could name the representative and 28 percent could name the senator (George Gallup, 1967). A recent Nebraska poll showed that 32 percent could name their legislator in the unicameral legislature (Welch and Comer, 1978). Several surveys in the last several years have shown that about 50 percent or slightly fewer could name their U.S. congressman, nearly 60 percent could name one U.S. senator, and almost 40 percent could name both senators (Jewell and Patterson, 1977, p. 303). It seems reasonable to suppose that the level of name recall for state legislators might be about half that for members of Congress (though there must be some respondents with personal knowledge of state legislators and no awareness of congressmen).

Although a question on name recall would appear to be an obvious beginning point for studying awareness of legislators, the question is seriously flawed; it asks both too much and too little information. The fact that a respondent can name the legislator tells us nothing about how he perceives or what he knows about the legislator. At the same time it is possible for a constituent to have read about a legislator or even spoken to him, to have a distinct impression about his accomplishments and liabilities, and to be prepared to vote for or against him and yet not to be able to remember the legislator's name when asked to do so by a poll taker. Recently students of congressional elections have begun to recognize that name recognition is more important than recall in trying to determine how much voters know about incumbents and other candidates (Abramowitz, 1975; Mann, 1978). The 1978 congressional survey showed that while only 50 percent of voters could recall the name of the incumbent member of the U.S. House, 94 percent of them could recognize his name and rate him on a feeling thermometer.[1] (The percentage of all respondents, not just voters, who could recognize and rate the incumbent was nearly 80 percent.)

Name recognition is a more valuable measure than name recall not only for studying respondents as voters but also for studying them as constituents. The attentive constituent who reads about a legislator, gets mail from him, or hears him speak at a meeting is likely to be able to recognize the legislator's name and be capable of making some judgment about him—whether or not he can pass a name recall test.

We do not have data on name recognition of state legislators. (In a national or statewide survey that would be mechanically difficult to collect.) But it is reasonable to assume, from a process of extrapolation, that as many as half the constituents should be able to recognize the name of their state legislator. Some caveats need to be added, however. In multimember districts where constituents have several legislators they may have a better chance of recognizing at least one, but probably very few could recognize all of those in a district with half a dozen or more members. In a metropolitan county divided into several single-member districts (for both houses) it seems very likely that many otherwise attentive constituents may forget which senator and which representative represents their district. Some are more experienced or attract more publicity than others. A constituent may contact one who is better known or is known personally to him, or one who seems more accessible or more likely to be sympathetic to the constituent's request. Constituents who attend meetings of citywide or countywide organizations may hear legislators speaking who represent other districts in the metropolitan area.

It is possible that many attentive constituents view the legislators from the county or the area collectively and may give little thought to which one is their representative until they look at the ballot. Living in a county with six representatives, I have heard friends who were well informed and very interested in state government and politics trying to recall which representative was in their district. One more pertinent fact is that persons frequently move from one location to another in a metropolitan county without any awareness of crossing legislative district lines. They may be very conscious of entering a new school district or moving into or out of the city, or into or out of a sewer district, but they never think about which legislative district they have entered or left.

In the third chapter I described the consequences of legislative district lines that do not coincide with political boundaries, particularly in rural areas. In such circumstances voters are often confused about who their representative is and sometimes contact the wrong one. If we are trying to construct detailed, precise measures of constituent familiarity and contact with their legislators, how do we count the constituent who maintains frequent contact with a legislator—reading about him, asking for assistance, and listening to him on the radio or at meetings—but who is in contact with the wrong legislator?

In those counties or communities where constituents have some form of contact with several legislators, it would be interesting to know how constituents distinguish among them, what factors lead to greater recognition and familiarity, and what proportion of constituents are mistaken about which legislator is elected from their district. Gathering such information would be difficult and expensive; before we attempt it, we need to collect much more basic information about recognition and contacts. We need to find out how many constituents have various degrees of familiarity and contact with at least one legislator. This not only is methodologically easier, but also may have greater substantive importance. In other words, it may be more useful to find out what kinds of awareness and contact constituents have with legislators than to find out whether constituents are contacting the proper member.

If we move from name recognition to other forms of contact, we have some solid evidence about members of Congress but very little data on state legislators. We might begin by recalling the somewhat impressionistic evidence gathered from interviewing state legislators. One of the assumptions underlying some of my questions was that state legislators would have difficulty in achieving visibility and would have to work hard to accomplish that. Many legislators, however, did not consider that to be a problem. They were loaded down with speaking requests, besieged by constituents wanting favors, and deluged by more mail than their limited staff could handle. Such members tended to be puzzled by my questions about their problems in achieving visibility. Some of these, however, recognized that most of the contacts came from only a minority of attentive, and often demanding, constituents. Others agreed that visibility was a problem and complained about the lack of constituent interest in issues. Some legislators cited the relatively large numbers of responses to their questionnaires as evidence that constituents were aware of them and interested in issues; other legislators cited very low response rates to draw the opposite conclusion. In short, the evidence from interviews is that some legislators are much more visible than others, the variation depending, among other things, on experience and the member's own efforts.

The best evidence on contact pertains to members of Congress; it comes from the 1978 congressional survey, which asked a wide range of questions, and from several other recent studies. In an effort to compare contacts with congressmen and state legislators, I replicated a number of these questions in surveys of Kentucky respondents, asking them about contacts with both congressmen and state representatives. The results are shown in Table 6 along with data from the 1978 congressional survey and one conducted in 1977.

The 1978 congressional study suggests that the proportion of constituents having direct contact with congressmen—face-to-face, in meetings, or by contacting a congressional office—is generally no more than 15 percent. On the other hand, roughly half remember getting mail from their congressman, and similar proportions have read about and have seen the congressman on television. The same survey showed that slightly fewer had firsthand contact with U.S. senators but slightly more had read about or seen them through the media. When the same questions were asked about U.S. representatives in a poll of a statewide sample of Kentucky citizens, the figures were consistently somewhat higher. There is no obvious reason for this; in fact, because the poll was conducted in 1979 when no election campaign was going on, I would have expected lower figures.

Several months later I asked a similar sample of Kentuckians about their contact with their "state representative in Frankfort." (We did

TABLE 6. Constituent Contact with Legislators (Percent Having Contact)

| Type of Contact | Kentucky Survey | | National Surveys | |
|---|---|---|---|---|
| | State Representative 1980 | U.S. Representative 1979 | U.S. Representative 1978 Survey | 1977 Survey |
| Met legislator personally | 23 | 20 | 14 | 8 |
| Attended meeting where legislator spoke | 16 | 19 | 12 | 26 |
| Talk with staff member | 12 | 13 | 8 | – |
| Received mail from legislator | 58 | 65 | 52 | 66 |
| Read about legislator in newspaper or magazine | 77 | 82 | 52 | 68 |
| Saw legislator on television | 61 | 69 | 43 | |
| Contacted legislator or his office | 20 | 24 | 15 | – |
| — To express opinion | 10 | 12 | 6 | – |
| — To seek information | 11 | 13 | 5 | – |
| — To seek assistance | – | – | 7 | – |
| Wrote letter to legislator | – | – | – | 29 |
| (N) | 671 | 746 | 2,299 | 1,537 |

Sources: Surveys conducted by the University of Kentucky Survey Research Center; National Election Studies (1979); Commission on Administrative Review, U.S. House of Representatives (1977), p. 835.

not identify, or ask them to identify, that representative because of the difficulties of doing so in a statewide poll.) The results indicated that Kentuckians have approximately as much firsthand contact with state legislators, both in person and through the media, as they have with their congressmen. It is not surprising that there is as much personal contact because state representative districts are much smaller than congressional districts and it is more likely that state legislators are known personally to constituents, outside the context of politics. But it is surprising that such a large percentage has received mail from state representatives (who lack secretarial staff and franking privileges) or has read about them or seen them on television. It seems likely that a number of respondents misunderstood the reference in the questionnaire to "your state representative in Frankfort" and gave answers pertaining to their congressmen; other respondents may not clearly distinguish between the two levels of representatives.

There are some data on the relative visibility of state and national legislators, and possible confusion between them, from a survey of residents in and around Lexington, Kentucky, conducted by a seminar of graduate students.[2] Responents were asked if there was a particular member of the state legislature (and of the U.S. House and U.S. Senate) who best represented their view. Only 9 percent were able to name a state legislator who represented their views. When the same question was asked about a U.S. representative, 20 percent named a congressman from Kentucky, while 5 percent named a senator from Kentucky or a congressman or senator from another state. When asked about U.S. senators, 17 percent named a senator from Kentucky, 12 percent a senator from another state (often presidential candidates), and 4 percent a Kentucky congressman. These answers suggest that state legislators are less visible on policy issues than national legislators, and that neither level is high. When asked what state legislator they would write to if they had a problem involving state government, only 16 percent named a state legislator, while some others mentioned a congressman or the governor. About one-fourth of the respondents said that they had written to a state or national legislator at some time, but only a very small proportion named a state legislator as the one.

Another fragment of information on contacts with state legislators comes from a mail survey of constituents conducted in the mid-1970s in four western states, and summarized in Table 7.[3] Respondents were asked a broad question about whether they had personally gone to see, spoken to, or written to their state legislator in the past few years about some need or problem. One-third or slightly more had done so in each of the four states, and 10 percent or more had done so more than once. Even more interesting are the reasons given for not having done so. Of those who had not, about one-fourth said there was no necessity to do so, but almost half thought it would do no good, and roughly 15 to 20 percent did not know how or thought they needed someone to help them make contact. If these rather general answers are reliable, legislators who want better communication with constituents not only need to become more visible but, more importantly, need to demonstrate that they can get things done for constituents.

Data on visibility of and contact with legislators from a few states are of limited value because they do not explain what factors cause variation in visibility and contact. We need data from a number of states and districts to answer questions such as these: Are legislators more visible in states where the legislature meets a larger proportion of the time? (Contacts were slightly less in Arizona and Colorado than in New Mexico and Utah even though the first two states have significantly longer sessions.) Within a state, are legislators more visible in the types of districts where media exposure is easier to obtain? Can variations in visibility among individual members be explained by their

seniority and by their efforts—such as newsletters and district offices—
to become visible?

It would be useful to find out more about that subgroup of citizens
who take the initiative in contacting state legislators, either to express
views on issues or to get information or assistance with personal problems. We know that the proportion of citizens who are likely to contact
any public official is small—perhaps 15 or at most 20 percent (Verba
and Nie, 1972, p. 31). But we have not distinguished between those
who seek to influence policy and those who want help on individual
problems, or between those who contact congressmen and those who
contact state legislators. A survey in Iowa conducted in 1966 (Patterson, Hedlund, and Boynton, 1975, p. 85) found that 10 percent of the
citizens said they had done something to influence the decision of the
state legislature often or several times, and another 17 percent had
done so once or twice. It also identified that much smaller group identified by legislators as "attentive constituents" who were knowledgeable and whose advice they might seek on issues. Perhaps we need to
identify more carefully the "semi-attentive constituents" who at least
occasionally initiate some contact with state legislators.

It would be useful to know something about public awareness of
the legislature as an institution, as well as of legislators as individuals.
From time to time national surveys have demonstrated that only a
small proportion of Americans know some of the most important facts
about Congress, and presumably state surveys would reveal that
knowledge of state legislators is even less. Some types of knowledge—
such as the exact number of congressmen or legislators—are of little importance to the citizen. It would be more valuable to find out whether
citizens know what they need to in order to understand and evaluate
the legislative process. For example, the 1966 Iowa study (Patterson,
Hedlund, and Boynton, 1975, p. 79) showed that almost two-thirds
knew which party controlled the House and the Senate in the state legislature, but only one-sixth knew which party the legislators from their
county belonged to. A Nebraska poll taken in 1978 showed that 63 percent of respondents knew that the state had a unicameral legislature,
but only 20 percent knew that legislators were elected on ballots without party designation; this latter percentage was only slightly higher
for those who had voted recently.[4]

Our understanding of constituents' awareness of their representatives would be enhanced if we knew more about their understanding
of the representative process: whether they lived in a single- or multimember district, how large the district was, whether the legislator had
a district office, and what types of services they thought a legislator

TABLE 7. Proportion of Respondents Who Have Contacted
State Legislators about Problem in Recent Years
(percentage)

| Number of Contacts | AZ | NM | CO | UT |
|---|---|---|---|---|
| Three or more | 10 | 16 | 11 | 12 |
| One or two | 24 | 23 | 24 | 27 |
| No contact | 66 | 61 | 65 | 61 |
| | | | | |
| Reasons for No Contact (as % of those with none) | | | | |
| Not necessary | 22 | 25 | 27 | 27 |
| Would not do any good | 49 | 48 | 49 | 40 |
| Did not know how or needed intermediary | 18 | 17 | 15 | 21 |
| Other reasons | 12 | 9 | 10 | 12 |

Source: Unpublished data provided by Helen M. Ingram,
produced by the Four Corners Regional Policy Project.

could perform for them. One of the startling findings of the 1977 national study conducted by Louis Harris for a congressional committee is that, when asked the population of the typical congressional district, the average response was under 2,900 and the median was 1,000. When asked how many letters the typical congressman got in a year, the average response was 1,350 and the median was 80 letters a year. As to how many requests for personal help a congressman gets annually, the average response was 328 and the median was 25.[5] In short, the public underestimates, by an enormous margin, the size of the congressman's job. One wonders what they might say about the scope of a state legislator's job.

## Public Expectations about Legislators

What do constituents expect from their legislators? Do they demand certain qualities or characteristics such as high education or lifetime residence in the district? What roles do they expect them to play, in terms of both representational and purposive roles? Is there any reason to believe that these expectations are growing as legislators become more active and more professional?

The level of public familiarity with state legislators appears to be low, based on the small amount of data available and assumptions that can be made from the somewhat fuller data on congressmen. It would be unrealistic to expect that persons who have little or no awareness of their legislators or of the state legislative process have given much thought to how those legislators ought to perform. Even for a person who is better informed, it is a safe assumption that many weeks or months often go by without his giving any thought to representational roles. Thus when we ask respondents questions about representation roles, we run the risk of getting answers (if we get any response at all) that do not reflect clearly thought-out and articulated opinions. Constituents may also be ambivalent about some representational roles, and it may be difficult to separate ambivalence from confusion or non-opinion.

With these caveats firmly in mind, we can explore the thinly scattered terrain of opinion surveys pertaining to expectations about legislators.

What attributes or characteristics do constituents expect their legislators to have? The best piece of evidence for state legislators comes from the 1966 Iowa study (Patterson, Hedlund, and Boynton, 1975, pp. 97-99). The qualities ranked highest by the public were, in order: be completely honest, study problems thoroughly, know the will of the people in the district, work hard, be interested in serving others. When all the characteristics were factor-analyzed, it was possible to measure the importance attributed to each factor by the weight given to the items in it. This analysis showed that the most important factors were: purposive activity (including interest in serving others, hard work, and study), community status (including knowing the district's wishes, being honest, and being influential in the district); a commitment to slow and deliberate change; and several aspects of experience and education. Attentive constituents in Iowa had almost the same priorities (p. 101).

At the heart of most debates over representation is the question of representional role: whether the legislator should follow his own judgment or the wishes of particular constituencies. One aspect of the process of representation that is at least theoretically important is the expectations of constituents. In judging whether a legislator is responsive to his district, one factor that obviously should be considered is whether constituents expect the member to follow demands of constituent groups or to follow his own conscience. In fact many of those legislators who profess to rely primarily on their own judgment claim that this is what their constituents expect.

Although the expectation of constituents is theoretically important, in practice we may have doubts about how many constituents have a clearly enough defined viewpoint to provide valuable guidance to the legislator. Even those constituents who understand the complexities of representational role may be ambivalent; they might expect the legislator to follow his own judgment except on matters of particular concern to them, or they may trust him to follow his own judgment because they are confident that he agrees generally with their own viewpoint. If the choices faced by legislators in practice are complicated and the answers must vary with the specific issues and demands, it may not be very helpful for a legislator to know that a small majority wants him to behave in a particular way.

There is evidence from the Iowa study (Patterson, Hedlund, and Boynton, 1975, p. 140) about the priorities chosen by the general public when asked about the choices of representational role that state legislators should make. Respondents in Iowa were confronted with a series of paired comparisons about the choices the legislators should make. The results showed a rather clear ordering of priorities: 1) A substantial majority ranked conscience—the member's judgment—above everything else; 2) A large majority ranked both district and state interests above the remaining factors (in choosing between these two, a small majority preferred state interests); 3) Although a few gave party interest priority over any of the above, most ranked it higher than the governor or interest groups; 4) The governor was ranked higher than interest groups by a majority.

A study of constituents in Utah, Arizona, Colorado, and New Mexico[6] showed similar though not identical results when respondents were asked to choose (in paired choices and rankings) the priorities a legislator should establish on issues: his own opinion, the views of voters in his district, the party, and the governor. The results showed that overwhelming majorities gave top priority to the views of the district. The views of the legislator ranked far above the party or the governor. Respondents in Colorado and Utah ranked party above the governor, while those in Arizona and New Mexico were almost evenly divided between them, with both ranking low.

The concept of purposive role was developed by Wahlke and his colleagues (1962, ch. 11) to describe the priorities that legislators assign to the job of being a legislator. Although they were thinking primarily of purposive roles related to lawmaking, the concept can be defined more broadly to include the allocative and service roles played by legislators. Earlier, we noted differences among legislators in the importance they attach to the lawmaking, allocative, and service roles, as well as in the efforts they make at communicating with constituents. We also noted the trend in most legislatures toward more allocative

TABLE 8. Reasons Cited by Constituents in Evaluating Congressmen

| Categories | Percentage | | | |
|---|---|---|---|---|
| | 1968 | | 1977 | |
| Constituency Service | 49.8 | | 37.7 | |
|   District service and conditions | | 30.8 | | 17.0 |
|   Constituent assistance | | 2.1 | | 12.6 |
|   Keeping constituents informed | | 16.9 | | 8.1 |
| Personal Characteristics and Reputation | 26.9 | | 35.6 | |
| Policy Matters | 11.2 | | 3.0 | |
| Group Treatment | 6.4 | | 3.7 | |
| Other Factors | 0.3 | | 10.4 | |

Source: Parker and Davidson (1979).

and service responsibilities. The question to be considered here is what the constituents think their legislators ought to be doing—what priorities they give to various responsibilities.

One way of measuring this, of course, would be to count the number of letters and calls pertaining to such functions as lawmaking and constituency service. Though this seems imprecise, the growing number of demands for constituency service is interpreted by many legislators as proof that many constituents give this high priority. We have also discussed the ability of legislators to set expectations for their constituents—making it clear that they want to concentrate on lawmaking, or that they are eager to serve individual constituent needs. It would be valuable to compare survey data from those districts with legislators who are primarily lawmakers and from ones with service-oriented members to determine whether there are differences in constituent expectations.

In the absence of survey data on the purposive role of state legislators, we may look briefly at survey findings related to congressmen. National surveys conducted in 1968 and 1977 by Louis Harris included questions on how respondents evaluated their congressmen and the reasons for that evaluation (findings summarized by Parker and Davidson, 1979). In 1968 respondents were asked, "How would you rate the service your representative gives in looking after this district in Washington?" In 1977 they were asked, "Overall, how would you rate the job the congressman who has been representing this area during the past two or three years has done?" That data (Table 8) show that the allocation, service, and communication roles of congressmen are more important than lawmaking or the policy role as a basis for evaluation. It would be misleading, however, to assert that the policy or lawmaking expectations for congressmen have become insignificant; rather it appears that most constituents find it difficult to evaluate the policy contributions of their congressmen. It does seem reasonable to conclude from these data that there is a broad recognition among constituents of the legitimacy and importance of the allocative and service roles.

What do these findings from surveys about expectations concerning congressmen tell us about what constituents expect of their state legislators? Obviously we should be cautious about speculating, in the absence of any data at the same level. Constituents appear to recognize a diversity of legitimate roles for congressmen, and there is no consensus about the relative importance of each. It seems likely that the allocative and service roles are widely accepted by constituents today because they are universally performed by congressmen, and it is possible that these roles would be less widely accepted by constituents at the state level because they are less universally performed.

## Public Evaluations of Legislators

If the level of public familiarity with state legislators is often low, and there is little information about public expectations concerning legislators, we should be cautious in drawing conclusions about how legislators are perceived and evaluated by the general public. There is some evidence, even at the state level, concerning such evaluations, although it is not precisely focused enough to permit us to measure the effects of particular behavior or activities of legislators. We will begin by examining the limited data on evaluations of individual legislators, and then look at evaluations of legislative bodies. Since my nine-state study did not include public surveys, I must rely here on other studies.

*Evaluating Individuals.* Earlier in this chapter I described some of the reasons why constituents who were reasonably attentive and well informed might be unable to identify their own legislator or legislators; particularly in metropolitan areas, they might be familiar with several members but unsure of which one represents their district. This same factor would obviously weaken the process of evaluation. Perhaps the least important aspect of evaluation is the absolute level of approval. A more important question is whether there is much variation within a legislature in how well individuals are evaluated. If so, what types of activities are correlated with high evaluations, and what characteristics or behavior are cited by those who approve or disapprove of a member?

We do not have data on allowing comparisons among legislators in a state, or comparable data on individual evaluations across state lines. Even the comprehensive Iowa study (Patterson, Hedlund, and Boynton, 1975, p. 97) did not provide such individual comparisons, but it did ask respondents what characteristics of legislators are most important and to what extent legislators actually have these characteristics. The most important characteristics (honesty, studying problems, knowing district's will, working hard, serving others) were ranked fairly high in terms of how many members had them; however, the characteristics perceived as most common among legislators were judged to be less important: party loyalty, friendliness, influence in the district, and prestige in the community.

A fragment of evidence about the evaluation of individual legislators comes from the Minnesota Poll in 1971. Less than one-third of those polled were able to evaluate the representative; of these, 42 percent rated him as excellent, 33 percent fair, and 23 percent poor.[7] The figures are less significant than the fact that these ratings were higher than those given to the performance of the legislature as an institution.

The possibility that constituents may evaluate their own representative more favorably than the institution is supported by data from Congress. Parker and Davidson (1979) reported, in the 1968 and 1977 surveys referred to earlier, that constituents were much more positive in their evaluation of their own representatives than they were of Congress because they were using different criteria to evaluate their representatives collectively and individually. As an institution, Congress was judged on the basis of policy, relationships with the executive, and style and ethics; these evaluations were often unfavorable and by 1977 had become heavily unfavorable. Individual congressmen, however, were judged on the basis of various aspects of constituency service (communication, and service and allocative roles) and personal attributes; they ranked very favorably on these criteria. Only a few constituents evaluated congressmen in policy terms, and these judgments were often unfavorable. (These conclusions by Parker and Davidson resulted from analysis of responses to open-ended questions about why respondents evaluated Congress and the congressman as they did.)

These findings demonstrate that respondents may use different criteria for evaluating institutions and individuals; if this occurs on the congressional level, we might expect it to occur at the state legislative level. Congressmen are able to provide enough services to their constituents and districts, and to publicize them well enough, to create a strongly positive image about their accomplishments, and a strongly favorable personal image. Whether most state legislators, with fewer (but increasing) opportunities, have been able to create such a positive image remains an unanswered question.

These findings are reinforced by the 1978 survey of congressional elections. Jacobson (1981) reports that among the respondents who voted (and therefore might be considered attentive constituents), 71 percent ranked the congressman's job performance as good or very good; 65 percent of those who initiated a request to the congressman were very satisfied with the results; and 31 percent could recall something specific that the congressman had done for the district. The 1978 study, like the one in 1977, showed that most of the specific things that voters said they liked about the incumbent congressman pertained to personal characteristics, attention and service to the district, experience, and performance, rather than items related to policy. Those who ranked the incumbent higher were more likely to vote for him.

If similar findings should result from asking constituents questions about state legislators, we would be able to conclude that the personal communications and service roles of legislators not only give them higher rankings than the legislature receives but contribute significantly to their reelection. Such studies, however, remain to be undertaken. The survey in four western states did show that, of those constituents who had contacted a legislator with a request, about one-fifth were very satisfied with the results, about 40 percent somewhat satisfied, and about 40 percent not very satisfied, a less impressive result than the congressional data.[8]

*Evaluating Legislative Institutions.* There are two comparative studies available of public evaluations of state legislatures: the first conducted in 1968, the second in 1980.[9] In each study, respondents were asked to choose among four evaluations: excellent, good, fair, and poor (in 1968 the middle categories were pretty good and only fair). Table 9 summarizes the evaluations, combining the 1968 and 1980 studies (and including two states—New Mexico and Nebraska—surveyed separately in 1980). The excellent and good rankings are combined, as are the fair and poor rankings, and the net difference between the two categories provides a summary variable of evaluation.

One obvious conclusion is that the evaluation of legislature varies substantially from state to state. It tends to be lower in the large industrial states, such as Massachusetts, New York, New Jersey, and California (but not in Illinois or Ohio); these are mostly states where the legis-

TABLE 9. Public Evaluation of State Legislatures
(percentage)

| State | Year | Excellent or Good | Fair or Poor | Net Evaluation |
|-------|------|-------------------|--------------|----------------|
| MA | 1968 | 32 | 57 | −25 |
|    | 1980 | 23 | 68 | −45 |
| CN | 1980 | 36 | 46 | −10 |
| NH | 1980 | 37 | 41 | − 4 |
| NJ | 1980 | 23 | 65 | −42 |
| NY | 1968 | 29 | 56 | −27 |
| PA | 1968 | 40 | 50 | −10 |
| DE | 1980 | 33 | 54 | −21 |
| IL | 1968 | 44 | 46 | − 2 |
| MN | 1968 | 49 | 41 | + 8 |
| IA | 1968 | 48 | 33 | +15 |
| OH | 1968 | 55 | 34 | +21 |
| NM | 1980 | 36 | 51 | −15 |
| SD | 1968 | 49 | 43 | + 6 |
| NE | 1978 | 47 | 53 | − 6 |
| CA | 1968 | 33 | 51 | −18 |
| FL | 1968 | 37 | 50 | −13 |
|    | 1980 | 44 | 35 | + 9 |
| NC | 1968 | 51 | 36 | +15 |
| KY | 1980 | 38 | 48 | −10 |
| AL | 1968 | 52 | 31 | +21 |
| LA | 1968 | 47 | 43 | + 4 |
| TX | 1968 | 46 | 42 | + 4 |

Sources: The 1968 data are found in Black, Kovenock,
and Reynolds (1974); the 1980 data come largely from
the cooperative polling project conducted by Rutgers
University, University of Connecticut, University of
New Hampshire, Delaware State College at Dover,
Clark University, Florida State University, and
University of Kentucky.

lature is more professional and meets for longer sessions. Perhaps the more a legislature is in session, the more the public is aware of conflicts and controversies and the less respect it has for the institution. Some of the least popular legislatures are ones with strong legislative parties, and therefore more partisanship in the legislature, which may lead to lower evaluations. In the two states where we have data from both time periods, the Massachusetts legislature has become less popular and the Florida one more popular.

Before drawing any conclusions about the characteristics of legislatures that lead to high evaluations, we should recognize that public impressions of a legislature are likely to vary over time, depending presumably on both the policy outputs and the operating style (such as partisan conflict) of the body. We need data on evaluations for each state over several points in time before we can make interstate comparisons with any confidence. Evidence of variations in public attitudes toward the legislature comes from Minnesota and Iowa, where questions on evaluation have been asked over a number of years. [10] In Minnesota the net evaluations (measured as in Table 9) varied from + 8 percent to –37 percent in polls taken from 1965 to 1974; in fact the highest figure was in 1968 and the lowest in 1971. In Iowa the net evaluations ranged from + 15 percent to –44 percent in polls conducted between 1959 and 1972; in that state the shifts occurred even more quickly—with rankings of + 9 percent in 1966, –44 percent in 1967, and + 15 percent in 1968.

Obviously these percentages, even when compared across states or across time, can tell us very little in the absence of information about the reasons for public evaluations. What aspect of the legislature's image or activities has the greatest influence on public appraisals? Do partisan or legislative-executive conflicts erode evaluations? The 1980 study of seven states permits some modest conclusions about the correlates of legislative performance evaluation. Respondents were asked to evaluate the governor as well as the legislature, and in most states the governor ranked higher. When these two rankings were cross-tabulated, between 61 and 79 percent of the respondents were consistent in their rankings for both (based on combined excellent-good and fair-poor rankings). In other words, substantial majorities do not distinguish between the quality of performance of the governor and legislature.

One obvious question to ask is whether constituents are influenced by their own partisan preferences in making evaluations. Table 10 provides data from the 1980 seven-state study on evaluations by Republicans, Democrats, and independents of both the governor and the legislature. The results are somewhat surprising. In every state except Florida and Massachusetts there are fewer partisan differences in evaluating the legislature than in evaluating the governor; apparently voters are more likely to think of the governor as a partisan figure, or are unfamiliar with the partisan majority in the legislature. (All governors except in Delaware were Democrats; the Democrats controlled the legislature in all states except in New Hampshire, which had an evenly divided Senate and a Republican House.)

In almost all states the lowest evaluation of the legislature came from independents. The differences among partisans in evaluation of the legislature were remarkably small in all states except Massachusetts and were not always in the expected direction. Gubernatorial evaluations tended to follow partisan lines, in some states (such as New Jersey, Delaware, and Kentucky) very sharply.

It seems obvious that the next questions on the agenda for those who study the evaluation of legislatures should explore the reasons for the evaluation and for variations in the ratings that occur in one state over a few years. We need to know whether evaluations are based on policy outputs, perceptions of legislative style (are the members honest and efficient?), or other factors. From our perspective, in studying individual legislators, it would be valuable to know whether favorable (or unfavorable) impressions of the respondent's own member lead to comparable evaluations of the legislative institution.

We conclude our review of public perspectives of representation essentially where we began. Our understanding of this topic is handicapped by the shortage of data, but what we have learned suggests that most citizens have relatively little contact with legislators and poorly defined expectations concerning them. The most intriguing and unanswered question is whether respondents judge legislators, like congressmen, largely in terms of their accessibility and service to constituents.

## Representation and Trends in State Legislatures

State legislatures have been in a stage of transition. Twenty years ago, in all but the largest states, the legislatures—and their members—were almost invisible, meeting for a few months every two years and then disappearing from public view. High turnover in many states compounded the problem of invisibility for many members. Although we lack evidence that public perceptions of legislators have changed over this period of time, some change seems almost inevitable. The longer sessions, greater interim activity, increased staffing, and other trends have enhanced the importance and increased the visible activity of the

TABLE 10. Evaluation of the Legislature and Governor in Seven States in 1980 by Party Identification of the Respondent (percentage)

| State | Levels of Evaluation | Governor's Performance | | | | Legislature's Performance | | | |
|---|---|---|---|---|---|---|---|---|---|
| | | All | R | D | I | All | R | D | I |
| MA | Exc–Good | 23 | 34 | 27 | 17 | 23 | 17 | 27 | 21 |
| | Fair–Poor | 74 | 60 | 71 | 80 | 68 | 73 | 64 | 71 |
| | Net | −51 | −26 | −44 | −63 | −45 | −56 | −37 | −50 |
| NJ | Exc–Good | 31 | 23 | 38 | 27 | 23 | 24 | 29 | 16 |
| | Fair–Poor | 65 | 75 | 59 | 68 | 65 | 64 | 62 | 71 |
| | Net | −34 | −52 | −21 | −41 | −42 | −40 | −33 | −55 |
| KY | Exc–Good | 46 | 40 | 52 | 43 | 38 | 44 | 40 | 29 |
| | Fair–Poor | 36 | 44 | 31 | 40 | 48 | 42 | 48 | 59 |
| | Net | +10 | − 4 | +21 | + 3 | −10 | + 2 | − 8 | −30 |
| DE | Exc–Good | 62 | 73 | 60 | 55 | 33 | 33 | 40 | 28 |
| | Fair–Poor | 34 | 23 | 39 | 37 | 54 | 55 | 49 | 60 |
| | Net | +28 | +50 | +21 | +18 | −21 | −22 | − 9 | −32 |
| CN | Exc–Good | 53 | 56 | 59 | 49 | 36 | 37 | 35 | 36 |
| | Fair–Poor | 44 | 42 | 38 | 49 | 46 | 45 | 43 | 51 |
| | Net | + 9 | +14 | +21 | 0 | −10 | − 8 | − 8 | −15 |
| NH | Exc–Good | 49 | 45 | 53 | 50 | 37 | 40 | 33 | 36 |
| | Fair–Poor | 37 | 42 | 36 | 36 | 41 | 43 | 44 | 40 |
| | Net | +12 | + 3 | +17 | +14 | − 4 | − 3 | −11 | − 4 |
| FL | Exc–Good | 64 | 65 | 65 | 61 | 44 | 42 | 49 | 40 |
| | Fair–Poor | 27 | 21 | 26 | 31 | 35 | 33 | 35 | 37 |
| | Net | +37 | +44 | +39 | +30 | + 9 | + 9 | +14 | + 3 |

Source: The data come from the cooperative polling project conducted by Rutgers University, University of Connecticut, University of New Hampshire, Delaware State College at Dover, Clark University, Florida State University, and University of Kentucky.

legislature as an institution. They have presumably also increased the visibility and the political strength of individual legislators.

As state legislators, and their members, grow more professional, they begin to resemble the Congress and its members. Consequently, the findings of recent years about congressmen and how they represent their districts are becoming pertinent to state legislators. Recent scholarship has highlighted the growing electoral strength of congressmen and has suggested that this derives in part from their opportunities to provide services for their districts and constituents—and to publicize these activities. This provides a comparative framework for examining trends in state legislative representation.

There is clear evidence that turnover is declining in state legislatures. This is partly due to a decline in voluntary retirements; fewer legislators seek that office with the intention of serving only a couple of terms. There also appears to be a decline in the proportion of legislators being defeated in elections, although systematic longitudinal data are lacking to make that assertion with much confidence. It does appear that legislators are increasingly developing enough political strength to win reelection in the face of hostile political trends. Moreover, most legislators campaign on their own with relatively little help from the party. Incumbency has become a significant force in legislative elections, and a major reason is that legislators have increased chances to make a favorable impression on voters through their performances.

The longer sessions, increased staff and facilities, and declining turnover are increasing the professionalization of legislatures, and the gap between the most professional and the least has probably declined, though that gap is still substantial. The legislative world in California is still very different from that in Kentucky, and we must never lose sight of this when we are tempted to generalize about state legislatures.

We have found that the importance of good communication with constituents is widely recognized by legislators. When the legislature provides sufficient resources, most of them are prepared to use relatively sophisticated techniques for maintaining such communication. We have also found that the practical problems of communicating are very much affected by the character of district boundaries, including both geographic differences and the contrasts between at-large and single-member districts. Moreover, those district boundaries that are drawn with little regard to existing communities and political subdivisions frustrate the communication process, making the component of representation more difficult.

Interviews with legislators demonstrate that it is unrealistic to discuss the problems of policy responsiveness in the abstract, without regard to issues. One conclusion from the interviews is that legislators seldom are under serious pressure with regard to traditional economic issues, because they find it easy to judge constituent opinion and usually share that opinion. The troublesome issues are few in number and remarkably uniform from state to state. They are the newer social issues, often very emotional ones, and they are troublesome not only because many constituents feel strongly about them but because the supportive constituencies are often divided on such issues. I have suggested that the most useful way of analyzing representational style is to define three styles: the legislator who is typical of the district, the one who makes his own judgment about district interests, and the one who is particularly sensitive to demands from the district. Moreover, it is possible, and very common, for a legislator to follow more than a single style simultaneously in representing the district. Finally, it is important to recall the emphasis placed by legislators on explaining their position to constituents, and the belief that it is possible to win respect from those who disagree with you if you are willing to explain your views.

We have found that legislators generally assume responsibility for seeking a greater allocation of resources for their districts—although this role may be more important and time-consuming in states where it is a traditional role. There is substantial variation among legislators in their commitment to serving individual constituents—partly because of state traditions and available resources, partly because of the personal priorities of legislators. A substantial number of legislators fully recognize the political advantages of constituency service and work aggressively to increase their case load and advertise their availability. As resources are increased for staff and district offices, in particular, this role is likely to grow. One consequence is likely to be an increase in the ability of legislators to gain the visibility and the favorable image that will enhance their electoral advantage.

How are these findings about the legislator and representation related to broader legislative trends? I have emphasized the growing political power and independence of the individual legislator. Alan Rosenthal (1979) argues that there is an underlying tension or conflict between the legislative institution and individual legislators. The individuals want more opportunities for political advancement; they want to be leaders rather than followers; and they want more individual staff members instead of having to rely on centralized or committee staff. One consequence may be that it is more difficult to reach legislative decisions if independent legislators become reluctant to follow party or committee leadership. Legislators may devote more time to their district or to laying the foundation for political advancement than to legislative chores. The more able legislators may move more rapidly to seek higher office—although it is not clear that any such trend is accelerating.

These criticisms are often leveled at Congress these days—that the needs of the institution are being sacrificed to the personal demands and political priorities of members. There are still many states where legislators have no individual staffs, except perhaps a secretary, and where other resources remain very limited. In such states, Rosenthal's criticisms would seem to be premature, but his underlying point is a valid one. The new generation of legislators—brighter, more ambitious, with greater political skills, devoting more time to the job—are making demands for greater independence and more resources to do their job. These demands represent a challenge to the established norms for running the legislature, and they may interfere with the goal of strengthening the legislative institution.

The lengthening of legislative session and the increase in interim activity have made the job of the member at least a half-time one in most states, while in some states a substantial proportion of members have become virtually full-time legislators. The growth in constituency service and the increasing attention to communication in the district have contributed to this trend. In a few states—like Ohio—there is a continuing debate among members about whether the job should become a full-time one and whether members should be paid accordingly. A number of members vigorously resist these trends and preach the virtues of the "citizen-legislator."

It was obvious from my interviews that it has become increasingly difficult for members to serve half-time. On the one hand, the pressures of the legislative job push the members to enlarge their commitment of time beyond 50 percent. On the other hand, members learn that it is very difficult to be a 50-percent teacher, or businessman, or lawyer. It is even more difficult to maintain an outside career when you can devote only 30 to 40 percent of your time to it. I believe that this frustration with part-time careers leads many members to leave the legislature after two or three terms—either to run for an office that is full-time or to return to a full-time career outside of politics. The picture of the modern legislator who is politically independent, actively involved in the district, and effective as a policymaker is somewhat misleading because these multiple roles and activities demand a commitment of time that may be unrealistic in states with part-time legislators. One reason legislators want personal staff is because they lack the time to fulfill the demands made on them. But an expanding personal staff will probably lead to more activities by the legislator rather than to a decline in the member's work load.

I have tried to shed some light on the legislator's political base by describing campaigns and collecting data on electoral outcomes, but much more needs to be learned about state legislative elections. Longitudinal data on the variables affecting outcomes are particularly necessary. In the past, the outcome of state legislative races appear to have been determined largely by traditional party loyalties in the district and short-term partisan trends. Reapportionment, by increasing the proportion of metropolitan and particularly suburban districts, has reduced the proportion of districts with strong party loyalties. At the same time, there is evidence that party identification generally has less impact on voting decisions. Obviously, if party loyalty is becoming less important, an incumbent legislator, or a skillful nonincumbent candidate, has a better chance of winning votes from both partisans and independents.

These trends away from partisanship in legislative voting coincide with extensive efforts by the national Republican party to recruit and support legislative candidates in a number of targeted districts in 1978 and 1980. Moreover, both parties (but particularly the Republicans) have embarked on sophisticated, computer-based efforts to redraw legislative district boundaries to their political advantage. Although there is doubtless a substantial political advantage to skillful gerrymandering, the exercise is based on the assumption of relatively stable party loyalties. If an increasing proportion of voters are casting votes without regard to party, we may wonder whether there could be a declining marginal utility to partisan gerrymandering. Alternatively, the expanded efforts by state and even national political parties to protect and support their legislators might make the members more dependent on the parties then in the recent past.

Political scientists in the past have provided us with reasonably comprehensive information about roll-call voting in many state legislatures. They have identified certain types of issues on which partisan alignments occur and have shown that partisanship is stronger in state legislatures with closer two-party balance and in those where each party represents distinctly different and relatively homogeneous interests. There have been very few such studies in the last decade, and consequently we do not know whether partisan voting has been affected by recent legislative trends. If legislators are winning elections with less support from party organizations and less reliance on traditional party voters in the past, we might anticipate a decline in cohesive party voting. Moreover, some of the more controversial issues divide the supportive constituencies that would normally reinforce the legislator's support for his party's position. We have noticed that legislators are not often very specific about representing the distinctive interests of their supportive constituency. If legislators believe that their reelection depends less on traditional partisan supporters and more on voters who can be attracted by efficient constituency service and effective communication techniques, they may be less motivated to support the legislative party on controversial roll calls. This is only a hypothesis, but we need some up-to-date studies of voting in state legislatures to determine whether the conventional wisdom needs to be revised in the light of these trends at the district level.

The general thrust of most interviews with legislators has been that, except for a few types of issues, the task of representing constituency interests is not a difficult one, because relatively few issues are salient to significant constituent groups, and on those salient issues the interests of the constituency are usually clear. There are some trends in state government that may complicate the situation. The basic problem is that in many states the tax revenues are not keeping up with the growing demand for, and cost of, state services. The public pressure to reduce, or at least limit the expansion of, tax revenue has not been accompanied by any significant public willingness to give up state services. At the same time the Reagan administration is seeking to return a number of functions to the state and to reduce federal aid for state programs. The conflicting demands for lower taxes and more services have spelled political disaster for some governors. Individual legislators are less often the focal point for these conflicting pressures, but they are not immune from them. Particularly in districts with many state institutions or state-supported constituents, these pressures are likely to be felt by legislators.

One consequence of greater pressures on limited tax resources is that legislators may be less successful in gaining programs and projects for the district. It is possible, of course, that legislators can claim as much credit for keeping an existing project going as for gaining a new one. There is no reason to expect any decline in the constituency service role of legislators. In fact, if more state employees are dismissed or more persons are threatened with the loss of state services, there will presumably be more appeals to legislators for exemptions and other forms of assistance. The growth of demand for constituency service and the growth of staff members for individual legislators are likely to go hand in hand. The constituency service role is likely to be more accepted by legislators than it is today.

The demands on state legislatures are likely to become greater and more difficult to reconcile as the issues become more complex. This means that individual legislators will face more difficult pressures at the same time that they are acquiring more assistance and resources and the job of being a legislator is gaining more importance. The process of representation at the state legislative level is becoming more complicated and more interesting. The recent research on several dimensions of congressional representation suggests hypotheses that ought to be tested and methodological paths that can profitably be followed to better understand state legislative representation. The fifty state capitols and the thousands of legislative districts offer ideal laboratories for testing these hypotheses and gaining such an understanding.

# Appendix: Criteria for Selection of States and Methodology

A number of factors were considered in choosing the nine states for interviews, and these are summarized in Table A 1. It seemed to me that there might be significant differences in the way legislators represented their constituents between the most and the least professionalized bodies. I defined professionalism in terms of long sessions, high salaries, and low turnover of members. As the table shows, I chose three states that ranked generally high—California, Massachusetts, and Ohio; three that were in the middle range—Colorado, Tennessee, and North Carolina; and three that ranked low in professionalism—Texas, Indiana, and Kentucky. I also sought variation in the degree of two-party competition in the legislature and some geographic spread. (Table A 2 describes the partisan balance in the nine states.) Indiana and North Carolina were included partly because they represent the states that have some multimember districts. Massachusetts was chosen partly because the size of the House was cut from 240 to 160 and the size of districts was correspondingly increased, beginning with the 1979 session; it seemed interesting to inquire about the consequences of this change for representation.

Other states could have been chosen that would provide the desired variation in the variables, but several specific considerations led to these nine. In 1967 I had conducted interviews among metropolitan state legislators in six of these states in a study of the effects of changing district systems, and it seemed useful to return to states where I had done previous research. Moreover, the inclusion of Kentucky, Tennessee, Indiana, and Ohio made it possible to travel by automobile and return home for weekends.

Carrying out interviews over a nine-month period, from mid-September 1978 to early June 1979 required careful attention to the schedule of legislative sessions. Most states did not have a legislative session in the last months of 1978. The choice of Kentucky enabled me to conduct interviews of legislators in various parts of that state during September and October; some members were interviewed in Frankfort

TABLE A 1. Characteristics of Legislatures Included in Study

| Characteristics | CA | MA | OH | CO | TN | NC | TX | IN | KY |
|---|---|---|---|---|---|---|---|---|---|
| Length of sessions | long | long | long | medium | medium | medium | short | short | short |
| Salaries | high | high | high | upper medium | upper medium | lower medium | lower medium | upper medium | lower medium |
| Turnover of members (1970–75) | low | low | low | medium | medium | high | medium | high | high |
| Party competition (1953–76) | 2 party | limited 2 party | 2 party | 2 party | limited 2 party | 1 party dominant control | 1 party control | 2 party | 1 party dominant |
| Types of districts | single | single | single | single | single | multi & single | single | multi & single | single |

TABLE A 2. Partisan Control of the Governorship and
Legislature, 1961-1980 (in number of years)

| State | Governorship | | Senate | | | House | | |
|-------|---|---|---|---|-----|---|---|-----|
|       | D | R | D | R | Tie | D | R | Tie |
| TX | 18 | 2 | 20 | 0 | | 20 | 0 | |
| NC | 16 | 4 | 20 | 0 | | 20 | 0 | |
| TN | 14 | 6 | 20 | 0 | | 18 | 0 | 2 |
| KY | 16 | 4 | 20 | 0 | | 20 | 0 | |
| MA | 8 | 12 | 20 | 0 | | 20 | 0 | |
| CA | 12 | 8 | 18 | 0 | 2 | 18 | 2 | |
| IN | 8 | 12 | 8 | 12 | | 4 | 16 | |
| OH | 6 | 14 | 6 | 12 | 2 | 8 | 12 | |
| CO | 8 | 12 | 2 | 18 | | 6 | 14 | |

during interim committee meetings. Ohio reconvened its legislative session in November, making it possible to interview a majority of the members then, and the rest in early January.

A decision was made early in the research design to interview only members of the House (or Assembly) and to omit senators. I did not have time or resources to interview a good sample of members from both houses; I knew that several cross-state studies in recent years had included only senators; and it seemed to me that I might find greater variation in pertinent variables among districts in the lower house. As a practical consideration, it seemed likely that representatives would be more accessible than senators.

Within each state I sought interviews with a sample of one-fourth to one-third of the representatives, or a total of twenty to thirty interviews; in larger houses I expected a larger total and a smaller percentage. Table A 3 shows that the number of interviews obtained was very close to these goals in each state except North Carolina and Massachusetts. My original research plan had included only eight states. Later I decided to add Massachusetts in order to provide one more highly professional state legislature, get better geographic balance, and include the state where there had been a recent change in the size of districts. I divided the time originally allocated to North Carolina between that state and Massachusetts, and as a result had a lower proportion of interviews in those two states.

Within each state, I tried to interview a cross-section of representatives, paying particular attention to geographic and partisan distri-

TABLE A 3. Proportion of House Members Interviewed

| State | Number Interviewed | Total Members | Percentage |
|-------|--------------------|---------------|------------|
| CA    | 19                 | 80            | 23.8       |
| MA    | 15                 | 160           | 9.4        |
| OH    | 28                 | 99            | 28.3       |
| CO    | 23                 | 65            | 35.4       |
| TN    | 27                 | 99            | 27.3       |
| NC    | 16                 | 120           | 13.3       |
| TX    | 34                 | 150           | 23.3       |
| IN    | 26                 | 100           | 26.0       |
| KY    | 33                 | 100           | 33.0       |

bution and urban-rural balance. I also sought legislators with varying degrees of seniority, but generally excluded freshmen because (particularly in the first months of a session) they would not have had enough experience to answer many of the questions. With a few exceptions, the samples who were interviewed were quite representative on these dimensions. (Republicans were underrepresented in California; in North Carolina rural legislators were underrepresented because I was particularly interested in exploring representation in the large multimember districts in metropolitan areas.) In choosing the specific members who were approached for interviews, I paid some attention to probable accessibility (not trying to contact the busiest leaders, for example) and make initial contacts with more members than the number I needed to interview. Only rarely was I turned down flatly, but in some legislatures (particularly late in the session) it was difficult to make contacts and set up firm appointments in a brief period. I spent an average of two weeks in each legislature (briefer in North Carolina and Massachusetts); if more time had been available, I probably would have been able to talk to most of those whom I sought.

The interviews were tape recorded (with very few exceptions), and were typed up in considerable detail although not always verbatim. The interviews were semi-structured and open-ended; the questions asked and the amount of time devoted to each topic varied, depending on such factors as the member's experience and the type of district he represented, as well as the points that he chose to emphasize. Members were promised anonymity and are not quoted by name.

# Notes

## Chapter 2

1. The election data are drawn largely from official statistics published in each state, usually by the office of the Secretary of State. In some cases records of primary elections were more difficult to obtain; in North Carolina this required consulting unpublished records in the Secretary of State's office, and in Texas files were examined in the headquarters of the Democratic party.

2. It is difficult to calculate winning percentage margins in multimember districts in a way that would be comparable to similar calculations for single-member districts. In the multimember districts of Indiana the following method was used: If there were twice as many candidates as there were seats in a district, the percentage was found by dividing the vote of each winning candidate by the total vote for all candidates, and multiplying that by the number of seats in the district. If the number of candidates was less than twice the number of seats, a slightly different method was used. The average vote for all losing candidates was calculated. This figure was added to the denominator as many times as there were missing candidates, before the percentage was calculated. The following examples may clarify the procedure.

*6 candidates for 3 seats*

Votes for winners: $\dfrac{510 + 520 + 550}{490 + 480 + 450}$ X 3 = Winning margins: 51%, 52%, 55%

Votes for losers:

*5 candidates for 3 seats*

Votes for winners: $\dfrac{510 + 520 + 550}{490 + 480 + (485)}$ X 3 = Winning margins: 50.4%, 51.4%, 54.4%

Votes for losers:

The purpose of doing this is to provide an approximate measure of the closeness of each winner to the losers and avoid inflating the margins of winners. Even if there are only seven candidates for six seats, for example—and all but one are assured of victory—each winner must get enough votes to defeat the loser.

3. The data on campaign spending by legislative candidates was gathered by me from political scientists in a number of states for the *Comparative State Politics Newsletter*. For the specific data included here, from Tennessee and North Carolina, thanks are due to Steven Williams and to E. Lee Bernick, respectively. Data from California was drawn from California Fair Political Practices Committee (1979). That agency provides unusually detailed published figures on campaign financing for legislative as well as other races.

4. The calculation of general election margins in multimember districts in Indiana and North Carolina is the same as that used for primary elections in Indiana.

## Chapter 6

1. An earlier paper on variations in constituent service roles appeared in *State Legislatures* (Jewell, 1979).
2. See Johannes (1980) for a study of the causes of variations in the load of casework carried by members of Congress.
3. See, however, an article on causes of turnover in the California legislature (Price and Bell, 1980).

## Chapter 7

1. The information used in this chapter related to the 1978 congressional election survey comes from the codebook (National Election Studies, 1979) and from several papers that use that survey (Mann and Wolfinger, 1980; Jacobson, 1981; Hinckley, 1980).
2. Information on the survey was provided by Deborah Gona, a member of the seminar. A total of 311 respondents were polled; the sample was drawn systematically from the telephone directory covering Lexington-Fayette County and two adjoining counties.
3. This information comes from unpublished data provided by Helen M. Ingram, produced by the Four Corners Regional Policy Project; other data from the survey is found in Ingram, Laney, and McCain (1980).
4. The data on Nebraska comes from a survey conducted by the Bureau of Sociological Research of the University of Nebraska-Lincoln, reported by Welch and Comer (1978).
5. See Commission on Administrative Review, U.S. House of Representatives (1977), 2: 825.
6. See note 3.
7. Press release of the Minnesota Poll, *Minneapolis Tribune*, September 16, 1971.
8. See note 3.
9. Data for 1968 are reported in Black, Kovenock, and Reynolds (1974) and are summarized in Jewell and Patterson (1977), p. 318. They come from a thirteen-state study of state and national elections. Data for 1980 come from a cooperative polling effort in seven states involving the following universities: Rutgers University, University of Connecticut, University of New Hampshire, Delaware State College at Dover, Clark University, Florida State University, and University of Kentucky. Data are also reported from separate polls conducted by the University of Nebraska (Welch and Comer, 1978) and for New Mexico by Zia Research Associates.
10. Jewell and Patterson, 1977, p. 318.

# References

Abramowitz, Alan I. 1975. "Name Familiarity, Reputation, and the Incumbency Effect in Congressional Elections." *Western Political Quarterly* 28: 668-84.

Barber, James David. 1965. *The Lawmakers*. New Haven: Yale University Press.

Bell, Charles C., and Price, Charles M. 1975. *The First Term: A Study of Legislative Socialization*. Beverly Hills, Calif.: Sage Publications.

Black, Merle; Kovenock, David M.; and Reynolds, William C. 1974. *Political Attitudes in the Nation and States*. Chapel Hill, N.C.: Institute for Research in Social Science, University of North Carolina.

California Fair Political Practice Committee. 1979. *Campaign Contribution and Spending Report: November 7, 1978, Election*. Sacramento.

Citizens Conference on State Legislatures. 1971. *State Legislatures: An Evaluation of Their Effectiveness*. New York: Praeger.

Clausen, Aage R. 1973. *How Congressmen Decide: A Policy Focus*. New York: St. Martin's Press.

———. 1977. "The Accuracy of Leader Perceptions of Constituency Views." *Legislative Studies Quarterly* 2: 361-84.

Commission on Administrative Review, U.S. House of Representatives. 1977. *Final Report*. vol. 2, "Survey Materials." 95th Cong., 1st sess. House Doc. 95-272.

Council of State Governments. 1980. *Book of the States, 1980-81*. Lexington, Ky.

Cover, Albert D. 1977. "One Good Term Deserves Another: The Advantage of Incumbency in Congressional Elections." *American Journal of Political Science* 21: 523-542.

Cover, Albert D., and Mayhew, David R. 1977. "Congressional Dynamics and the Decline of Competitive Congressional Elections," in *Congress Reconsidered*, edited by Lawrence Dodd and Bruce Oppenheimer. New York: Praeger, pp. 54-72.

Davidson, Roger H. 1969. *The Role of the Congressman*. New York: Pegasus.

———. 1970. "Public Prescriptions for the Job of Congressman." *Midwest Journal of Political Science* 14: 648-66.

Dexter, Lewis A. 1977. "The Representative and His District," in *New Perspectives on the House of Representatives*, edited by L. Peabody and Nelson W. Polsby. 3d ed. Chicago: Rand McNally.

Dye, Thomas R. 1961. "A Comparison of Constituency Influences in the Upper and Lower Chambers of a State Legislature." *Western Political Quarterly* 14: 473-80.

Easton, David. 1965. *A Systems Analysis of Political Life.* New York: Wiley.

———. 1975. "A Re-Assessment of the Concept of Political Support." *British Journal of Political Science* 5: 435-57.

Elazar, Daniel. 1972. *American Federalism: A View from the States.* 2d ed. New York: Crowell.

Elling, Richard C. 1979. "The Utility of State Legislative Casework as a Means of Oversight." *Legislative Studies Quarterly* 4:353-80.

Eulau, Heinz. 1978. "Changing Views of Representation," in *The Politics of Representation,* edited by Heinz Eulau and John C. Wahlke. Beverly Hills, Calif.: Sage Publications, ch. 2.

Eulau, Heinz, and Karps, Paul D. 1978. "The Puzzle of Representation: Specifying Components of Responsiveness," in *The Politics of Representation,* edited by Heinz Eulau and John C. Wahlke. Beverly Hills, Calif.: Sage Publications, ch. 3.

Eulau, Heinz, and Prewitt, Kenneth. 1973. *Labyrinths of Democracy: Adaptations, Linkages, Representation, and Policies in Urban Politics.* Indianapolis: Bobbs-Merrill.

Eulau, Heinz, and Wahlke, John C. 1978. *The Politics of Representation.* Beverly Hills, Calif.: Sage Publications.

Eulau, Heinz; Wahlke, John C.; Buchanan, William; Ferguson, Leroy C. 1978. "The Role of the Representative: Some Empirical Observations on the Theory of Edmund Burke," in *The Politics of Representation,* edited by Heinz Eulau and John C. Wahlke. Beverly Hills, Calif.: Sage Publications, ch. 6.

Fenno, Richard F., Jr. 1978. *Home Style: House Members in Their Districts.* Boston: Little, Brown.

Fenton, John. 1957. *Politics in the Border States.* New Orleans: Hauser Press.

———. 1966. *Midwest Politics.* New York: Holt, Rinehart, and Winston.

Fiorina, Morris P. 1974. *Representatives, Roll Calls, and Constituencies.* Lexington, Mass.: D.C. Heath Lexington Books.

———. 1977a. "The Case of the Vanishing Marginals: The Bureaucracy Did It." *American Political Science Review* 71: 177-81.

———. 1977b. *Congress—Keystone of the Washington Establishment.* New Haven: Yale University Press.

Flinn, Thomas A. 1964. "Party Representation in the States." *American Political Science Review* 58: 60-71.

Francis, Wayne L. 1965. "The Role Concept in Legislatures." *Journal of Politics* 27: 567-85.

Friesema, H. Paul, and Hedlund, Ronald D. 1974. "The Reality of Representational Roles," in *Public Opinion and Public Policy,* edited by Norman R. Luttbeg. 2d ed. Homewood, Ill.: Dorsey Press, pp. 413-17.

Gallup, George. 1967. *Gallup Opinion Index* 20: 17-19.

Gove, Samuel K., Carlson, Richard W. and Carlson, Richard J. 1976. *The Illinois Legislature.* Urbana: University of Illinois Press.

Grau, Craig H. 1981. "Competition in State Legislative Primaries." *Legislative Studies Quarterly* 6: 35-54.

Gross, Donald A. 1978. "Representative Styles and Legislative Behavior." *Western Political Quarterly* 31: 359-71.

Grumm, John. 1965. "The Systematic Analysis of Blocs in the Study of Legislative Behavior." *Western Political Quarterly* 18: 350-63.

Hadley, David J. 1977. "Legislative Role Orientations and Support for Party and Chief Executive in the Indiana House." *Legislative Studies Quarterly* 2: 309-35.

Hamm, Keith E.; Harmel, Robert; and Thompson, Robert J. "The Impact of Districting on County Delegate Cohesion in Southern State Legislatures." Paper presented at the annual meeting of the Southern Political Science Association.

Hevesi, Alan G. 1975. *Legislative Politics in New York*. New York: Praeger.

Hinckley, Barbara. 1979. "House Reelections and Senate Defeats: The Role of the Challenger." Paper presented at the annual meeting of the Americal Political Science Association.

———. 1980. "The American Voter in Congressional Elections." *American Political Science Review* 74: 641-50.

Ingram, Helen M.; Laney, Nancy K; and McCain, John R. 1980. *A Policy Approach to Political Representation*. Baltimore: Johns Hopkins Press.

Jacobson, Gary C. 1981. "Incumbents and Voters in the 1978 Congressional Election." *Legislative Studies Quarterly* 6: 183-200.

Jewell, Malcolm E. 1967. *Legislative Representation in the Contemporary South*. Durham, N.C.: Duke University Press.

———. 1969. *Metropolitan Representation: State Legislative Districting in Urban Counties*. New York: National Municipal League.

———. 1970. "Attitudinal Determinants of Legislative Behavior: The Utility of Role Analysis," in Allan Kornberg and Lloyd D. Musolf, eds., *Legislatures in Developmental Perspective*. Durham, N.C.: Duke University Press, ch. 13.

———. 1979. "Legislative Casework: Serving the Constituents, One at a Time." *State Legislatures*, 5: 14-18.

Jewell, Malcolm E., and Olson, David M. 1978. *American State Political Parties and Elections*. Homewood, Ill.: Dorsey Press.

Jewell, Malcolm E., and Patterson, Samuel C. 1977. *The Legislative Process in the United States*, 3d ed. New York: Random House.

Johannes, John R. 1980. "The Distribution of Casework in the U.S. Congress: An Uneven Burden." *Legislative Studies Quarterly* 5: 517-44.

Kingdon, John W. 1977. "Models of Legislative Voting." *Journal of Politics* 39: 563-95.

———. 1981. *Congressmen's Voting Decisions*. 2d ed. New York: Harper and Row.

Kirkpatrick, Samuel A. 1978. *The Legislative Process in Oklahoma*. Norman: University of Oklahoma Press.

Kuklinski, James H., with Elling, Richard C. 1977. "Representational Role,

Constituency Opinion, and Legislative Roll-Call Behavior." *American Journal of Political Science* 21: 135-47.

LeBlanc, Hugh L. 1969. "Voting in State Senates: Party and Constituency Influences." *Midwest Journal of Political Science* 13: 33-57.

Macartney, John D. 1975. "Political Staffing: A View from the District." Ph.D. dissertation, University of California, Los Angeles.

McCrone, Donald J., and Kuklinski, James H. 1979. "The Delegate Theory of Representation." *American Journal of Political Science* 23: 278-300.

Mann, Thomas E. 1978. *Unsafe at Any Margin: Interpreting Congressional Elections.* Washington, D.C.: American Enterprise Institute for Public Policy Research.

Mann, Thomas E., and Wolfinger, Raymond E. 1980. "Candidates and Parties in Congressional Elections." *American Political Science Review* 74: 617-32.

Matthews, Donald, and Stimson, James. 1970. "Decision-Making by U.S. Representatives," in *Political Decision-Making,* edited by S. Sidney Ulmer. New York: Van Nostrand Reinhold.

Mayhew, David R., 1974. *Congress: The Electoral Connection.* New Haven: Yale University Press.

Miller, Warren E. 1961. "Policy Preferences of Congressional Candidates and Constituents." Paper presented at the annual meeting of the American Political Science Association.

Miller, Warren E., and Stokes, Donald E. 1963. "Constituency Influence in Congress." *American Political Science Review* 57: 45-56.

National Election Studies. 1979. *The American National Election Study, 1978.* Ann Arbor, Mich.: Inter-University Consortium for Political and Social Research.

Parker, Glenn R., and Davidson, Roger H. 1979. "Why Do Americans Love Their Congressmen So Much More Than Their Congress?" *Legislative Studies Quarterly* 4: 53-62.

Patterson, Samuel C. 1961. "The Role of the Deviant in the State Legislative System: The Wisconsin Assembly." *Western Political Quarterly* 14: 460-72.

———. 1968. "The Political Cultures of the American States." *Journal of Politics* 30: 187-209.

Patterson, Samuel C.; Hedlund, Ronald D.; Boynton, G. Robert. 1975. *Representatives and Represented.* New York: John Wiley.

Pesonen, Pertti. 1963. "Close and Safe Elections in Massachusetts." *Midwest Journal of Political Science* 7: 54-70.

Pitkin, Hanna F. 1967. *The Concept of Representation.* Berkeley and Los Angeles: University of California Press.

Price, Charles M., and Bell, Charles G. 1980. "Why the Voluntary Exodus of So Many Assembly Members?" *California Journal* 11: 365-66.

Robeck, Bruce W. 1972. "Legislative Partisanship, Constituency and Malapportionment: The Case of California." *American Political Science Review* 66: 1234-45.

Rosenthal, Alan. 1979. "Separate Roads: The Legislator as an Individual and the Legislature as an Institution." *State Legislatures* 5: 21-25.

Schlesinger, Joseph A. 1966. *Ambition and Politics: Political Careers in the United States.* Chicago: Rand McNally.

Shin, Kwang S., and Jackson, John S. III. 1979. "Membership Turnover in U.S. State Legislatures: 1931-1976." *Legislative Studies Quarterly* 4: 95-104.

Sorauf, Frank J. 1962. *Party and Representation.* New York: Atherton Press.

Uslaner, Eric M., and Weber, Ronald E. 1977. *Patterns of Decision-Making in State Legislatures.* New York: Praeger.

Verba, Sidney, and Nie, Norman H. 1972. *Participation in America: Political Democracy and Social Equality.* New York: Harper and Row.

Wahlke, John C. 1978. "Policy Demands and System Support: the Role of The Represented," in *The Politics of Representation,* edited by Heinz Eulau and John C. Wahlke. Beverly Hills, Calif.: Sage Publications, ch. 4.

Wahlke, John C.; Eulau, Heinz; Buchanan, William; Ferguson, LeRoy C. 1962. The Legislative System. New York: John Wiley.

Weissberg, Robert. 1978. "Collective vs. Dyadic Representation in Congress." *American Political Science Review* 72: 535-47.

Welch, Susan, and John, Comer. 1978. "Nebraskans and Their Legislature." Unpublished paper.

# Index